POLITICS IN THE
AMERICAN DRAMA

POLITICS

IN THE

AMERICAN

DRAMA

Caspar H. Nannes

1960

The Catholic University
of America Press

Washington 17, D.C.

To Mom, Dad, and Sue

FOREWORD

It is a general article of faith with everyone who knows politics that anything that can help the public to become more thoroughly educated in this supremely important field is greatly to be encouraged. When the instruction can be as entertaining and at the same time as factual as Caspar Nannes' study of politics in the American drama, the end is well served.

Here in astute analysis are the principal depictions of politicians and the political society that have reached the popular stage since the 1890's. Some are stereotypes, others hit closer to reality; all are informed with their creator's desire to show the country how its affairs are run and to make some comment, usually critical, upon the process. Yet from them all emerges a basic idealism which in the most severe inspires protest and in the most friendly strengthens approval. And from them, too, emerges an entertaining insight into the changing attitudes of America toward the men who hold public office and conduct the affairs of government.

It is here, perhaps, that this pleasant survey provides the most for the general reader, for it serves as an introduction to plays that stimulate interest and direct attention to the political process. Here is the pointed mockery of *Of Thee I Sing* and *I'd Rather Be Right*, the vigorous good citizenship of *State of the Union*, the acrid bitterness of *Both Your Houses*, the dark burden of *They Shall Not Die*, and many another drama built upon politics. Each has its place in the unfolding story of American political sophistication, and Mr. Nannes has done an excellent job of analyzing them and putting them in proper perspective in that story.

To the citizen who wishes to learn more about the development of American politics, and who hopes to be entertained in the process, this survey is recommended. Just as the plays themselves often instruct painlessly, so does Mr. Nannes' book: a good introduction, an interesting analysis, a sound recapitulation of changing decades as they have been reflected in a changing drama.

Allen Drury

PREFACE

Man is a political animal who has always been fascinated by politics. Through the centuries he has expressed this absorption in many ways, and the theatre was one of the most appealing to man as author and audience. The great Greek satirist, Aristophanes (450-385 B.C.) turned his bitter shafts upon politics and politicians in plays that still have current application. His *Lysistrata*, a virulent anti-war drama, has been revived numerous times within our own century.

Subsequently playwrights in other periods and other countries utilized the theatre to support or to criticize the governments and party leaders of their own day. In the United States plays appeared sporadically from colonial times on, but political dramas did not reach the Broadway stage in significant numbers until the last decade of the nineteenth century. Still another forty years were to elapse before this genre was produced in quantity. "It is a pity that no great dramatist turns to politics for inspiration," Dr. Arthur Hobson Quinn lamented about nineteenth century American playwrights in his *A History of the American Drama from the Beginnings to the Civil War*.

This, then, is the basic reason why the relationship of politics to the drama has been, on the whole, by-passed by scholars. Here and there articles on the subject have appeared, each to meet a particular need. Occasionally a history of the American drama has devoted part of a chapter, rarely a complete chapter, to the topic. But a detailed study showing the close relationship of politics and the theatre is lacking.

Politics in the American Drama attempts to fill that gap. The book will limit itself to those plays produced on the New York, that is the Broadway, stage from 1890 until the end of 1959. Its fundamental aim is to point out that playwrights and theatrical producers were alert during these years to the dramatic possibilities of contemporary political events.

Setting criteria for the inclusion of some plays and the omission of others was difficult. No rigid rule could be applied, for there are too many twilight zones where the importance of politics to the plot is debatable. A basic requirement demands that the major action of a play revolves around the political theme. The latter may be divided into several classifications, of which one or more may be present during a play. The dramas may deal directly with (1) candidates running for office, corruption in government, specific political issues; (2) outstanding political figures such as Franklin Delano Roosevelt, Woodrow Wilson, or Fiorello La Guardia; (3) political philosophies, such as Naziism, Fascism, or Communism, or (4) political situations.

An effort will be made to develop clearly the background out of which a play came. Playwrights are inadvertently historians of their era, putting contemporary emotions concerning controversial issues and personalities of the period onto the stage. That will be a corollary theme, for the significance of a plot cannot be fully appreciated until the issues, and frequently the historical characters, are properly put into perspective. When this is done, the living relationship of politics to the drama is achieved.

Perhaps more stress should be laid upon this aspect. Political plays are essentially aimed at a contemporary audience that instantly recognizes the characters, situations, issues, or philosophies upon which the story is built. This immediacy may be a major reason for the ephemeral quality of most political dramas. Only a few—*Winterset, Born Yesterday, The County Chairman,* for instance—retain their appeal for later periods.

The plays in *Politics in the American Drama* were selected as examples fitting the requirements set up. Their artistic worth was a secondary consideration, though usually some evaluation of a play's quality is suggested. The primary standard was a production's reflection of what interested the American people at a particular time. Since many political plays quickly reached "hit" proportions, they indicated that dramatists and producers had tapped a rich source of appeal to theatregoers. This vein reached flood tide in the nineteen-thirties when the twin dangers of a debilitating depression and an approaching world conflict inspired playwrights to write dramas developing these themes. During the nineteen-forties and nineteen-fifties political subjects furnished the plots for numerous plays, but not quite in the same number as the nineteen-thirties.

May 15, 1960
Washington, D. C.   Caspar H. Nannes

ACKNOWLEDGMENTS

The efforts of many people enter into the creation of a book. To thank properly all who helped would be impossible. The fact that each name is not recorded only emphasizes my debt to so many. But a few must be singled out. My heartfelt appreciation goes to John McAleer for his keen direction of the manuscript; to Lloyd M. Hampton for his confidence in the work and his astute and imaginative suggestions; to Mrs. Rona Solberg, whose sprightly observations led to approaches that might have been overlooked, and to John Goodwin for his courteous placing at my disposal the facilities of the Virginia Theological Seminary library.

Special thanks must go to Mrs. Catharine F. Seigel for her alert, careful, and brilliant examination of the manuscript. The final shape of the book owes much to her perspicacity and devotion to accuracy.

I am grateful to the following publishers and authors for their permission to quote from the plays and books listed below:

Appleton-Century-Crofts, Inc.—From *Twentieth Century United States,* by Jeannette P. Nichols. Copyright 1943, Jeannette P. Nichols. By permission of Appleton-Century-Crofts, Inc.

Bobbs-Merrill Company, Inc.—From *George Ade,* by Fred C. Kelly. Copyright 1947, used by special permission of the publishers, The Bobbs-Merrill Company, Inc.

E. P. Dutton & Company, Inc.—*Washington Cavalcade,* by Charles Hurd; *This Man LaGuardia,* by Lowell M. Limpus and Burr W. Leyson. By permission of E. P. Dutton & Company, Inc.

Samuel French, Inc.—*Men Must Fight,* Copyright 1959 (in renewal), by Reginald Lawrence and S. K. Lauren; *The Racket,* Copyright 1955 (in renewal), by Mrs. Howard Fithian Kingman; *Still Waters,* 1953 (in renewal), by William Elliott; *The Man of the Hour,* by George H. Broadhurst; *The Lion and the Mouse,* by Charles Klein; *Glorious Morning,* by Norman Macowan; *The Seventh Trumpet,* by Charles Rann Kennedy; *Birthright,* by Richard Maibaum; *The Gentleman from Athens,* by Emmet Lavery.

Harcourt, Brace and Company—*The Letters of Lincoln Steffens,* edited by Ella Winter and Granville Hicks.

Sidney Kingsley—*Darkness at Noon.*

CONTENTS

1

TWO WORLDS: PAST AND PRESENT

TWO MEN streaked across the political heavens fifty years apart, and in so doing inspired plays expressing the ethos of their times. One was Senator Preston B. Plumb of Kansas. The other was Wendell Willkie.

Both were political mavericks who flouted party lines on important occasions. Senator Plumb, a Republican, supported Horace Greeley in the presidential campaign of 1872. Willkie had been a committeeman at the Democratic convention of 1924 before becoming a Republican during the New Deal era. Each man had personal charm, color, and crowd appeal. Senator Plumb satisfied the easterner's conception of a western Congressman. He was raw-boned, open-hearted, and outspoken. He acted naturally and modestly in the Nation's Capital and quickly became popular with official and unofficial Washington. Plumb was also a serious-minded senator, intent on proving that his 1877 election was not a mistake. His re-elections in 1883 and 1889 were earned by hard work, wholesome enthusiasm, and real accomplishment. Willkie skyrocketed out of Indiana to

steal the 1940 Republican nomination for president from the
party professionals by unorthodox, but effective tactics. There
was something about the rugged Hoosier that inspired intel-
lectuals and working men alike to rally around him.

Senator Plumb was a national figure; Willkie a world personality. The times had something to do with the difference.
The plays each man inspired, *The Senator* and *State of the
Union,* reflected their periods and revealed a partial reason for
the somewhat limited reputation of the Kansas Senator and the
global recognition of the Indiana industrialist. *The Senator*
opened at the Star Theatre on January 13, 1890. *State of the
Union* gave its first Broadway performance November 14, 1945,
in the Hudson Theatre. The headlines in the *New York Times*
for those two days suggest the radical change in outlook that
had taken place in our country. The 1890 headlines read:

OHIO'S NEW GOVERNOR
IOWA'S LEGISLATIVE FIGHT
SENATOR QUAY'S PLANS
THE RIVALS FOR THE SITE
ANGRY RIOTERS IN LISBON

The 1945 headlines read:

ATTLEE IN ADDRESS TO CONGRESS ASKS WORLD
UNITY IN UNO
HURLEY ASSERTS RED PLOT TO OUST CHIANG
US, BRITAIN SHARE PALESTINE INQUIRY
SACKARNO SHELVED BY INDIES REPUBLIC
1,000 NAVY MEN RIOT IN HONOLULU
DeGAULLE ELECTED UNANIMOUSLY
BUT VOTE MASKS PRESIDENCY RIFT
$1,350,000 ASKED FOR UNRRA BY TRUMAN
FAIRLESS REJECTS SCHWELLENBACH BID
TO PAY TALKS TODAY
O'DWYER TO FACE JURY IN "SHOWDOWN" ON
"LAXITY" TODAY

Only one headline in 1890 was concerned with overseas controversies, and that dealt with the violent reaction of Portuguese mobs to an English ultimatum demanding that the Iberian country leave certain parts of Africa. The other headlines were all domestic, with the fight between Chicago and New York for the 1893 World's Fair featured. The change by 1945 is evident. A British prime minister appeals to Congress for a strong United Nations to save civilization "in the terrible light of the atomic bomb." His appeal is underlined by headlines indicating trouble in China, Russia, Palestine, Indonesia, Hawaii, and France. Domestic difficulties are added to this roll call, with Secretary of Labor Schwellenbach trying to bring peace to the United States Steel Corporation and its employees.

There was obviously more than a half-century date difference between 1890 and 1945. During those years a way of life had died, and a new one had been born. The world, without shrinking physically, had become immeasurably smaller. Improved means of communication and transportation had succeeded in making one continent's political headaches the political headaches of every other continent. No longer could a nation worry only about its own troubles. The difference was apparent in both plays. *The Senator* was a provincial play meant for an insular audience. *State of the Union,* national in theme and international in implications, was written for an audience presumed familiar with important political names and situations on a world basis.

This assumption on the part of later dramatists was a valid one. The American of 1890 was far removed from international concerns. His newspapers, the chief source of information for the general reader, gave niggardly space to foreign events. It was only the educated person who turned to the periodicals for more detailed explanations. But by 1945 the ordinary citizen could hardly escape national and international news—in the newspapers, on the moving picture screen, over the radio, and on television. Current history was ever present, and the humblest citizen could speak with authority about names and places and

situations thousands of miles away. In addition, Washington
had become the key city of the world. "World War II made
Washington two cities," Charles Hurd in *Washington Cavalcade*
observed. "It became the actual ruling center with an unassail-
able power over the entire United States. It became, too, with
all the reluctance imaginable, the first city of the world."[1]

The enormous difference in political awareness between the
audiences of 1890 and those of 1945 was reflected in the tone,
language, and plot of *The Senator* and *State of the Union*. Not
only was the former written for an insular audience, but it had
only one aim—to amuse. *State of the Union* sought to instruct
as well as to entertain.

The Senator was written by David Demarest Lloyd and
Sydney Rosenfeld. For some years critics debated which author
deserved more credit for the play. Scholarly accounts differed.
One view held that Lloyd, who died before *The Senator* was
produced, had completed the work except for minor details.
A different explanation claimed that Lloyd wrote the first two
acts and Rosenfeld the last two. The latter's account is the
only one available, but it does seem to be an honest one. Asked
"What portion of *The Senator* is your work?" he answered:

> Well, it would hardly be fair for me to point out, as
> Mr. Lloyd is not alive to corroborate my statement.
> I will say, however, that I did what I should have done
> under any circumstances. I rewrote the entire play, in
> order to avoid anything like patchwork. Consequently,
> the dialogue is in my own vein, and a number of new
> characters were introduced by me.[2]

The plot suggests what political knowledge audiences in
1890 were supposed to possess. Senator Rivers, in love with
Mabel Denman, undertakes to help her father receive compensa-
tion for a ship his father had lost seventy-three years earlier
while fighting the British. Subplots include Rivers' fight against
unnamed railroad interests, several minor love affairs, and
maneuvers by second-rate politicians for political preferment.

Perhaps the sharp transition from the New York of 1890 to the Washington of 1945 may be best measured by an interchange between the real life Senator Plumb and William H. Crane, who, as Senator Rivers, was impersonating Plumb on the stage.

"Mr. Crane," Plumb said, "I never wore a silk hat in my life, and my creditors wouldn't know me for myself in a headpiece like that."

The actor impulsively threw the hat into a corner, but immediately hastened over and picked it up.

"Senator," Crane explained, "people in New York wouldn't recognize the Senator without his stovepipe. When I go to Washington, the Senator will appear in a plain felt hat."[3]

The Senator was an instantaneous hit. It ran for more than a hundred consecutive performances on Broadway and attracted large audiences elsewhere for many years. In 1910 a sequel by Miss Martha Morton, *The Senator Keeps House,* also proved popular. Crane took the leading role in this play.

Lloyd's death at the age of thirty-eight was a real loss to the American theatre. He wrote four highly successful plays within six years, each showing marked improvement in technique and understanding. His first play, *For Congress* (1884), was a satire on district nominating conventions and on Congress. Rosenfeld rewrote and produced it in 1895 at the Columbia Theatre, Brooklyn, as *The Politician.* A friendly, kindly man of serene manner and grave conduct, Lloyd died in September, 1889 of a heart attack. The *New York Tribune,* where he worked intermittently for twenty years, called him "an accomplished man of letters, a constant and faithful friend, a serene, unsullied and noble soul."[4]

Writing political drama was a natural evolution for Lloyd. He lived twice in Washington, the first time in 1871 as secretary to Chief Justice Salmon P. Chase of the United States Supreme Court and the second time, ten years later, as correspondent for the *New York Tribune.* These periods of residence gave him the

necessary background and inspiration to write political plays.
Those he wrote read easily and act naturally, but a friend
observed, "Audiences which have been convulsed with merri-
ment over his bright dialogue and grotesque situations could
have no idea of the toil and mental anxiety which had been
involved in the creation of his plays."[5]

Lloyd's partner, Sydney Rosenfeld was the George
S. Kaufman of his day. The Virginia-born writer served a
newspaper apprenticeship in New York. He became editor of
the English magazine, *Puck* when only nineteen years old.
By the time he died at seventy-six, Rosenfeld had written forty-
one plays and numerous musical comedies.

But the real attraction for the socially elite opening night
audience was William H. Crane. "There was a large contin-
gent of intimate friends of Mr. Crane [present]," the *New York
Tribune* critic observed the next day:

> The part of the Senator is a capital one for Mr. Crane.
> His incessant spirit carried the piece last night. Mr.
> Crane has fine power, acute knowledge of character,
> great comic vim and an adroit faculty for comic in-
> flection of the voice and for quiet satire. All these good
> gifts are shown in his new character, and therefore he
> will much augment his popularity in the play.[6]

Two others contributed greatly to the play's success. They
were Mrs. Georgiana Drew Barrymore, mother of Ethel,
Lionel, and John, and Miss Jane Stuart. Mrs. Barrymore was
an outstanding hit, one critic describing her as "handsome as a
picture, exquisitely dressed, brimming over with fun and an
actress to the tips of her fingers. She captured her audiences
and kept them in roars of laughter."[7] Miss Stuart, daughter of
the Commissioner of Public Works of New York, had the
sprightly role of Josie Armstrong, daughter of the Secretary of
State. As Josie, her word coinages anticipated those of Walter
Winchell. "Love is all a delusion, a scootlum of the brain,"
she tells an admirer. "A scootlum is a limpgoggle," she explains,

adding later that her hectic home life makes "existence simply one cross jigger." Something wonderful is "thrilloquent."

These were the things that pleased the 1890 audience. *The Senator* also included a Chinese character, conventional on the stage of that period. He was another of the popular one-dimensional foreign characters frequently portrayed in those days: the fat Dutchman, the brogue-ridden Irishman, the long-nosed Jew, the excitable Frenchman, the humorless Englishman. The Chinese character in *The Senator* always carried a note-book, into which he promptly recorded his impression of America. "The American government consists of four departments," he wrote. "The rolling of logs, the pulling of wires, the laying of pipe and the pulling of legs." He had good reason to record the "rolling of logs," for the Senator was rolling plenty to get the Denman claim passed. "Just make a memorandum," Senator Rivers told his secretary:

> The next session I've got to vote for a new court house for Senator Griffin, two new granite roof houses for Senator Allen and a new court house with mansard roof for Senator Dooley . . . talk about log rolling. I've rolled enough logs since I've been pushing the Denman claim to build a new railroad.

New York of *The Senator* still recalled the "Little Old New York" of song and legend. The theatrical district had its center around Broadway and Fourteenth Street. Uptown was Forty-second Street and way uptown where the substantial burghers lived was Harlem. Brooklyn was the home of churches and cemeteries, and civic and other doings there were recorded by the *New York Tribune* in a column called "Affairs in Brooklyn."

The theatres, the plays, and the players of those years have gone, and most of them have been forgotten. *The Senator* was housed in the Star Theatre at Broadway and Thirteenth Street. The theatre was torn down long ago to make way for office buildings. On the day *The Senator* opened, Robert Mantel

was thrilling audiences in *The Corsican Brothers* at the Fourteenth Street Theatre, Fourteenth Street and Sixth Avenue.
A rising young actress, who had gained quite some renown
within a comparatively short time, was performing in *Ingomar*
at the Fifth Avenue Theatre, Broadway and Twenty-eighth
Street. Her name was Julia Marlowe. Charles Hoyt's *A Midnight Bell* was enjoying a successful return engagement at the
Bijou Theatre, Broadway and Thirtieth Street, and the popular
operetta, *The Brigands* by Offenbach, was the feature at the
Grand Opera House, Eighth Avenue and Twenty-third Street.

Hugh J. Grant was Mayor of New York. Tammany Hall boss
Richard Croker was having his troubles with insurgent leadership rows in several districts and with the sermons of the Rev.
Dr. Charles Henry Parkhurst. Tammany Hall, which in 1945 was
staging an uncertain comeback with the election of William
O'Dwyer as mayor, was, in 1890, at a low ebb. Recent state
elections had gone overwhelmingly against the Hall, and committee memberships announced by the New York State Senate
and Assembly Republican leaders on January 13 did nothing to
assuage Tammany's unhappy state.

*   *   *   *   *   *   *

The Broadway of *State of the Union* was quite a different
street from that of *The Senator*. New York by now had become
the leading metropolis of the nation and perhaps of the world.
Skyscrapers made canyons of the city's streets; rapid transit
was living up to its name with fast-moving street buses and
underground subways replacing the slow-moving trolleys of the
earlier day. The "horseless-carriage" had come to stay; stream-
lined autos had replaced the pleasure carriages, and quick-start-
ing auto trucks, the plodding dobbins of the milk-wagon.

Mayor Fiorello LaGuardia—he of "the hat," the diminutive
barrel build, and the fire-chasing enthusiasm—ruled New York

with a temperamental and capable hand. He was soon to give way to Mayor-elect William O'Dwyer and a newly organized Tammany Hall. But the city residents were less concerned with municipal affairs than with the atom bomb and relations with Russia. The theatre district had also changed. The entertainment world had moved into the Times Square area, and new faces, new plays, and new theatres had taken the place of the old. *Life with Father,* a period piece of "Little Old New York," was in its seventh year at the Empire Theatre at Fortieth Street and Broadway. *I Remember Mama, The Late George Apley, Up in Central Park,* and *The Red Mill* also recalled the earlier days, each with a modern touch. New York was jerked rudely into the war period with *The Rugged Path,* and closed its eyes somewhat by enjoying *The Voice of the Turtle. Oklahoma, Carousel,* and *Bloomer Girl* were entertaining those who fifty-five years earlier would have gone to a minstrel show.

Moving pictures, unknown to entertainment seekers in 1890, were helping make Broadway "the Great White Way." They brought with them huge and palatial theatres: the Paramount, Roxy's, Strand, and Capitol among others. Sound pictures had long ago replaced silent films, and technicolor was no longer a curiosity. Shirley Temple, a child star more than thirty years after *The Senator* opened, had grown up and was being kissed on the screen for the first time—jolting the middle-aged into the realization that they were no longer young. The change in singing techniques from 1890 to 1945 was personified by Frank Sinatra, whose engagement at the Paramount Theatre was marked by numerous "bobby-soxers" swooning in the aisles as he sang, "Nancy," "Falling in Love with Love," and "It All Depends on You."

State of the Union also emphasized the passing years by its sophisticated approach, clever dialogue, and outspoken study of the contemporary political scene. Howard Lindsay and Russel Crouse, authors of *Life With Father* and other hits, wrote the play. They had met in 1934 after Crouse had written a musical comedy about doings on a pleasure ship. But before the show went into rehearsal the "Morro Castle" fire disaster had occurred, and the musical was shelved. Crouse and his backers were reluctant to lose the fruits of months of work. A mutual friend introduced Crouse to Lindsay. The two men rewrote Crouse's book, which was produced as *Anything Goes* and became a smash musical comedy hit.

The two writers came to the theatre by devious paths. Lindsay, an experienced actor, had left Harvard to go on the stage. He studied one year at the American Academy of Dramatic Arts, spent four years touring with a road company, and five years with Margaret Anglin's repertory company in New York. During World War I he served overseas and returned to write successful plays, the most popular before his partnership with Crouse being *She Loves Me Not* (1933). Crouse was a former Ohio newspaperman who served in the Navy during World War I. On his discharge he decided to try his luck on Broadway, writing three books and two musicals. One musical was *Hold Your Horses,* written for the popular comedian, Joe Cook.

Lindsay and Crouse were started on *State of the Union* in 1944 through a suggestion from Helen Hayes that they write a play about a presidential candidate. The idea took root, and after eighteen months of work, the writers brought *State of the Union* to New York. Two well-known moving pictures stars were featured in the play. Ralph Bellamy, who appeared on the New York stage before going to Hollywood in 1931, played the role of presidential candidate Grant Matthews. Matthews' sharp-tongued and idealistic wife, Mary, was portrayed by Ruth Hussey, a Pembroke College graduate who had also been on the Broadway stage before going to Hollywood in 1937.

State of the Union was inspired by Wendell Willkie, just as Senator Plumb had furnished the inspiration for *The Senator.* But the resemblance ended there. *State of the Union,* critical, though not cynical, had a message for its audiences. It called upon Americans to take politics away from the politicians and into their own hands. Matthews tells Mary after deciding to withdraw from the race for president that his withdrawal "doesn't mean I'm out of politics. Nobody can afford to be out of politics. I'm going to be yelling from the sidelines; you've got to be yelling; everybody's got to be yelling. I'm going to be in there asking questions, and I'm going to see that people get the answers."

The play charged politicians with preventing candidates from doing what they want to do and from saying what should be said. Political boss James Conover warns Matthews as the latter sets out on a preliminary speaking tour to "keep whatever you have to say pretty general. Don't be too specific." A cartoon in a Washington newspaper during the 1948 pre-Republican convention period indicated how most candidates followed this advice. The sketch has a Senator Snort telling two newspapermen, "What other candidate can match my fearless record—just name an issue that I've been afraid to dodge."

The professional politician also advises Matthews to avoid Minneapolis. "I wouldn't speak there," Conover suggests. "You might stir up trouble. That's Stassen territory. The local boys would resent it and you might start a backfire." When Stassen announced in 1947 that he was going into Ohio for delegates, followers of the late Senator Robert Taft charged the former Minnesota governor with "splitting the party's unity."

State of the Union insists that the American people will respond to a candidate who tells them what he stands for, regardless of the consequences. "Don't kid yourself," newspaperman Spike Mac Manus says. "This guy does something to people. I've been on a lot of campaigns. They don't shake hands with Grant to say they've shaken hands with him. They're up there with a light in their eyes—they practically mob him." When Willkie toured the country in the months preceding the Republican convention of June, 1940, he produced similar reactions. "Willkie Clubs" spontaneously sprang up everywhere. They weren't the carefully nurtured clubs professional politicians organize for their candidates. They were closely-knit groups manned by amateurs who had a crusading light in their eyes.

The plot revolves around Grant Matthews, a self-made wealthy business man who has caught the imagination of the people and the attention of the political bosses by his outspoken comments on current domestic and foreign issues. Influential James Conover sees Grant as a potential presidential candidate and enlists the help of other important political leaders in the drive to nominate him. He appeals to Kay Thorndyke, newspaper publisher who is having an affair with Grant, and Mary, Matthews' estranged wife, to bury their rivalry and take part in the campaign. Conover urges Mary to make the speaking tour with her husband, pointing out that Americans insist on their presidential candidates being happily married and taking their wives along on these trips. He tells Mary the most important thing is to kill the gossip about Matthews and Kay Thorndyke. "We haven't got a chance unless we do," Conover declares. "The American people like to think of a married candidate as happily married. They want to see him and his wife together. They like to see them make the campaign together. It's an American tradition."

Conover's move proves a mistake, for Mary not only blasts the politicians for their self-seeking motives but finally opens Matthews' eyes to the degree he has deteriorated in pursuing the nomination. Grant eventually rebels against the continual demands that he compromise his principles, and he tells Conover that he is going to speak out and that he is no longer a candidate for president:

> I promised myself when I went into this that I'd appeal to the best in the American people. The only advice I've ever had from any of you was to appeal to their worst . . . We have some damn good men. There are some wonderful men in the Senate and in the House, too—Democrats and Republicans. But damn it, Jim,

there aren't enough of them to shape party politics.
So, to get votes, both parties are out to buy the American public. I can't do that, Jim. So I'm afraid I can't
be of any use to you.

State of the Union, which later became a popular moving picture, was called by the *New York Herald Tribune* critic Howard
Barnes "a literate and amusing comedy which speaks out loud
about things that need stating." He adds that the authors "have
written wisely and well" and have "fashioned a political satire
which is as good humored as it is pertinent."[8]
Professor Quinn observed that the playwrights had taken an
important step by the "breaking down of a cliche concerning
political plays. . . . Heretofore producers had been afraid to
mention the actual names of parties for fear of offending someone. How much more reality was given to the use of 'Democrat'
and 'Republican'—and no one was offended."[9]
Before 1890 there were comparatively few plays dealing
with political subjects. Professor Quinn, widely regarded as one
of the country's leading authorities on the American drama, in
his *A History of the American Drama from the Civil War to the
Present Day* observed, "We have not had many serious studies of
our politics, largely because of managerial dread of controversial subjects."[10] But there were enough plays before 1890 to
provide a base upon which later dramatists could build. Such
productions as J. Horatio Nichols' *The Essex Junto* (1802);
Penn Smith's *The Eighth of January* (1829); George L. Aiken's
popular dramatization of Harriet Beecher Stowe's novel, *Uncle
Tom's Cabin* (1852); Edward Harrigan's *The Mulligan Guard
Nominee* (1880); and Charles Hale Hoyt's *A Case of Wine*
(1882), were forerunners of the twentieth century political
drama.
The building of such a genre was helped immensely by the
numerous sources of information available to the public after
1890. Newspaper circulations zoomed to incredible figures
during the decade in response to the flamboyant methods pur-

sued by Joseph Pulitzer and William Randolph Hearst. Working men and women who had never read a newspaper before snatched eagerly at the spectacular journalism provided by Pulitzer and Hearst. Then, in the first ten years of the twentieth century, came equally colorful articles in popular magazines exposing unsavory phases of American life. These skyrocketed magazine sales. When newspaper and magazine circulations began to level out, the moving picture brought a new impetus. This was especially true of newsreel shorts, with their visual information about happenings in foreign lands. Then followed the radio, which brought news from distant lands into the home and shop. And now there is television to bring a pictorial presentation of world events into the living room.

"Sharpening news emphasis kept everyone at least a little informed on the trend of events, brought establishment of news theatres in some large cities and became a prime instrument for influencing public opinion," the historian Jeannette Nichols observed in her *Twentieth Century United States* survey of American life.

These sources of information naturally gave the average man a knowledge of world affairs his forefathers did not possess. They inevitably raised the level of his interests and undoubtedly influenced dramatists to write plays having political plots. Before 1890, with notable exceptions such as *Uncle Tom's Cabin,* political plays were a managerial gamble for the prospective audience was sharply limited. But after that date the many new sources of information added an ever increasing number of people conversant with political affairs, and playwrights and producers were anxious to take advantage of this fact. A *State of the Union* produced in the nineteenth century probably would not have lasted a week. Brought to Broadway near the mid twentieth century, its 765 consecutive performances made the play the forty-fifth longest running show in the history of the New York stage.

2

POLITICS,
MELODRAMA, AND
THE NINETIES

O N A summer evening in 1891 an American
journalist in Havana looked down from his hotel room upon a
small park. There he saw a group of men, carrying guns and
other weapons, preparing to drill. "Those are the Volunteers,
the most vengeful of all the men here who wear the uniform, or
rather the livery, of the mother country," he later wrote.

> They are not soldiers, but clerks with business houses,
> waiters in restaurants, barkeepers, etc., of Spanish
> descent or birth, who love to gloat over the natives by
> a show of military power and insult them with their
> guns and by the assumption of authority. In Havana
> alone there are 14,000 of them, and they are masters.
> They hate the Cubans, and are hated by them in
> return.[1]

The smoldering hatred between the natives of Cuba and their
Spanish overlords was eventually to erupt into a bloody civil war.
For the Cubans the insurrection grew out of long years of abuse
—years of paying incredibly heavy taxes, of cruel rule, of

15

notorious flouting of the islanders' wishes. In the city of
Havana not one Cuban was on the Board of Aldermen; censor-
ship of the press was absolute; Spaniards were carried on the
pension roles so many years one writer commented "it would
appear that the granting of a pension insures immortality."[2]

The rising tide of native resentment exploded on February 24,
1895, when the Cubans, under the leadership of Maximo Gomez
and Antonio Maceo, revolted against their Spanish masters. An
estimated 60,000 rebels —"one-third well armed, one-third
tolerably equipped, and the others very poorly provided,"[3] —
conducted a guerrilla warfare that by the end of 1896 gave them
control of "three-fourths of Cuba inland."[4] In October of that
year Martinez Campos, Spanish Governor-General of Cuba, was
replaced by General Valeriano Weyler, whose reputation for
ruthlessness in warfare was widespread. He quickly lived up to
his reputation. Within a short time more than 400,000 natives
were thrown into "reconcentrados," the Cuban version of World
War II concentration camps. They were "penned in like cattle"
and "deprived of home and with little clothing, they lay upon
the earth, with foul air, foul water and foul food, until
emaciated and diseased, they died like flies."[5]

The American people responded quickly and angrily to
newspaper reports of these atrocities. Festivals were held to
raise money for the rebels. Public figures demanded that something drastic be done. Theodore Roosevelt contemptuously declared that President McKinley's policy of inaction showed he
had "no more backbone than a chocolate eclair."[6] The theatre
produced plays about Cuba and Spain calculated to arouse the
emotions of their audiences. Tension between Spain and the
United States rapidly grew more taut. Two dramatists, sent
to Havana by the noted theatrical producer, William A. Brady,
to gather material for a play, had a harrowing experience. The
evening following their arrival they went for a ride in a carriage.

> On the return suddenly a faint hissing was heard on the
> sidewalk, which was repeated and accentuated from

the opposite side. The driver looked around nervously and urged on his horse. Two men darted into the road and ran after the carriage, hissing as they went. They were joined by others. The crowd commenced to murmur. The men in pursuit cried out 'Muerte Americano. Muerte tio Sam,' and called to the driver to stop. Instead, he whipped his horse unmercifully, and turning sharply into a side street, comparatively deserted, succeeded in outrunning the mob, and reached the hotel in safety.[7]

The Last Stroke, by I. N. Morris opened at the Star Theatre on March 23, 1896. Cuban flags were hung throughout the theatre; cries of "Cuba Libre" were heard time and again. The play's melodramatic plot revolves about an American fighting for the Cuban rebels, and a Spanish spy who has designs on the girl the American loves. The excited audience could barely contain itself during the performance. When the American consul on the stage said, "No, we don't want diplomacy. Where would America have been if we had had diplomacy instead of Bunker Hill," the audience rose to its feet and shouted approval. At the end of the second act a pretty girl threw a small Cuban flag on the stage. Immediately a grey-haired man in a box leaped to his feet and called for three cheers for Cuba. They were heartily given. A critic voiced the current feeling by declaring "the play does not pretend to literary distinction but it carries its atmosphere of thrill and heroism cleverly, and must prove most successful so long as the Cuban enthusiasm continues to circulate in the veins of America."[8]

A year earlier H. Guy Carleton's *Ambition* had been performed at the Fifth Avenue Theatre with Nat Goodwin in the leading role. It was a political drama whose thinly disguised sympathy for the Cuban insurrectionists appealed to the audience. The play was considered by many to be a rebuke to the course President Cleveland was then pursuing. One critic dissented from the favorable verdict on the play and on Goodwin's performance. He said the story mixes up the

Sugar trust, the independence of Cuba, international
relations and a presidential nomination in an inex-
tricable and unintelligible hash. Common sense, custom, everything is sacrificed for the sake of winning
a laugh, or a little applause for the cheapest kind of
'jingo' sentiment.[9]

But he was in the minority, for contemporary American feeling
towards Cuba refused to allow other considerations to inter-
fere with its expressions of sympathy and partisanship. Other
than artistic values invaded the theatre in this area; art bowed
before politics in the race for audience popularity. Among the
plays inspired by the situation were *Cuba* (1896), and *For
Liberty and Love* (1897), both replete with spies, love, and
sympathy for the rebels' cause.

*   *   *   *   *   *   *

"All women are not always lovely, and the wild women never
are," an anti-suffrage leader wrote in 1891. "Political firebrands
and moral insurgents, they are especially distasteful, warring as
they do against the best traditions, the holiest functions, and
the sweetest qualities of their sex."[10]

Woman suffrage and prohibition—these were two emotional
domestic issues of the political scene in the 1890's. Partisans
substituted emotion for reason, and practical politicians were
probably more fearful because of that fact. During these years
most easterners viewed woman suffrage as "an aberration of the
wild and woolly West."[11] Wyoming, in 1890, was the first state
to give women the right to vote and hold office, though as a
territory it had given them those rights as early as 1869.
Colorado followed suit in 1893, and Utah and Idaho in 1896.
But distaff demands for franchise equality were not received
favorably by most of the nation. Perhaps the strongest opposition came from the women themselves. Mrs. Lynn Linton
declared "the clamor for political rights is woman's confession

of sexual enmity" and predicted that "women in politics meant the disruption of the home."[12] Another enemy of woman suffrage was so unchivalrous as to declare that all females seeking the vote were "ugly women, old maids and disappointed wives."[13]

But the women had their defenders. An Army general listed the arguments against woman suffrage and termed them frivolous. "Women, it is said," he wrote, "are weak, foolish, frivolous, dependent; they can't fight; they have other and more important duties to attend to; they have all the rights they ought to have now; they are protected by men's votes, and so forth, but the real and only reason is they are women."[14]

The theatre hardly touched the subject. Where it did, the treatment was one of comedy. Charles H. Hoyt's *A Contented Woman* (1897), expressed the popular feeling on the subject. His comedy, written especially for his beautiful second wife, Mrs. Caroline Miskel-Hoyt, has a wife enter a mayoralty contest against her husband because she incorrectly sewed a button on his shirt. The usual humorous complications, with a political background, take place before peace is restored to the Holme household.

*   *   *   *   *   *   *

In December, 1890, a Norwich, Vermont, restaurant owner was found guilty of violating the state prohibition law and sentenced to serve sixty years in jail. It was a stiff sentence for selling 715 glasses of beer, but George F. Kibling was a victim not so much of the law as of the crusading prohibition advocates behind it. These advocates were intensely aware of the political value their movement had. As early as 1884 their small but vital voting power changed a presidential election. In that year the Prohibition Party nominated John Pierce St. John, governor of Kansas from 1879 to 1883, for president. His defeat was a foregone conclusion, but his vote proved that the Prohibition

Party had to be carefully considered by both major parties in future campaigns. "St. John was often referred to, after the campaign of 1884, as 'the man who beat Blaine'; and it is questionable that his vote in New York deprived the Republican Party of votes enough to have changed the result in the electoral college."[15]

The enthusiasm of prohibition followers for their cause had a distinctively religious tinge. "A Prohibition convention has a very religious cast to it throughout," a contemporary observer said. "It is a custom to hold a prayer and praise meeting for several hours preceding the convention proper; and it is not unusual, in New York State, at least, for the delegates to hold enthusiastic prayer-meetings in the coaches of trains, much to the surprise of the other passengers."[16] Strong church support for prohibition was emphasized by the formation of the Anti-Saloon League, the Prohibition Party's political action committee, on June 4, 1893, in the First Congregational Church at Oberlin, Ohio.

Arguments for and against prohibition raged in the periodicals of the period, but it is doubtful if the drinking man was greatly disturbed. Local and state option were the goals of the day, and if a man lived in a dry community it did not take long to reach a wet one. But one person really concerned with the laws and their over-zealous enforcement was Charles Hoyt. A native of Concord, New Hampshire, Hoyt served two terms, 1892 and 1893, in that state's legislature. While there he became familiar with the Kibling case, and was so incensed that he wrote *A Temperance Town* (1893), in protest. Within the sharp and sometimes melodramatic comedy, Hoyt laid bare the tactics of prohibition followers during the period. One of the best known, Carry Nation, became the subject of a play, *Carry Nation* (1932), many years later. Her penchant for wrecking saloons by using an axe on the furniture was a highlight of the play.

2. POLITICS, MELODRAMA, AND THE NINETIES

The religious basis of Hoyt's play was expressed in the person of the Rev. Ernest Hardman. He was one of those seeking to trap the leading character, Fred Oakhurst, owner of a drug store, into selling liquor illegally. Oakhurst was finally induced to sell whiskey on the plea it was for the buyer's dying mother. Once the deal was completed, the buyer turned on Oakhurst and had him arrested. In the fabulous 1920's, prohibition agent Izzy Einstein used similar tricks to trap unsuspecting speakeasy owners. Once, Einstein later wrote, he became a football player to accomplish his goal:

> On a Saturday in November, I got together a little group of good men and true, and we rigged ourselves out in football togs, smeared with fresh mud. And faces to match. In this regalia, we burst into the place announcing with a whoop that now, with the last game of the season over and won, we could break training. Would any saloonkeeper refuse drinks to a bunch of football players in that state of mind? This fellow didn't anyhow. And he discovered that his season was ended, too.[17]

Perhaps the most important aspect of Hoyt's play was his view of the moral problem underlying the issue. A leading character, Launcelot Jones, declares, "If a man ain't born a man, you don't make him one by law. When I quit drinking, I'll do it because I want to, and not to please the whim of a lot of cranks like you. As long as you try to reform me by law, I'll drink. And I'll get it, too, and no darn country legislature can stop me, either." This was the moral problem facing prohibition in the 1890's; it was the same moral problem that made prohibition enforcement impossible during the 1920's.

*   *   *   *   *   *   *

Dramatists of the decade seized upon other political situations as the bases of their slight plots. One issue having a

mid-twentieth century ring was the fear of some Americans
about the increasing Catholic influence on American government during the 1890's. They were worried about the presence
of the great James Cardinal Gibbons in nearby Baltimore. In
The Capitol (1895), by Augustus Thomas, a priest asks a
friend whether, "with the only American cardinal at Baltimore,
with the Papal legates residing here, the inference is inevitable
that the Church of Rome attempts to influence American legislation." To which query the friend answers, "That inference is
inevitable." But an historian of the period later noted "Cardinal
Gibbons of Baltimore was supporting the American Constitu-
tion and the doctrine of separation of church and state with
an enthusiasm which tended to make the American Church
national."[18]

The play, which deals primarily with the efforts of a
representative to become a senator, touches on the religious
problem when the question of appointing an ambassador to
Italy arises. The logical man for the post is a Catholic, but
intolerant pressures force the eventual choice of a Protestant
after the Catholic aspirant withdraws in favor of harmony.

The press has always been an important factor in the nation's
political life. In 1891 Augustus Pitou, noted actor and producer of the period, wrote *The Power of the Press,* in collabora-
tion with G. H. Jessup. It showed how the press used this power
when a newspaper favored a pardon for a man unjustly sentenced to jail.

Many political plays of the 1890's centered around elections
and the campaigns of candidates in office. *A Tammany Tiger*
(1896), by A. Gratton Donnelly, revolves about two men running for office who are in love with the same girl. For us, the
best part of the play lies in its historical sidelights. "A true picture of Madison Square on an election night is reproduced in the
third act," a critic observed. "The big bulletin with its calcium
light spreading the returns is also in evidence."[19] For a middle
twentieth century electorate which receives its election returns

mainly by radio in the home or at comfortable clubs, this is a record of the past and should take its place alongside the descriptions of torchlight parades and platform debates between candidates.

McFadden's Row of Flats (1897), by E. W. Townsend, based on a series of popular dialect stories written by the author for the *New York Journal,* still provides a vivid picture of Irish life in New York during the 1890's. The unimportant plot revolves around the efforts of Tim McFadden and Jacob Baumgartner, opponents for the office of alderman, to induce Terrence McSwatt to vote and break a tie. McFadden makes love to Mrs. Murphy, convinces her McSwatt would make a good husband for her daughter, Mary, and receives McSwatt's vote in return for his good efforts. *McSorley's Twins*, (1897), by an unknown author, also used the big city Irish neighborhood background and an aldermanic campaign for a musical comedy having "catchy airs and fetching dances and clever specialties."[20]

The Village Postmaster (1898), by Alice E. Ives and Jerome H. Eddy, is a refreshing comedy set in a small New Hampshire town. Seth Huggins, postmaster and owner of the town's general store, promises that his daughter will marry the political boss provided Huggins is nominated to the state legislature. Through a series of double-dealings by the boss, Huggins calls off the marriage and decides he would rather have his daughter happy than be elected to the legislature.

How political influence can be used to frustrate justice is the theme of *New York* (1897), by Andrew C. Wheeler and Edward M. Alfriend. The main thread of the complicated plot reveals how Dr. Follin Sanger shields his wife, Kate, who has killed her betrayer. Dr. Sanger, a power in city politics, is able to prevent detective John Wilder from bringing Kate to justice until near the end of the play. Then, when Wilder has the means to force Kate's arrest, a sentimental appeal to him carries the day. The play, based on a novel by Wheeler, *The Toltec Cup*, had a good run.

A musical comedy using politics as background was *Kate Kip, Buyer*, by Glen MacDonough (1898). The slight plot related the efforts of two towns to be chosen as the state capital by the legislature. The casting of May Irwin enlivened the play. Miss Irwin, popular and irrepressible, "beamed upon the audience and sang coon songs. The audience beamed back and applauded soulfully."[21] Her most popular song was "When Yo' Ain't Got No Money Yo' Needn't Come Around." The musical, a critic stated, had further merit, for "even the Federation of Women's Club would have to admit the play was perfectly clean."[22]

The plays of the 1890's reveal the widespread political immaturity of the audience to whom the playwrights were appealing. Though there were plays on the Cuban situation, woman suffrage, and prohibition, none of them came to hard grips with these problems. The plays about the Cuban rebellion were primarily ones using the explosive international question as an excuse for presenting a melodramatic plot. These plots, with very little effort, could substitute any other situation and be as effective theatrically. In contrast to such plays as *Watch on the Rhine* (1941), and *There Shall be No Night* (1940), melodramas like *The Last Stroke* indicate an almost childish immaturity in their approach to grave problems.

There was also a complete ignoring of current issues or personalities in plays dealing with elections. Dramatists merely used political situations and themes as a convenient base on which to build a plot. A serious study of politics by the drama had not yet arrived. That was to be the task of playwrights in the coming twentieth century.

3

THE FIRST DECADE

PENNSYLVANIA Avenue opposite the
White House was crowded with people the night of February 24,
1902. They watched as carriages drawn by prancing horses
swept through the gates and circled the impressive driveway
before the Executive Mansion. They gaped and whispered as
important looking men and splendidly gowned women stepped
from the carriages to attend a dinner for Prince Henry of
Prussia. He had been sent as a special emissary to Washington
by his brother, Emperor Wilhelm II. It was the first time a
Hohenzollern had visited the United States bearing official
greetings from his Imperial Majesty overseas.

Americans were thrilled with the visit. It was only ten years
earlier that European countries had accorded the United States
diplomatic recognition as a major power. Now a great con-
tinental nation had come courting Miss Columbia and seeking
the favor of Uncle Sam. This was in a very true sense America's
"coming out" party. Much had happened in the intervening
years to warrant Europe's changed attitude toward the United
States. One event that enhanced America's world prestige was
the action of President Cleveland in forcing England to negotiate

with the United States over settling the boundary dispute between
Venezuela and British Guiana. America's firm stand against
England in 1895 and the eventual settlement of the dispute in
1899 told the world a new power had come into the international
family. Even more important in this respect was the one-sided
victory of the United States over Spain. If proof were needed
that America had become a first-class power, here it was.

In the wake of these successes, the United States embarked on
a program of imperialism beginning in the last years of the nineteenth century and continuing into the first decade of the new
century. The historian, Jeannette Nichols observed that:

> Improvement was a prominent objective among bene-
> ficent persons . . . protection was the object of military
> strategists . . . prestige was the object of those who
> proclaimed that the United States had 'come of age'
> as an acknowledged world power . . . profit was the
> object of producers and investors. With these objec-
> tives, others became entangled, heterogeneous, oppor-
> tunistic.[1]

The results of this imperialism soon appeared. Around the
Caribbean the countries of Cuba, Puerto Rico, Santa Domingo,
Haiti, Nicaragua, and the Virgin Islands became either depend-
encies or protectorates of the United States. In 1903, Theodore
Roosevelt "took" Panama. Dr. Nichols noted the treaty that
Panama signed, giving it $10,000,000 in gold and $25,000,000
annually, enabled the United States to "build and fortify a canal
and to possess a zone ten miles wide across the isthmus. The
United States promised to maintain Panama's independence but
received other rights which virtually made Panama a pro-
tectorate."[2]

This course of empire did not please all Americans. It greatly
displeased many as evidenced in several plays on Broadway.
William Jennings Bryan and Adlai Stevenson made it one of the
major issues of the 1900 campaign, but William McKinley and
Theodore Roosevelt won the fight. The nation was fascinated

by its new role as a great power and gave imperialism hearty approval. But among those opposing the new trend was a young newspaper correspondent, George Ade. In July, 1900, Ade went to the Far East where he ran into stories from other correspondents about the strange negotiations American representatives were having with Jadji Jamalol Ki-Ram, the Sultan of Sulu or Jolo, an archipelago of 400 islands forming the southern central portion of the Philippines. The Moros were the dominant race on the islands, and Ki-Ram was "an untamed Moro chieftain who was trying to adapt himself to Uncle Sam's rules and by-laws without giving up any of his beloved native customs."[3] One custom Ki-Ram did not give up easily was polygamy. When pressed to do so, it was rumored that he had offered to settle the problem by taking two small wives for one large wife. Ade returned to write *The Sultan of Sulu*, called by Mark Sullivan "one of the best of American musical comedies of any time."[4] The comedy was a satire on America's imperialistic ventures, particularly of our country's desire for prestige and its self-satisfaction with the American way of life. One song illustrates the mood of the comedy:

> No longer than a hundred years ago
> We lived in humble style,
> Our methods were particularly slow,
> Our manners juvenile.
> Not counted in the list of powers,
> Or looked upon as worth a rap,
> But now what place as proud as ours
> For we intend to fill the map.
> To fill the map,
> To fill the map,
> To fill the map.

Perhaps Ade was thinking, in the opening scene, of some acquisitions the United States made as a result of the Spanish-American War. In the play, a visiting American battleship first sends a shell screaming into the native village and then lands a force under Lieutenant Budd. Budd immediately takes over the island, informing the natives that the United States now owns the land.

"How come?" he is asked.

"We bought it off the Spanish," Budd replies.

"But the Spanish didn't own the island," a bewildered native protests.

"That is exactly why they were so willing to sell out," Budd informs him. "We paid $20,000,000 for you."

Now, Budd tells the conquered leader, we are going to make you a governor, "the noblest work of a campaign committee," instead of a sultan. And in order to be sure he will govern correctly in the American way, Budd hands the sultan a volume on "the laws and customs of Arkansas" as a guide. It isn't long before other American customs creep into the island picture. The sultan objects to tipping his colored slaves, but Budd warns him, "Be careful, Governor. Don't antagonize the colored vote." Nor should one forget the union vote, he advises, for the island is quickly oganized by union workers. *The Sultan of Sulu* ran for more than 200 successive performances that season. It opened December 29, 1902, at Wallack's Theatre. Years later Ade met Ki-Ram again, but the writer did not tell the Moro chieftain that he had been the central figure of a musical comedy.

*   *   *   *   *   *

By the time Theodore Roosevelt became president in 1901, a noted historian declared that the United States had become to many people " a government of the corporations, by the corporations and for the corporations."[5] Wealth had stepped in to run municipal, state, and national government; the laws seeking to hold trusts, railways and big business in check were being openly evaded, and the nation was permeated with a rampant materialism penetrating every branch of industry and society. A "public be damned" attitude on the part of big business and its minions in public life was indicative of the times. Lincoln

Steffens only a few years later pointed out that while the ordinary businessman was too occupied to take part in politics, the big businessman was "very busy and very business-like in politics. He is a self-righteous fraud, this big businessman," Steffens declared. "He is the chief source of corruption, and it were a boon if he would neglect politics."[6]

The reaction to this was the "muckraking period," which ran its high tide from 1902 to 1908. Three important articles appeared in the January, 1903 issue of *McClure's Magazine*: Ida Tarbell's, "The History of the Standard Oil Company"; Ray Stannard Baker's, "The Right to Work," and Steffens', "The Shame of Minneapolis."

"We did not plan it so," S. S. McClure, publisher of the magazine, said later. "It is a coincidence that this number contains three arraignments of American character such as should make every one of us stop and think."[7] Coincidence or not, McClure was alert enough to notice the responsive public reaction. The muckraking era, a period of exposure of American business practices by magazine writers, had begun. Ida M. Tarbell's *The History of the Standard Oil Company* appeared in 1904 and is generally regarded as the first important book in this area. Other works to follow Miss Tarbell's were Thomas W. Lawson's *Frenzied Finance*, 1904; Upton Sinclair's *The Jungle*, an exposition of unsanitary conditions in the meat packing houses of Chicago, 1905; Ray Stannard Baker's *The Railroads on Trial*, 1905; and David Graham Phillips' *The Treason of the Senate*, 1906.

Roosevelt was the man who gave the exposurists the title "muckraker," which they later wore as a mark of distinction. He first used the term at a dinner of the Gridiron Club, an organization of Washington newspapermen, on March 17, 1906. The Club's annual dinner, completely off the record, is frequently addressed by the President or candidates for the presidential nomination. The reaction to the term, taken from the man with the muckrake in Bunyan's *Pilgrim's Progress*, was so favorable

that the phrase-minded Roosevelt used it publicly at the dedica-
tion of the House Office Building on April 14, 1906. The title
stuck to all exposurists, but Dr. Nichols warned that "differences
must not be overlooked. The factual Steffens, unlike Lawson
and his tribe, was supplying home truth which was sadly lacking
in current texts on American government. With him it was
special privilege, whether applied to big business or little business, which was the basic evil."[8]

Ida M. Tarbell was one of those whose facts could be trusted.
She first broached the idea to McClure in 1890 of using the story
of a typical trust to illustrate how and why the clan grew. Why
not, he suggested, use "the greatest of them all—the Standard Oil
Company?"[9] The original plan called for 25,000 words divided
into three installments. The completed job ran to nineteen installments, and when published in book form filled two volumes.
The articles started in *McClure's Magazine* the latter part of
1902 and were completed in 1904, when they were published
in book form.

One side result of the series was Charles Klein's play, *The Lion
and the Mouse*. The playwright was inspired by Miss Tarbell's
work to dramatize the trust question and did it so convincingly
that the play became one of Broadway's all-time successes,
running for 686 performances. After seeing the show, George
M. Cohan said to Sam Harris, "Well, Charles Klein might as
well go shoot himself. He'll never write another hit as big
as that."[10]

Klein wasn't so sure of the play's success, and particularly of
how it would be received on the road. "I won't be satisfied until
I hear every seat in the house but one is taken," he told his friend
William C. DeMille.

"Which one?" DeMille asked.

"The one behind the post," Klein replied. "Nobody wants
that."[11]

Klein, an English-born law student who came to America to
write plays, had the satisfaction of hearing a critic call *The Lion*

and the Mouse "the most typically American play of the last ten years."[12] At least two of his other plays, *The Third Degree* and *The Music Master*, were great hits. By 1909 he had made more than $500,000 from his plays. He was at the top of his fame and improving in technique and understanding when he went down with the "Lusitania" in 1915. In *The Lion and the Mouse,* Klein dramatized the relationship of captains of industry to Washington politics, and the influence of the first upon the second. That the love interest got the upper hand toward the end of the play does not affect its value as a commentary on conditions during the period. The plot revolves around the love of a magnate's son, Jefferson Ryder, for Shirley Rossmore, daughter of a judge who had ruled against the trusts in an important action and was now marked for impeachment. Shirley, whose relationship to Judge Rossmore is unknown to the Ryder family, has written a book, *The Great American Octopus,* obviously a stage counterpart of *The History of the Standard Oil Company.* She takes a position in the Ryder household, charms all its members until the magnate, John Burkett Ryder, calls off impeachment proceedings in the United States Senate.

Roosevelt said in 1906 that E. H. Harriman, the railroad magnate, had boasted "he could buy a sufficient number of Senators and Congressmen or state legislators to protect his interests, and when necessary he could buy the Judiciary."[13] David Graham Phillips in his *Cosmopolitan* articles on "The Treason of the Senate" charged that seventy-five of the ninety members of that body served the interests of the railroad, beef and sugar trusts, the Standard Oil Company, and the steel monopolists before they did those of the public. Klein dramatizes this situation in two ways. He first has Ryder initiate impeachment proceedings in the Senate against Judge Rossmore through Senator Roberts. After Shirley Rossmore has convinced Ryder to drop his antagonism, he calls Roberts in and tells him that the impeachment must be called off. Roberts, in dismay, stammers, "Ryder, it can't be done—we can't retreat now . . . we

can't march up a hill and march down again. . . . The United
States Senate is not the King of France . . . the Rossmore impeachment must go through."

"No," Ryder tells him, "The Senate must yield to public
opinion . . . we'll go together on a special train to Washington.
Don't you see it will be doing the proper thing, you know—
yielding to public opinion, and just think how easy it will make
it for your brother's Erie Canal proposition."

The alleged inside information captains of industry obtained
concerning Congressional action is developed in an exciting
scene. Ryder and his son, Jefferson, have had a disagreement
over the latter's feelings for Shirley. The father, irked by his
son's attitude, tells him to run along. "I have to study the advance report of the Inter-Railway Commerce Commission and
get it back to Washington tonight," he says.

His son is shocked. "Do you mean to say that you see it before
the Senate?" he asks.

"Take a tip from Washington, my boy," Ryder senior says,
"and jump with the cat. At present, I'm the cat."

Burkett Ryder was probably a composite of many captains of
industry, but Henry Rogers stands out as the nearest actual
prototype. Certainly the description of Burkett fits this identification. Rogers, called by Miss Tarbell "the first public relations
counsel of the Standard Oil Company," was about sixty years old
the first time she met him, "a striking figure, by all odds the
handsomest and most distinguished figure in Wall Street."[14]
Their meetings read like a chapter from a dime novel. The
Standard Oil Company had learned Miss Tarbell was going to
do a series of articles on the company's history, and the heads
had decided it would be best to have one of them confer with
her. Rogers was the one selected. The introduction was arranged by Mark Twain and S. S. McClure, the first meeting taking place in January, 1902, at Rogers' home at 26 East 57th
Street. Subsequent meetings were held in Rogers' office at 26
Broadway. Miss Tarbell never saw anyone but Rogers and his

private secretary at those meetings. She met the secretary near a little-used entrance of the office building. They slipped through an empty courtyard into a deserted hallway, and went furtively up to the magnate's office. Here the two fenced through innumerable meetings, Miss Tarbell seeking for the information necessary for her project, and Rogers trying to put the best light on what he gave her.

The stage meeting between Shirley Rossmore and Burkett bears a close resemblance to those described by Miss Tarbell in her autobiography. Even Burkett's astonishment at Miss Rossmore's characterization of a captain of industry as "the greatest criminal the world has ever produced" parallels Rogers' inability to understand Miss Tarbell's contempt for these leaders of industry. Rogers somehow expected admiration from the writer for the ruthless methods used by these titans of finance; Burkett likewise expected admiration instead of condemnation.

A theme which runs through many political plays, that men hold office at the pleasure of those who put them there, appears in *The Lion and the Mouse*. Ryder explains that Judge Rossmore's removal from the bench is a necessity, for "if this man goes back on the bench every paltry justice of the peace, every bench official will think he has a special mission to tear down the structure that hard work and capital has erected." Edmund Breese played John Ryder; Grace Ellison, Shirley Rossmore; and young Richard Bennett, Jefferson Ryder. Bennett was praised "for always being determined without ever indulging in heroics."[15]

*   *   *   *   *   *

Two plays directly concerned with life in Washington appeared during the decade. One was a musical comedy which poked fun at political goings-on in the Nation's Capital, and the other was a serious play about graft-laden bills in Congress.

Gus and Max Rogers were two of the best known musical comedy comedians of their day. Their farce was broad and aimed at "belly laughs," and their material fitted in with their approach. Their *Rogers Brothers In . . .* musical comedies were as popular during this period as the *Road To . . .* moving pictures of Bing Crosby and Bob Hope became some years later. *The Rogers Brothers in Washington* (1901), another in their long series of plays, reveals what the American people then thought of Congress. The musical comedy plot, by John J. McNally, is slight. By the terms of a will, Alf has to be elected to Congress as a Republican in a heavily Democratic district in order to marry Judge Bradley's niece. Gus and Max also decide to run for Congress. The campaign provides the line on which the jokes and situations are hung.

A running commentary on Congress persists through the comedy. "How would you like to be a member of Congress?" one comedian asks.

"I'd rather be something honest," the other replies. Gus and Max soon enter into a discussion of their platforms, "something where you tell everybody that you mean what you don't think." Campaign promises furnish the next subject.

Gus declares, "Imperialism is all right if it pays," and Max asserts his belief "in free silver, free gold, free speech, free schools, free lunch, free Ireland, and free seats in the park." Even the third-term issue raised its head in 1901—Gus heartily endorsing McKinley's "determination not to accept a third term."

Other issues appear pell mell in the swift succession of satiric comments. "Are you going to settle the Trust before you leave Congress?" Max asks Gus. On being told that he is, Max says, "You are going to stay there all your life, ain't you?" Even the pressure groups, represented here as in *State of the Union* are brought into the play by a woman who wants a contribution, and before Gus and Max can refuse, they have pledged a $200 donation to the Young Women's Rescue League. Another issue of the period in international politics was reciprocity. Gus gave his day a classic definition of it: "Reciprocity is where you give a man something you don't want in exchange for something that he doesn't need and is of no use to you."

The Sunday blue laws and the way they were evaded are suggested in the song, "Get Next to the Man with a Pull":

> If the owner you are of a neat little bar,
> Which on Sunday becomes a hotel,
> Where the sandwiches gay are of *papier mâché*
> And the celluloid crackers look swell,
> Some greenhorn policeman may camp on your trail,
> A new man who is not very foxy.
> But if you are next to a man with a pull,
> You can prove that the whiskey is moxie.

George Ade's *The County Chairman* was a genial study of small-town politics. In many respects this is the finest play on the subject yet to come out of the American drama. There is a charming love story, a graphic portrayal of a political boss, and a dramatic presentation of his methods woven into the play. With Maclyn Arbuckle taking the part of Jim Hackler, the political boss, and Willis P. Sweatnam running off with honors in the minor part of Sassafras, the play quickly became a hit. Produced November 24, 1903, at Wallack's Theatre, it has since become a part of those dramas that live in other periods than their own. *The County Chairman* was revived by the Players Club of New York, with Charles Coburn in the title role, on May 24, 1936 in honor of George Ade's seventieth birthday. Will Rogers starred in the moving picture version in 1935.

Jim Hackler, the central character, is a typical political boss. He knows all the tricks and uses them with complete cynicism. Hackler goes to the county convention determined that Tillford Wheeler shall be nominated to oppose Judge Rigby for prosecuting attorney. The convention opened, he later tells his followers in his home town, with everyone agreeing "on a harmony program an' then [we] started in to fight. First ballot about noon. Pomeroy 38, Jackson 35, Hackler 20."

"But Jim," a friend asks, "I didn't know you was a candidate."

Jim laconically replies that he wasn't, but said a few friends insisted on voting for him, "just enough to keep Jackson and Pomeroy from knockin' the persimmon." He then recounts the roll call of hung ballots, "15 ballots, 20—25—30—everybody tired an' hot, an' hungry, but too all-fired stubborn to give in."

About four o'clock that afternoon, with everybody hungry and tired and impatient to start for home, one of the other leaders comes to Hackler and says, "Jim, we need a compromise candidate."

The county chairman observes "it comes to me like a flash— Tillford Wheeler . . . well, we touched off the fireworks. There was an explosion, a stampede, an' a hurrah. An' when the dust was cleared away, Tillford Wheeler had 78 votes—Tillford Wheeler nominated."

In his volume on the 1920's, Mark Sullivan relates in detail how Warren G. Harding won the nomination for President. The big fight that year was between General Leonard Wood and Governor Frank O. Lowden of Illinois. As the Republican convention wore on, neither candidate could get a commanding lead over his opponent. Finally the leaders gathered at night in the now famous "smoke-filled room" to choose a compromise candidate. The tactics followed by Harding's campaign manager and by Hackler, one on a national and the other on a local level, were practically the same. The final result also proved equally gratifying to each.

In other ways, too, Hackler is the big-time politician writ small. Wheeler is upset about a pamphlet circulating through the county, "the most malicious pack of lies I ever read."

Jim takes the paper and tells him to read it again:

> It says you're a psalm singer and wear a white necktie. Well, will that hurt you with the Methodists and Baptists? It says you're an enemy of personal liberty. Won't that make votes for you among the temperance people? It says you've no property. Two-thirds of the voters are broke—they'll sympathize with you. That

kind of attack will do you good, and I knew it when I
sent it out.

Hackler is a true politician in his desire to win. Wheeler balks
at printing a story accusing Judge Rigby of stealing money be-
longing to an estate the Judge administered. "I don't want the
office if I can't get it by clean and dignified methods," Wheeler
declares.

"My boy," Hackler replies, "the day after election people
don't ask 'Did you make a clean and dignified contest?' The only
question is, 'Did you win?' That's politics—in a nutshell."

In Kaufman's *Of Thee I Sing* nearly thirty years later, Wintergreen's election to president is followed by a telegram of congratulations from his opponent, "Heartily congratulate you on
your splendid victory and charge fraud in Indiana, Illinois,
Nebraska, Montana, Washington, Ohio and Nebraska." At one
stage in *The County Chairman* the returns inspire a discouraged
Wheeler to say, "Jim we're done for. We can't carry those other
townships."

Hackler turns the remark away, "Pshaw, that's no way for a
politician to talk. Claim everything until the last precinct is in
and then holler 'fraud.' "

The hit of the show was not Maclyn Arbuckle, though he did
an exceptional job as Hackler, but Willis Sweatnam, the black-
face comedian of an earlier day. The story of how the latter
was hired for his role deserves retelling. During the years that
Ade was a Purdue University student, he frequented the theatre
at Lafayette, Indiana. One of his heroes was Willis Sweatnam,
who periodically passed through the town in a minstrel show.
During rehearsals for *The County Chairman*, director George
Marion told Ade that Sweatnam was in need of a job. "You
know," Ade said, "there's a ne'er-do-well white-trash character
in this play. Why couldn't I rewrite that part and make him a
black-face character? Then we could give Sweatnam a job."[16]
Never was a kind deed more fully repaid. Sweatnam as Sassafras
Livingstone for years attracted large crowds to the play.

* * * * * * *

Looking back on this century's first ten years, it is interesting to observe that the theatergoers liked music with their politics. No less than eight musical comedies dealing with political themes reached the Broadway stage. Of these more than half proved popular. *The Rogers Brothers in Washington*, already described, was one of the eight. George M. Cohan, who more than thirty years later was to star in *I'd Rather Be Right*, wrote, directed, and played in three of the eight shows—*The Governor's Son, Running for Office,* and *George Washington, Jr.*

It was *The Governor's Son* that enabled the dancing Cohans of the vaudeville circuit to make the big step to legitimate musical comedy. The play was fashioned out of a vaudeville skit the family had been playing for years, and when it landed on Broadway at the Savoy Theatre the night of February 25, 1901, papa Jerry J. Cohan, mother Helen F. Cohan, and sister Josephine Cohan were right up front with son George. The plot was inconsequential—the trouble a governor's son gets into and its political repercussions—and the reviews only halfhearted. But all agreed that George was a "real comedian . . . he made an undeniable hit last evening" and Josephine "earned much applause by her graceful dancing—in which she has few equals— and looked pretty and acted sweetly."[17]

George had better luck with *Running for Office* (1903). The plot was an old one. Two young people, who had never seen each other, were betrothed by their families. This situation was injected into the doings centering around a mayoralty campaign. George Cohan, as author, director, and actor, again carried off the honors. One critic observed that he was "a comedian of original methods and scores his points with an air of ease that is delightful."[18] Papa Cohan also scored a hit as a "prohibitionist who doesn't prohibit himself from taking an occasional drink." In the song hit of the show, "If I Were Only Mr. Morgan," the singer related the many things he would do if he were the financial tycoon.

Cohan ventured into new fields in 1906 with *George Washington, Jr.* The complicated plot has a Washington background, with bribery and corruption in the Senate as its major theme. It is interesting to observe that this was the year David Graham Phillips' articles on "The Treason of the Senate" were appearing in *Cosmopolitan.* It is not too far fetched an hypothesis to suggest that Cohan, ever alert to public taste, seized upon the popular interest aroused by these "muckraking" articles as the starting point of his plot. One reviewer had the acumen to point out that Cohan "seems fully to have established his theory of the melodramatic musical comedy."[19] But in breaking new paths "the song-and-dance man" did not forget his songs. Two of his most popular compositions, "You're a Grand Old Flag" (originally 'Rag') and "I Was Born in Virginia," were part of this hit show.

The popular new trend in musicals soon had many imitators. In April of the same year, Joseph E. Howard wrote *The District Leader,* which he called a "musical comedy-drama." The plot, unusually complicated, involved an election, a campaign manager who turns traitor on the eve of the election for state senator, an opium-drugged brother of the heroine, and a newspaperman who wins through for the right man. Howard's "imitation of either the Harrigan-and-Hart style of play or the later George M. Cohan concoctions," proved to be "simply a tiresome hash of incidents, characters and songs, poorly constructed and in general poorly played."[20]

Patsy in Politics must have been fun. This 1907 anonymous musical comedy places a stranded vaudeville troupe in a small New England town. It involves the troupe in an election campaign, with bellboy Patsy Bolivar of the hotel running against his boss for town supervisor, and further mixes things up by adding some hilarious early prohibition situations. The high point of the comedy is reached when a stuttering servant reports that the man whose vote would break the tie was "dead . . . drunk," with no one waiting long enough to hear the word "drunk." The hotel owner wins the election when the final report from Hog Hill shows that of the seven men eligible to vote, six were too drunk to vote and the seventh voted for hotel owner Hemlock. Women temperance advocates were satirized in the character of Jerusha Pickens. Billy B. Van, as Patsy Bolivar, made the most of his opportunities for comedy. Two hit songs from the play were "Back to Old Broadway" and "Much Obliged to You."

*   *   *   *   *   *   *

Three plays dealing with political pull during the decade were *The Next of Kin, The Power of Money,* and *A Citizen's Home.*

The Next of Kin (1909), was written by Charles Klein, author of *The Lion and the Mouse.* Its melodramatic plot showed how politically powerful lawyers were able to delay legal proceedings so long that a poor man could not win his case. Paula Marsh's uncle conspires with political boss Bascom Cooley to defraud Paula of an estate left by her father. The girl's lawyer, an honest man, explains the difficulty of fighting such a combination:

> How can one man, or a dozen men, break up a well-organized system? Ex-Judge Cooley, your uncle's lawyer, is a prominent member of the inner political circle that controls judicial destiny. He presented the petition to a judge who received his nomination from this very organization. The granting of the petition will give him complete control of your fortune.

When the lawyer appears to be getting results in spite of the opposition, the conspirators arrest him for borrowing on securities a client had left in his charge. Paula tries to escape to New Jersey, is caught at the ferry, and placed in an insane asylum. However, money can fight money, and it is the heroine's luck that Todhunter Chase falls in love with her and brings his wealth and political influence to bear in her favor.

Owen Davis' *The Power of Money* (1906), exposed the political tactics that a large concern used to put a smaller rival out of business. However, of most interest was the unexpected appearance of William Randolph Hearst and Theodore Roosevelt, impersonated by actors whose names were not announced on the program, as saviors of the small businessman. Hearst, then in the midst of a bitter struggle for the governorship of New York, was advised by a critic that he "could not do better than distribute free seats to the wavering voters."[21]

From politics and pull to politics and history was an easy step for audiences of the century's first ten years to take. Act I in Thomas Dixon's dramatization of *The Clansman* (1906), his novel of the reconstruction period in the South, gives a graphic picture of conditions in a southern state during the elections of 1867. Unfortunately, Dixon allowed his feelings to dominate his pen and the play as a whole distorted history "for the distinct object of reawakening sectional prejudices."[22] The dramatization was an extremely poor and amateurish piece of writing, far removed in quality from the novel, which later served as the basis for the famous motion picture, *The Birth of a Nation.*

Winston Churchill's stage version of *The Crisis* (1902), on the other hand, retained "all the charm of the novel—which is to say it is very charming indeed."[23] The play telescoped the novel's story so that the nation's political crisis resulting from the election of Lincoln in 1860 bore strongly on the love affair of a southern girl and a northern boy in the border city of St. Louis. There is a genuine effort by the playwright to induce better understanding between the sections. Clarence Colfax, cousin of the southern girl, and Stephen Brice meet near the end of the play. "Brice," Clarence says, "you are a good fellow, if you are a Yankee. I wish there were more like you."

Brice takes Clarence's extended hand and replies, "Thank you, Colonel Colfax. It's a great pity that we men of the North and you of the South didn't know each other better some years ago, sir."

A third play whose political background is set in an historical situation was *Sam Houston* (1906), by Clay Clement. Houston as governor of Texas refuses to accept secession of the state from the Union. A committee favoring secession calls on Houston and tells the old warrior he is no longer governor of Texas. The play ends as Houston, bowing to the committee's decision, takes the Texan and American flags from the wall, wraps himself in them and leaves the room.

*   *   *   *   *   *   *

In *The Nigger* (1909), Edward Sheldon dramatized the delicate question of race, love, and politics in the South. Phil Morrow, recently elected governor of a southern state, has become an ardent advocate of prohibition because the indiscriminate use of liquor had resulted in race riots involving drunken Negroes. He forces a prohibition bill through the legislature and is determined to sign it when his cousin, owner of a large distillery firm that would be put out of business if the act went through, demands Morrow veto the measure. The Governor refuses, and Clifton Noyes then tells Morrow he has colored blood in his veins. Noyes threatens to publish the news in the papers unless Morrow vetoes the bill. The latter, engaged to Georgiana Byrd and on the threshold of a brilliant career, nevertheless signs the bill. He later reveals his blood taint at a large public meeting of soldiers who had gathered to honor Morrow for putting down the race riots.

The Nigger is a powerful study of a "nigger-hating" white man who suddenly learns colored blood courses through his veins. The temptation to hide his taint so he could marry the girl he loves and to keep the high political office he has just won provides the play with several intensely dramatic scenes. Those between Morrow and Noyes are charged with electricity. This is especially true of the one in which Noyes tells Morrow how he had only recently forced the information about his birth out of the colored mammy in the house. The scenes between Morrow and Georgiana are moving and pathetic. Guy Bates Post played the title role in the original company. After seeing the play, George M. Cohan told Sam Harris, "Now that Sheldon, that fellow, Sam, is better than Gus Thomas ever dreamed of being, better than Gene Walter or Paul Armstrong or anybody. . . ."[24]

Charles Klein's *Hon. John Grigsby* (1902), was a play about politics in 1894 with the leading character obviously modeled on Abraham Lincoln. Grigsby is nominated for judge by politicians who believe that they can control him on the slavery issue through his friend, Mrs. Marston. The latter, unknown to Grigsby, pays the lawyer's debts so the sheriff doesn't have to sell Grigsby's office furniture to satisfy his creditors. Grigsby wins the election, but thinking that the nomination has been won through Mrs. Marston's putting up money for him, he decides to resign. All ends well, however, when the lawyer learns that the money has been advanced after he was nominated. Frank Keenan played the part of Grigsby and Taylor Holmes that of John Grigsby, Jr.

Romance was mixed with politics in *A Square Deal* by Edward A. Rose. The play, whose title was taken from Theodore Roosevelt's "A Square Deal" slogan, is a serious study of state politics. Veteran politician Hannibal Hawkins withdraws from the race for state senator so his young protege, Clinton Hargrave, can win the election and the young girl they both love. After the ballots are counted, Hawkins leaves for the Pacific Coast. On his return he learns that Hargrave has joined with the old political machine crowd and is helping them push a vicious land grab deal. To fight the bill, Hawkins runs for a state senatorial seat that had just become vacant, and he wins. A penitent Hargrave now speaks against the land bill and is instrumental in defeating it. But Hawkins wins the girl.

* * * * * * *

Playwrights of the first decade gave tremendous impetus to the American political drama. They roamed over almost every aspect of the nation's political life and expressed their views in practically every dramatic form. In addition, they produced three plays worthy to stand alongside the best of our later works in this genre. *The Lion and the Mouse, The County Chairman*, and *The Nigger* have become part of the dramatic heritage of our country and could still be presented with profit.

The dramatists in the extent of their wide range provided guide posts for later playwrights. They hit hard at unethical political influence in *The Lion and the Mouse*, lampooned American foreign policies in *The Sultan of Sulu*, fortified the citizen's inalienable right to poke fun at Congress in *The Rogers Brothers in Washington* and other musical comedies, treated with gentle, but nonetheless pointed, criticism some accepted political methods in *The County Chairman*. These authors also brought to the theatregoer of their decade the unholy alliance between politicians and unscrupulous self-seekers after money in *The Next of Kin*. Finally, in *The Nigger*, the dramatist presented on stage in moving terms the racial question that is currently one of the nation's most serious problems. In the range of their interests and the excellence of many of their plays, the playwrights of this era mark an important milestone in the development of the American political drama.

4
THE SHAME
OF THE CITIES

THREE MONTHS after Lincoln Steffens had been hired as managing editor of *McClure's Magazine* he was called into the publisher's office. "You don't know how to edit a magazine," blunt-spoken S. S. McClure told him. "Get out into the country and see what you can find."

Steffens did. He went to St. Louis, and spoke to the man in the street, the respectable businessman, the professional politician. His search took him to Minneapolis, Pittsburgh, Philadelphia, Chicago, and New York. His inquiring mind and pleasant personality brought confidences from those seeking to uncover corruption and from those trying to hide it. Ten years earlier he had naively revealed the quality which brought these confidences. "I wrote a long, careful article on the week's banking business," he said in a letter, "and saw all the big bankers. My acquaintance is becoming more and more personal with these men and they confide in me, saying they know I will report them accurately and without exaggeration."[1] This he did on his 1903 tour.

What Steffens had to report was municipal corruption. In St. Louis he found political corruption, and the titles of his two articles—"Tweed Days in St. Louis" and "The Shamelessness of St. Louis"—indicate the nature of the money-grabbing activities by politicians there. In Minneapolis the police department was riddled with graft, and Steffens called this report "The Shame of Minneapolis." In Pittsburgh the political and industrial leaders worked hand in hand for their mutual benefit and the mutual despoilment of the citizenry. It was, however, a citizenry aware of the low estate to which political life had fallen—"Pittsburgh, A City Ashamed." Philadelphians were like sleek, well-fed cats, "Corrupt and Contented." In Chicago, "Half Free and Fighting On," Steffens found earnest efforts to combat municipal graft, and in New York, with former Columbia University president Seth Low giving that city its best administration in years, the roving reporter saw "Good Government to the Test."

Political corruption wasn't new to the American people. It had probably come to America from Europe with the first adventurers who pictured themselves as officeholders. Our politicians had early developed their own particular devices for making easy money, and will probably continue to develop additional ones. The American people had been apprised of political corruption in municipal politics before Steffens told them in his 1903 *McClure's Magazine* articles. But this was the first time that they were made conscious of it as a national phenomenon. They became aware of it because Steffens had the gift and the will to make them aware of it. "Care like hell," he used to tell newspapermen. "Sit around the bars and drink, and pose, and pretend, all you want to, but in reality, deep down underneath, care like hell."[2] Steffens cared. And he had the ability to dramatize his feelings to the people. In a colorful and pungent style he made the nation acutely aware of *The Shame of the Cities* (1904).

One result of Steffens' crusade was the appearance on the Broadway stage of several plays dealing with municipal corruption. In 1906 *The Man of the Hour* and *The Stolen Story* became "hits"; a year later *The Undertow* played to capacity houses while *Friends of Labor* did fairly well; in 1909 *The City* brought the cycle to an end. Why the cycle should have come to an end is a curious commentary on the inability of the American people to follow through on recurrent imperfections. Certainly there were flagrant examples after 1910 as well as before of municipal corruption, examples which called for stage records. But there are few evidences that the playwrights thought so.

Ten years before this cycle began, in 1895, the corruption and brutality of the New York Police Department, exposed by the Lexow Committee of the State Senate, inspired Harrison Grey Fiske and Charles Klein to write *The District Attorney* (1895). The play centered around the ruthless methods Tammany leaders used to get rich. One critic observed that the play impressed "the spectator as a drama written expressly to meet that public curiosity which the details of the recent legislative inquiry excited."[3] Another noted with obvious satisfaction that the play was "an immediate and indisputable success."[4]

So was George H. Broadhurst's *The Man of the Hour* (1906), which came on the scene when *The Shame of the Cities* was still fresh in the minds of the public. Broadhurst told the story of a fighting young mayor's efforts to prevent the city's political boss from jamming through a traction grab steal. One critic remarked:

> There are considerable resemblances to be found between Bennett and the present mayor of New York, Horrigan and the present leader of Tammany Hall, and between the "Borough Franchise Bill" and a certain gas franchise that disturbed the public mind about two years ago. To make the resemblance more emphatic, the orchestra plays "Tammany" as the audience is leaving.[5]

The mayor of New York in 1906 was George Brinton McClellan. A graduate of Princeton and a "silk-stocking" New

Yorker, McClellan was chosen by Tammany boss Charles Francis Murphy in 1903 as "window-dressing" to oppose Seth Low for mayor. But by 1906 the mayor had proved to be a man with a mind and a will of his own. He broke with Murphy over the vice and gambling in the city. In January of that year Mc-Clellan knowingly committed political suicide by declaring, "I am unalterably opposed to Charles Francis Murphy and everything he stands for."[6] He retired from politics in 1909, served overseas as a lieutenant colonel in the American Army during World War I, and died November 30, 1940 in Washington, D. C. "He left behind a record for efficiency and honesty that forms one of the few bright pages in New York officialdom of that era."[7]

Charles Francis Murphy was the last of the great Tammany leaders. Steffens in his magazine report on New York had said, "There is a new boss in Tammany, a young man, Charles F. Murphy, and unknown to New Yorkers. He looks dense, but he acts with force, decision, and skill. The new mayor will be his man."[8] Steffens guessed wrong here, but his additional observations proved correct. "As a New Yorker, I fear Murphy will . . . stop the scandal, put all the graft in the hands of a few tried and true men, and give the city what it would call good government. . . . I don't fear a bad Tammany mayor; I dread the election of a good one."[9]

Tammany had a long history of franchise grabs. In 1871 "Boss" Tweed had the so-called Viaduct Railroad Bill introduced. This measure compelled New York to take $5,000,000 worth of stock in the company, exempted the firm from taxes, and set up a street grading and widening program that would cost the city from $50,000,000 to $65,000,000. Gustavus Myers in his *The History of Tammany Hall* pointed out that "associated with Tweed as directors were some of the foremost financial and businessmen of the day. The complete consummation of this almost unparalleled steal was prevented only by the general exposure of Tweedism a few months later."[10]

Another traction franchise grab precipitated the 1884 battle between the Broadway Surface Railroad Company and the Broadway Railroad Company for the right to run street cars on Broadway. The ensuing scandal centered on the buying of alderman votes for $22,000 each. The exposure ended that franchise threat. But in 1892 the "Huckleberry Franchise" bill for a street railway in outlying New York went through, "Boss" Croker masterminding the deal.

The Man of the Hour is an invaluable source of information on the smooth workings of a well-oiled political machine. Probably the first rule of such an organization is the unquestioning loyalty to the leader of those put into office. Mavericks are not wanted. In the play a district leader has defied Horrigan, so the boss explains to a henchman, "I've got to get him for the sake of discipline. If he can defy me and win, others might think they can—so—I've got to get him." Even the highest officeholders are not exempt from boss rule. Mayor Bennett, refusing to sign the traction grab bill in the play, is bluntly told by Horrigan to sign "or your political career ends right now. You think you're on top and that you can stay on top without the man who put you there. But you can't. I can pull you down just as easy as I put you up, and I'll do it unless you sign that bill." The withdrawal of McClellan from politics in 1909 was a contemporary illustration of a boss' power. Present illustrations of the same psychology are expressed in *State of the Union* when political boss Conover tells Grant Matthews, "In this country we play politics—and to play politics you have to play ball."

With their power the bosses and their intimates were convinced that the law could not touch them. Despite the fall of Tweed, "Honest" John Kelly, and Croker from power, the belief persisted in the ranks that the leaders were safe from punishment. *The Man of the Hour* ends on possibly the most cynical note in the American drama. Wainwright, a prominent business leader teaming with Horrigan on the franchise steal, has been exposed and faces criminal prosecution. He is worried. "What's the matter with you, Wainwright?" Boss Horrigan asks. "Brace up and come along. So long as you have money—don't worry. The woods are full of investigations, and subpoenas, and indictments, but I notice there are damn few rich men in jail even today."

But the power of Tammany did not lay entirely in its high-pressure tactics. It was built upon a firmer foundation of good organization, distrust of reformers by the people, and a willingness to help the poor immigrant get a job and become a naturalized citizen when the rest of the world was kicking him around. The immigrant was welcomed by the Tammany clubs and he used them as centers for social activities. The newcomers to America could go there for dinners and entertainment when other places shut them out.

"The leaders and their captains have their hold on the people because they take care of their own," Steffens wrote in explaining the power of corrupt bosses.

> They speak pleasant words, smile friendly smiles, notice the baby, give picnics up the river or on the Sound, or a slap on the back; find jobs most of them at the city's expense, but they have also newsstands, peddling privileges, railroad and other business places to dispense; they permit violations of the law and, if a man has broken the law without permission, see him through the court. Though a blow in the face is as readily given as a shake of the hand, Tammany kindness is real kindness, and will go far, remember long, and take infinite trouble for a friend.[11]

In *The Man of the Hour* Phelan, the district boss, played by George Fawcett, proudly tells a friend:

> I turkey 'em in the winter and picnic 'em in the summer. They're the days of my life, Miss. I've had as many as 2,500 at one of 'em—most of 'em women and children; women who never get a breath of fresh air and children who never see a blade of grass except when I take 'em out. It's a happy day when I down a man who's again' me, it's a happy day when

I help a man who's for me, but the happiest days for me are my picnic days.

Probably when the twentieth century history of New York politics is written, the decline of Tammany as a political power may be traced to the disappearance of the immigrant and of his need of the clubhouse as a place to meet. Perhaps then Phelan's power in the play as a district boss will prove a period curiosity piece for the future reader.

* * * * * * *

The Undertow by Eugene Walter was a companion piece to *The Man of the Hour*. It posed the same question that many who have fought the public's battle and then were turned away probably have asked themselves, "Does it pay to fight for the general welfare against an entrenched political machine?" It was probably the question Mayor Seth Low asked himself when he was defeated by George B. McClellan in 1904, after having given New York an outstandingly honest and capable administration. It was probably the question McClellan asked himself following his break with Boss Murphy and his decision to retire from public life. It was the question asked time and again of crusading reporter Dick Wells in *The Undertow*. The play, which opened April 22, 1907, occupied the Harlem Opera House almost half-way between the rejection of Mayor Low in 1904 and the foreshadowed enforced retirement of Mayor McClellan in 1909.

"The dirty-faced mob is the most treacherous in the world," a fellow worker told Dick Wells:

> Take it from me, Dick. If you stick to this game the time ain't very far off when they'll stick the double-cross on your back—red hot—and let you sizzle until you yell for help. Go ahead and grab Mary, a good job, and a good salary, and let the other fellow take care of himself.

On February 14, 1892, the minister of the Madison Square Presbyterian Church rose to address his congregation. Unknown to him newspaperman W. E. Carson was sitting in the crowd. Carson had come to the church by chance. As the speaker kept going further into his sermon, Carson's casual attitude changed. He soon reached for the pencil in his pocket and the blank paper he always carried. The minister continued talking, holding his audience with the fervor and the eloquence of his speech. The reporter wrote steadily, his eyes dancing with excitement. The next day New York was startled by reading what has since been called "one of the most famous and effective pulpit utterances in American history."[12] The Rev. Dr. Charles Henry Parkhurst woke that Monday morning to find himself famous, much quoted, and widely attacked. Tammany-owned New York officeholders, he had declared the day before, were nothing more than "polluted harpies that, under pretense of governing this city, are feeding day and night on its quivering vitals . . . [they are] a lying, perjured, rum-soaked, libidinous lot."[13] The Hall was not long in striking back, "Where's your proof?" it demanded. "Produce your evidence."

Dr. Parkhurst did not have the kind of evidence that would stand up in court. Some members of his congregation became frightened, timorous. There was talk of curbing their impetuous pastor. Dr. Parkhurst said nothing, but his stubborn New England conscience was aroused. "Produce your evidence." "Where's your proof?" He set out to get it. For the next month Dr. Parkhurst, to the gibes of critics and the vicious cartoons of Tammany-influenced newspapers, went into saloons, dance halls, gambling dens, houses of prostitution. On March 13, a month less a day following the first sermon, he rose to speak in his pulpit. This time he had the evidence, affidavits which proved beyond doubt the truth of his charges.

Dr. Parkhurst's campaign against corruption in New York was a major factor influencing the formation of the Lexow Committee by the New York State Senate two years later. The Committee's voluminous report more than vindicated the minister. The police department of New York, it declared, was responsible for

> graft, brutality, blackmail, protection of disorderly
> houses, protection of gambling, swindling, abortion-
> ists, and other crimes . . . the evidence, taken as a
> whole, indicates that the department was permeated by
> the influence of Tammany Hall; that district leaders
> influenced not only the appointment but the assign-
> ment of officers and that officers learned the only
> hope for advancement was in joining and contributing
> to Tammany Hall Associations.[14]

Of even greater importance for the city was a mass meeting held September 6, 1894, at Madison Square Garden Concert Hall. The meeting organized "a citizens" movement for the government of New York, "entirely outside of party politics, and solely in the interest of efficiency, economy and the public health, comfort and safety."[15] First step in the fight was the formation of a Committee of Seventy. Many important names were included in the list: A. C. Bernheim, Abram S. Hewitt, J. Pierpont Morgan, William J. Schieffelin, Jacob H. Schiff, Gustav H. Schwab, Cornelius Vanderbilt, John Crosby Brown, John Claflin, Everett P. Wheeler. The fight was on to elect a reform ticket in the 1894 elections. The Committee of Seventy proved able political fighters and elected William L. Strong, a Republican, as mayor and John W. Goff, a Democrat, recorder.

Seven years later, after Mayor Strong's fall from grace and the resurgence of Tammany, the battle had to be fought all over again. This time the fight made by William Travers Jerome, who was candidate for District Attorney, stole the campaign show from Seth Low. "Carrie [sic] Nation" Jerome, so-called by the opposition papers because of his raiding tactics on gambling and other illegal houses, was an unusual man in politics. Wealthy, outspoken, brave almost to the point of foolhardiness, he sailed into Tammany and its minions with vigor and aplomb. "His voice is harsh; his speech is blunt, to the verge at times of downright rudeness; and his gestures come as God pleases," an historian recorded. "But during his canvass he knew what he was talking about as he knew his ten fingers; he had, by inheritance, wit and fun, and the gift of telling a story; and, more

than all the rest, when in great earnest, he had the accent of
daring and sincerity."[16] It was in measure due to the "happy
warrior's" aggressive tactics—he received the sobriquet more
than twenty years before it was bestowed on Alfred E. Smith—
that Seth Low and the rest of the reform ticket were elected in
1901.

The Undertow was based on these campaigns. Wells, a
crusading young reporter, succeeds in electing a reform mayor
by outplanning and outsmarting the machine politicians of the
unnamed city, thinly disguised, but transparently New York.
The Mayor, Augustus Hoffman, puts himself into the power of
a newspaper publisher and political force. Faced with the
choice of signing a graft-ridden franchise bill or going to prison
on embezzlement charges, Hoffman signs the bill. The Committee of Seventy, aroused to an unreasoning anger, charges
Wells with conspiring to have the franchise bill signed and
reads him out of the party. Wells, in a stirring speech, tells the
committee members:

> You are about to send me before the world as a thief
> and a scoundrel—I hope that God Almighty will for-
> give you, for you are killing the last chance of a
> decent man fighting your cause. . . . I tried to lead you
> to better conditions, better homes and a decent stand-
> ing in the world and now . . . you stab me in the back.
> I have been warned that of all the ingratitude in the
> wide world that of the common people, the oppressed,
> the weak and the ill-treated, was the most scathing,
> cruel and unwarranted towards those who tried to help
> them. You have proved it. . . . I still have my con-
> science clear.

But the committee members, moving uneasily in their seats
and answering the vote call in low voices, read Wells out of
the organization. The reporter, however, proves the best man to
the end. He refuses to turn traitor and work for the opposition
publisher; instead, Wells and the girl he loves leave for parts
unknown as the curtain falls.

The methods used by the reform groups of 1894 and 1901 are pointed up in the play. "They came into the field today with as complete an organization as I ever saw," one astonished machine follower exclaims. "They knew every move we made and beat us to it."

"They challenged every repeater," another ward heeler complained. "Everyone, and they knew the law; every judge, every watcher, every teller they had had a complete set of instructions, the greatest ever, short and to the point. They couldn't go wrong."

The Undertow is a good play. With a few changes it could be fitted to any period in which machine control of a city has reached a point where the bosses are completely indifferent to the public interest. In this respect the play points to the future as well as to the past, for the lesson it has to teach is as good this year as it was in 1907. *The Undertow* is an advance on the plays of its own period and on those of the Nineties in that it is stumbling towards a basic philosophy of political conduct for the people. Here it stretches forth a hand towards similar plays to be studied later.

* * * * * * *

The Man of the Hour and *The Undertow* treated specific situations in the political life of New York that could be traced with more or less certainty. *The Stolen Story, The City,* and *Friends of Labor* were concerned with a more general approach to the problem of corruption in municipal politics.

Of these plays the best was *The City,* by Clyde Fitch. Fitch was America's leading dramatist at the time of his death in 1909, a few months before *The City* was produced in New York on December 22 of that year. He was chiefly concerned with character analysis, and in this play Fitch studied the deterioration of George Rand, Jr., under the pressure of seeking high office. The blame in some speeches was put upon the corroding effects of city life, but a further analysis reveals it is more Rand's desire to be governor of New York than his residence in a city which brings about his many compromises with truth. The story indicates the problem Fitch is probing. Rand, candidate for governor of New York, had promised his dying father to take care of his half-brother, George Hannock. Hannock, the illegitimate offspring of the older Rand's liaison with a now dead woman, is a morphine addict. Hannock is in love with Cicely, his half-sister. Neither knows they are related, but George Rand does. To prevent the marriage, Rand reveals the truth to dope-crazed Hannock, who shoots Cicely. Hannock then tries to kill himself but is prevented from doing so by Rand, who insists Hannock must suffer by standing trial for Cicely's murder. The dope addict then warns Rand that publication of their relationship would ruin his political chances, but by this time Rand has determined to leave the city and politics and start over again elsewhere with his fiancee.

The corroding effect of political ambition upon a man's character appears early in the play. Rand is told by a committee that he can have the gubernatorial nomination provided his past life is blameless. He feels that the actions of his illegitimate half-brother are his responsibility and so, to gain the nomination, hides the relationship. To keep the secret Rand bribes Hannock by making him his secretary. In still another situation Rand's frantic desire to be governor betrays him, though audiences today would wonder about the furor. Rand's sister and her husband have parted; they no longer live together. George pleads with Cicely to return to her husband until the campaign is over. "If your divorce comes out after my election, it needn't affect the party," he explains. Then, to condone his actions, Rand adds, "My acts will speak for themselves then. I intend to be square in office, and to succeed or fail by that standard. I don't mind failure, doing the right thing; what I can't stand is failure doing nothing without having had my chance."

The play has aged markedly. Some of its socio-moral

standards are no longer valid, and the characters' actions frequently are unbelievable. A situation ending the first act is very bad. Rand, Sr., who has died suddenly from a heart attack, is forgotten a few minutes after his death as George and Cicely discuss how many advantages there are to living in a city rather than a small town. *The City* was "wildly received" by the first night audience, many women becoming "hysterical during the thrilling episode of the second act" leading to the shooting of Cicely. A critic declared that the scene "owes its success to a purely morbid, ultra sensational coup, bodied forth in language exceeding the limit of all hitherto attempted freedom of speech on the American or any other stage."[17] The same critic observed that Walter Hampden's acting of George Rand was "in the main artistic, a well-restrained performance of a responsible role." Tully Marshall's interpretation of George Hannock was called "remarkable," the actor becoming "the drug-crazed maniac to the life."

Only a few short story writers have the gift of dramatic composition. Jesse Lynch Williams was not one of them. In *The Stolen Story* he wrote a short story masterpiece. His effort to make it into a play resulted in bad writing, incredible characters, and unbelievable situations. The short story is a delicate tale of a middle-aged, absent-minded newspaperman who periodically gets drunk. Despite this failing, he is always taken back by the editor after one of his drinking bouts. One day, however, he is not taken back, and a rival paper hires him. A big political scandal breaks, and the reporter covers the story. He gets it, but absent-mindedly returns to his old paper to write copy. The story then centers around the efforts of the assistant city editor, who immediately sees what has happened, to keep the reporter working at top speed so he won't remember he no longer works there. A spy for the rival paper works in the office and complicates the situation. But all ends happily with the reporter rehired on the paper he loves.

The play makes the vague political situation concrete. Here

Tammany loads with graft a bill, which well-meaning General Cunningham has pushed through the legislature to provide parks near New York's rivers. The gentle, modest reporter of the short story has been changed to a conceited young man. A love story between the reporter and the general's daughter is dragged into the play. The plot revolves around Tammany's willingness to use any bill for graft, and how the reporter foils its money-grabbing efforts. Once again, Tully Marshall is highly praised for the reality he brought to his role of assistant city editor.

Edward Sheldon's *The Boss* (1911), is not basically a political play but its treatment of the boss-worker relationship justifies a glance at the drama. The plot centers around Michael Regan, a labor leader whose insistence upon loyalty from his men stems from the same hard code Tammany leaders exerted upon their subordinates. In his vigor, hard-headedness, and ruthlessness as well as in his willingness to take the blame for the actions of a follower, Regan personifies the type of boss-organization worker relationship associated with most American political machines. The play is a powerful one, justifying the comment of a drama critic that "Edward Sheldon has broken loose with a third play that stands in the same emphatic rank with *Salvation Nell* and *The Nigger*."[18] It was well acted, for Holbrook Blinn as Regan and Emily Stevens as Emily Griswold gave memorable performances.

The plays in this chapter are essentially period pieces addressed to an audience concerned with the problems of municipal corruption. They have aged and it is doubtful that later audiences would enjoy them, although *The City* retains a literary appeal for the scholar. Despite this fact, the plays present in vivid terms a picture of the times difficult to match by other sources. There is an immediacy even in the reading now that substantiates the view that dramatists, unconsciously, are writing history in living terms for future generations to study.

5

WASHINGTON: COCKTAILS AND POLITICS

A TRAVELLER approaching Washington by plane from the South will immediately note three impressive structures in a direct line: the Lincoln Memorial, four-square and solid, as enduring as the greatness of the martyred President who sits in heroic proportions within its walls; the Washington Monument, a bright white shaft pointing finger-like heavenward, an arresting tribute to our nation's first President, and the Capitol, standing majestically upon high ground overlooking the city, the statue of Freedom surmounting its dome. To the last, come Congressmen from every state, selected by their fellow citizens to make the laws under which this nation is governed. In the main, the 437 Representatives and the 100 Senators are inspired by the highest ideals and endeavor to do their duty honestly and well. A few eventually turn cynical and even corrupt, but their number is small.

"The city of magnificent distances," Washington has been called, with justification. Since Pierre L'Enfant laid out the

District of Columbia in 1802 upon the marsh lands beside the placid Potomac, the city has grown politically as well as physically. Now the magnificent distances are more than geographical, for the influence of the Nation's Capital extends far beyond its earthly boundaries. Events have brought Washington from occupying a central position in a small, provincial country to a place where the world looks to it for guidance and leadership. Its lawmakers, too, have been forced to grow with the passing years, for their decisions in mid-twentieth century determine the fate of nations far removed from the District of Columbia.

This is Washington, and playwrights through the years have not been unaware of the city. But until the depression descended heavily upon our country in 1929, their plays had the straitjacket of provincialism stamped upon them. The dramatists had been bound by their own and the country's limited conception of what went on in the Nation's Capital, and these views were all too often far removed from reality. But history, starting with the depression and extending into the World War II years, brought about a great change in those writing for the theatre. They were now dealing with citizens more knowing and more inquisitive about the District of Columbia and the men who made our government's laws. The newspapers, magazines, moving pictures, radio, and television reported activities in the Capital on a scale never before attempted. The most remote citizen in point of miles had a quantity of information concerning Washington at his fingers' reach. This knowledgeable citizenry increased vastly the number of theatregoers interested in plays about the Nation's Capital, but they also made the task of the playwright more binding and exacting. Truth may be stranger than fiction, but when an author is appealing to an audience familiar with his subject, the job becomes infinitely more difficult.

If politics is the main business of Washington, certainly its favorite partner is the social whirl. The latter is more than a handmaiden of political success. It frequently is the maker of such success, and without a certain amount of social activity, few figures on the Potomac move beyond obscure elective or appointive government positions. As early as 1891 Charles Hoyt noted this phenomena in his comedy *A Texas Steer*. Its plot was inspired somewhat by the set formula for social activities upper echelon government figures had to follow in the decade preceding our century. Cabinet officers held open house on Wednesdays, Senators on Thursdays, and the Vice President on a day of his own choosing. How the practice started no one knew, but its importance could not be exaggerated.

"It would require considerable argument, if not endanger his position, for a Cabinet officer to disregard this unwritten law," a social historian of the period wrote.[1] But the terms of open house were far more generous than in later years. "Anyone bearing the passport of respectability and good breeding may present his card at the doors of the Cabinet household and receive a welcome from the inmates," the historian added.[2] There they were greeted by liveried butlers, ushered onto the reception line to receive a hurried "Happy to meet you" from the hostess, herded through the rooms, treated to tea or chocolate, sweet biscuits, salted almonds and bon-bons, and shunted out of the door to the street. "Had the headquarters of our national government been seated in the central city of trade and commerce, the official life might not have been able to assume the dominant social tone it has secured in Washington," the same writer somewhat snobbishly observed.[3]

It was into this social atmosphere that Maverick Brander and his family stumbled in Hoyt's *A Texas Steer*. Brander, elected to Congress over his protests, came to Washington with the cry, "I'm an honest man. What would I do in Congress?" The question has since been repeated in numerous plays and moving pictures, sometimes humorously and sometimes seriously. Under the guidance of his socially ambitious wife, Brander soon learned the answer. Before the play ended, he had become another pleasure-bent and grafting member of Congress, intent on staying in Washington under any circumstances.

Brander is spotted by Washington hangers-on before he has time to acclimate himself. Two parasites volunteer to guide him through the social and political pitfalls of the capital city. John Innitt promises to write his speeches, "on any side of any question." To Maverick's query about scruples, Innitt replies that he isn't bothered by them since "I've lived all my life in Washington." He demonstrates this ease of conscience by branding the Congressman's unwillingness to back a land-grab bill as "too sensitive," and then promptly shifts position after Maverick explains support of the measure "would rob me of 80,000 acres of cattle range."

In that case, Innitt declares, "Your conscientious scruples against the bill are entirely justified."

The perils of Washington social life crop up in a scene famous during its era. Brander is tricked into kissing a pretty young girl, who had told him Daniel Webster had kissed her mother and she, too, wanted to be kissed by a famous statesman. A photographer hidden behind curtains snaps the picture and Maverick, to forestall unpleasant publicity, buys the plate from him. "Tell me one thing," he asks the girl, "did it cost Daniel Webster $100 to kiss your mother?" Later, when a similar situation is shaping up, Brander hurriedly calls his daughter into the room and tells her, "Just come in and stay in. I'm beginning to think a Congressman should never be left alone."

The reader at first likes the hearty and bluff Maverick Brander, but the Texan soon slips out of character and never does get back. At the end he is an object of contempt rather than of admiration. But for the sheer good spirits of the unrelated situations and as a picture of Washington political life in the 1890's, *A Texas Steer* is still an enjoyable play. There is a description about office-seeking in the Nation's Capital that should be preserved. A minor character observes:

Office seekin' is a mighty poor business fo' most every-body. I seen bright young men who come here expect-ing office. Dey stops at de best hotels and take in de theaters. Den, a little later, dey stops at cheaper hotels an' gives de theater de gobye. Den it's a way down cheap hotel—clothes gettin' shabby—and on de faces a care-worn look. An' den a roomin'-house an' a bite at de free lunch, den a bench in de park, and den dey finds rest down in de Potomac. Marse Brander, dis is one fine town with its bro'd streets and sunshine, but it's a big graveyard, too.

The passing years did not make any change in the rela-tionship of social life and politics, as a keen observer pointed out in *Harper's* of January, 1917. Everybody talked politics and shoved forward socially by entertaining political figures. "Poli-tics—and Senators—are sometimes the fashion with this set, sometimes not," one observer noted. "Even now you can hear in Washington that an administration is or is not fashionable, and learn of politics when it is not at all 'the thing' to go to the White House."[4]

Political business—even international affairs—was fre-quently conducted during a social evening. There is the story of a Secretary of State who met the ambassador of a foreign country at a party. It was their first meeting. "The boys at the Department were telling me this morning," the Secretary said, "that there were some difficulties between your country and mine."

"Yes, yes," answered the astonished ambassador.

"Oh, that's all right," the Secretary went on. "I told the boys I didn't know much about it, but I was sure the trouble wasn't so serious as they thought. We'll fix it." And here he turned to where the ambassador's proud and distinguished wife stood, talking to Mrs. Secretary. "If your husband and I cannot get this straightened out," said he beamingly, "then you and mama must put your heads together and do it for us—that's all."[5]

The close relationship of the social and the political appears in two plays about Washington, *The First Lady of the Land* (1911), and *The Governor's Wife* (1912). The former, by Charles Nirdlinger, was a retelling of the Aaron Burr and James Madison rivalry for the hand of Dolly Todd. It also brings in Burr's Mexican escapade and the resulting treason charge, suggesting that Burr ventured the madcap effort as much to win Dolly Todd as to become President. The play ends with Burr's being arrested for treason, Dolly Todd's promising to marry Madison, and both vowing to stand by Burr. Lowell Sherman took the part of Madison and Frederick Perry of Burr. A critic observed, "Elsie Ferguson may not be the real Dolly Madison, but it is certain that the historical prototype could not have been more charming than she, and she has never looked more beautiful."[6]

The Governor's Wife, by Alice Bradley, emphasized the importance of social poise and position in Washington. Governor Slade desires to become a United States Senator. He believes he has outgrown the wife of his youth, and accuses her of failure to keep pace with him in their climb up the political ladder. He wants to divorce her and marry the daughter of a Senator. "When I have another house I want my friends to come there," he tells his wife. "I want . . . well . . . a head-quarters . . . that's what I want . . . headquarters. And I want a person at the head of my house that I can be proud of . . . like Strickland." The play was of and for its period. Mrs. Slade refuses to grant Slade a divorce. Miss Strickland, after an interview with Mrs. Slade, renounces the Governor and returns to her lover. Slade and his wife separate. Years later they meet again, and the old ties are resumed. Milton Sills, the famous moving picture actor of a later period, played the part of the young lover, Slade, in the play.

If in the next decade the country was in the throes of the fabulous Twenties, Washington was still living in the plushy Nineties. Compared to the exciting period of the war years just finished and to the crucial Thirties immediately ahead, the

Twenties in the Nation's Capital was a period of placid calm. It is true that the calm was broken somewhat by the "Teapot Dome" oil scandal, and the ensuing prosecution by Senator Thomas J. Walsh of Secretary of Interior Albert B. Fall, Secretary of the Navy Edwin W. Denby, and others. The scandal, with its charges of duplicity by high government and business officials, momentarily rippled placid Washington. It is also true that the Washington Conference for the Limitation of Armament in November, 1921 interrupted the complacency of the District of Columbia. But these and similar events were only passing phases in a city where the prosperity of the country allowed full attention to the icing on the cake of political living.

"From 1920 to 1932 Washington reached a point of political consciousness hardly less high than it was in Grant's administration, and a social level which represented the last hang-over of plushy Victorianism," a witness on the scene later recorded. "It was the overgrown village where a tail coat and white tie were more important than an idea. All but the most robust citizens of the radical states realized that there was no greater risk to political careers than questioning the stability of established things."[7]

Possibly this was the reason that the few plays about Washington mirrored the social emphasis of the Twenties. An historical play, *That Awful Mrs. Eaton* (1924), by John Farrar and Stephen Vincent Benét, shows how President Jackson tried to bludgeon Washington society into accepting controversial Mrs. Eaton, wife of his Secretary of War. The interweaving of the social and political is developed by opposition efforts to embarrass Jackson's policies by attacking him through Mrs. Eaton. The attacks prove baseless and fail, and the play ends with Jackson introducing Peggy Eaton as the hostess of an important White House function.

Her Way Out (1924), by Edwin M. Boyle, started out promisingly as an exciting social-political drama and then petered out into a melo-dramatic love story. Clever Mrs. Hamilton, of questionable past, is engaged by political leaders to tame newly-elected Senator Norcross, who is intent on pushing through a bill to nationalize the railroads. This note reflected the still current public interest in the railroads, which had been taken over by the government during the first World War and were returned to private ownership after the conflict ended. Mrs. Hamilton falls in love with the Senator, walks out on his enemies, but also refuses to marry him because of her past as owner of a bawdy house in New Orleans. To solve her dilemma, she takes poison and dies in the arms of Senator Norcross.

Most exciting of the social-political plays was the 1935 production of *First Lady,* by George S. Kaufman and Katherine Dayton. It came at a time when the nation felt the first lifting of the depression. The play brought a note of hope and optimism, of confidence in the future, and of conviction that the right people will guide the destinies of our country. That is the significant point in *First Lady,* for in the rivalry between Lucy Wayne and Irene Hibbard for social mastery of Washington and the struggle between Stephen Wayne and Carter Hibbard for the presidential nomination, the better people win. Lucy, with all her faults, is a finer woman than Irene, and Wayne is incomparably better equipped for the job of president than Hibbard.

First Lady was written with one eye on the coming 1936 presidential race. By the time it opened at the Music Box on November 26, 1935, the race was already well under way with the leading candidates jockeying for position. Public opinion polls in November placed Senator Borah of Idaho in the lead for the Republican nomination with Governor Alfred Landon of Kansas second, newspaper publisher Frank Knox third, and former President Herbert Hoover fourth. The boom for Landon had all Kansas excited. It was the first time that a Kansan had been given serious consideration for the presidential nomination. Nationally important Republican leaders converged on Topeka, and state politicians asserted, "Landon looks like the best bet." In fact, optimistic Kansans felt that their Governor must be all but on his way to the White House. This interest naturally made *First Lady* an appealing play to an excited public.

Another important change in temper from 1931 was reflected in the play. Roosevelt's theme song for the 1932 campaign, "Happy Days Are Here Again," was coming true. The New York Stock Exchange reported trading for November 16, 1935, the greatest since February, 1934: 3,948,000 shares changed hands with gains averaging from one to four points. Business had improved so much all around that Roosevelt, replying to a letter from Roy W. Howard, chairman of the board of the Scripps-Howard newspapers, said, "This basic [legislative] program has now reached substantial completion and the 'breathing spell' of which you speak is here—very decidedly so."[8] Roosevelt, of course, was referring to his broad New Deal program and especially to its more radical reform aspects.

The time had also come when the playwrights could relax and turn from the hard core of social problems to less urgent topics. Probably the most intriguing centered around politics in the Nation's Capital during the year preceding a presidential election. Washington is always more politically minded than any other city in the country. Even in off years the city is alive with politics; in a presidential year the place fairly hums with it. There is, moreover, another aspect interwoven with politics which sets Washington apart from any other city. Other communities have civic pride in some indigenous activity and set their lights around it;

> Washington having no other primary interest, made Society in capital letters its primary interest and wrapped this society around the banner of politics. . . . But while money counts for little in Washington, family for more, and culture and good manners for much, official connection counts for about everything. Official influence is absolutely necessary to social leadership or even social success.[9]

The struggle for political preeminence in *First Lady* is therefore tacked onto the struggle for social recognition. The battle never lets up in the capital, and the struggle could be set in almost any year. Perhaps the best publicized actual instance of the combination occurred when Charles Curtis came to Washington in 1929 as Vice President. Mr. Curtis was a widower. As Vice President, he presides over the Senate. At social functions, the Vice President outranks by one seat the Speaker of the House of Representatives. Mr. Curtis was aware of his need for a companion at official dinners. He brought his sister, Mrs. Dolly Gann, to Washington and announced that she was going to accompany him to official affairs and was to receive all the privileges due a wife of the Vice President. Whatever happened to Mr. Gann no one ever learned.

This started the battle. Nicholas Longworth was Speaker of the House at the time and his wife was Alice Roosevelt, daughter of Theodore Roosevelt. They refused to accept Mrs. Gann as a substitute Vice Presidential wife. Quickly the word got around that while Speaker and Mrs. Longworth considered Mrs. Gann a charming woman, a fine woman, and a clever woman, they refused to consider her a lady entitled to the privileges of a Vice President's wife. Mrs. Longworth refused to sit below Mrs. Gann. "You may laugh about it now, but that was a genuine crisis," an historian wrote.

> There are about a dozen dinners a year in normal times where the Vice President and the Speaker and their wives normally are invited together. This simply became impossible and even the White House schedules had to be revised. Mrs. Gann accepted invitations, but Mrs. Longworth declined them. Soon official hostesses accepted the fact.[10]

The situation in *First Lady* has many echoes of this competition. It adds to this social rivalry the contest between the ladies' husbands for the presidential nomination. This combination could not help but prove attractive to a public acutely aware of the struggle for the 1936 Republican nomination. In addition, *First Lady* included attacks on pressure groups, newspaper publishers, and political hypocrisy. All these are a part of presidential booms and campaigns. Mrs. Wayne accepts the support of pressure groups to get the boom started for Supreme Court Justice Hibbard. This aspect is satirized in Mrs. Creevy

as head of the women's "Peace, Purity and Patriotism League."
So effective is the maneuver that newspaper publisher Ganning
takes up the drive to nominate Hibbard seriously. Here, as in
State of the Union, the way pressure groups and newspaper
owners work together to promote a presidential boom is clearly
shown. The hypocrisy behind political attitudes, even of officeholders' wives, is expressed by Belle Hardwick. Mrs. Hardwick,
wife of a senator, tells a friend to take a cigarette:

> You could use them Mary—Cabinet members don't
> run for office. But our state. My dear, they have
> kidnappers, and rape, and more general hell-raising
> than you can shake a stick at, but their politicians'
> home lives must be pure. Caesar's wife was a hussy
> compared to what a Senator's wife from our state
> must be. If I smoked these at home, Tom would lose
> the election sure.

Jane Cowl played Lucy Wayne, Stanley Ridges was Stephen
Wayne, and Lilly Cahill took the role of Irene Hibbard.

From Hoyt's *A Texas Steer* to Kaufman and Dayton's
First Lady is a period of forty-four years. Physically Washington changed dramatically during that time, from a small country town to a large sophisticated city. The importance of the
Nation's Capital had also grown, and was destined to grow even
more. But as these plays, and others in this chapter, suggest, the
one unchanging factor in the city's life is the connection between
the social and political worlds. In President Jackson's day the
social battle lines had their repercussions in the political arena.
First Lady more than a hundred years later shared the same
situation. The plays about Washington reflect the social mores
current when each was written. Their one common denominator
is the important part social activities and relationships exert upon
politics in the city. This connection inevitably leaves an
impress upon the laws passed by Congress. For this reason,
if no other, plays about this side of Washington life have a
contribution to make toward furthering understanding by
Americans elsewhere of the numerous elements that go into the
milieu of their Nation's Capital.

6

CRUSADING TEENS
AND FABULOUS
TWENTIES

As THE early morning sun on August 13,
1913, crept over the New York State capitol in Albany, a man
arose in the Assembly chambers and called for a vote to impeach
the forty-second governor of the state. The demand climaxed
hours of speeches, delays, and conferences. Through the long
night assemblymen had been kept at their desks in anticipation
of this call. Some had put their heads on their arms and slept;
others wandered aimlessly around the chambers; others listlessly
read newspapers and magazines. On a few occasions the
Speaker of the House, Alfred E. Smith, had to bang his gavel
in order to awaken the members for a vote.

The long delay was contrived so Assemblymen could come by
train from New York and other places to vote on the impeachment proceedings. A little after 5 A.M., all the Assemblymen
who could be brought to Albany had arrived. A few minutes
later Majority Leader Aaron J. Levy called for the impeachment vote. At 5:16 A.M., the vote was completed, and Gov-

ernor William Sulzer was impeached, seventy-nine to forty-five, of having diverted campaign contributions to his own use and of having made false statements as to how these contributions had been spent. With the vote a promising and brilliant political career came to an abrupt halt. The impeachment brought a wave of protest from the city, state, and nation, newspapers and magazines charging that Tammany Hall's victory was a smashing blow at good government.

Sulzer's impeachment was the climax of a turn that saw a "safe" party man take seriously his campaign promises. Before his election as governor, Sulzer was a solid Tammany Hall man. He had served his party well in the Assembly from 1889 to 1894, and had continued to serve the party as a Congressman from 1894 to 1912. Shortly after his election as governor a magazine called Sulzer a loyal member of Tammany Hall, but noted that he "is identified by both his adherents and his opponents with the progressive wing of the Democratic Party." This judgment was borne out by Sulzer's record. In Congress, he supported such legislation as the direct election of United States Senators, progressive labor bills, and the short ballot. As early as 1898 Sulzer, who looked like Henry Clay and carried out that resemblance in his dress and gestures, was spoken of as a governorship possibility.

During the gubernatorial campaign of 1912, Sulzer repeatedly asserted, "My only boss is under my own hat," but Tammany Hall supporters smiled knowingly at the statement, and the opposition ridiculed it. But Sulzer meant what he said, for shortly after his inauguration he proposed legislation and named office appointees that quickly led to a break with Charles Francis Murphy, leader of Tammany Hall. The new governor made the break inevitable when he removed several of Murphy's favorites from state department posts. When Sulzer refused to appoint James E. Gaffney as state highway commissioner, the cleavage became irreparable. According to one source, Murphy sent Sulzer an ultimatum, "Gaffney or war." It was to be war. "If Sulzer is to fight Tammany, there must be real weapons and real blood, and at the end a corpse," the *Nation* of January 9, 1913 said. The Governor was to be the political corpse.

"The irreparable break came when the governor vetoed the primary election bills proposed by the legislature, and insisted on a thorough-going direct primary, which would mean the abolition of the party convention," the *Outlook* of October 18, 1913, observed. "At this point the Republican machine began to make common cause with the Democratic organizations, for the party convention is essential to the continuance of both."

Both parties teamed in producing the seventy-nine votes that found William Sulzer guilty of not making a full accounting of his campaign expenditures. In the light of the period's practices, the charges were absurd. An editorial in *Outlook* declared that two issues were present, "one concerns the guilt or innocence of William Sulzer; the other concerns the Invisible Government." The article asserted the offenses, "though undeniably grave," were not "of the sort that warrant even so high a court as the High Court of Impeachment to remove him from office." Invisible Government, most comment declared, won. The impeachment was political, brought about by the machines to save their powers.

Less than a year later, in April, 1914, *The Governor's Boss,* by James S. Barcus, reached the Broadway stage. Despite its forced happy ending—in the play the Governor fights successfully against impeachment charges—numerous details suggest the production was inspired by the Sulzer case. Governor Manville and "Boss" Haggerty fall out over political appointments to state offices. Manville refuses to appoint Jackson, Commissioner of Highways because he is "connected with your [Haggerty's] partner's contracting firm. The public have sanctioned the expenditure of a good many millions of dollars on roads, and if the people don't think it is spent honestly for roads, it would hurt me politically." Murphy's known practice of bringing Tammany into partnership with big business indicates an apparent parallel. "Political leaders became partners in business enterprises and then compelled the awarding of large contracts to their companies," one historian of political machines said.[1]

After Manville refuses to allow the lure of a presidential nomination to sway him, Haggerty laughs at the governor's statement that the people have their rights:

> I never thought you'd come to be a sentimentalist. That's mushy talk. The people haven't got nothin' to do with it. Never did have. It's the leaders that control politics—call 'em bosses if ye want—who cares, and that's the way the universe is run. Any man who believes in an Almighty God, believes in an intelligent despotism.

Haggerty then contrives to have Manville impeached. From here on the play becomes melodrama, with the girl who was betrayed by the boss' son using a concealed moving picture to show the boss bribing assemblymen to vote for the impeachment. The play ends with the Governor triumphant. It did not work out so well in real life.

Another form of political corruption, the importance of big corporation approval for political advancement, appeared in *A Man of Honor* (1911), by Isaac Landman. Judge Amos Kingsley is slated to receive the nomination for governor of Montana when it is learned his son has embezzled a mining company's funds. An important decision effecting the company is to be given by the Judge, and William Price, president of the corporation, tries to force a favorable verdict by using his knowledge of the embezzlement. Kingsley, however, refuses to change his adverse findings, even though it means the loss of the nomination. But all turns out well when the president's daughter forces him to change his stand by indicating that she was involved in the embezzlement through her love for the Judge's son. The connection between big business and politics appears several times, particularly during the talks between the Judge and Price. In one conversation Price tells Kingsley, "Then I will speak plainly. (*Pause*) I'll give you the nomination—if you give me the decision in the Wills-Consolidated case . . . others whose standing on the bench is as high as yours have done it." But the Judge, being a man of honor, kicks Price out of the house instead.

* * * * * * *

"Child labor must go," an article in *Cosmopolitan* for November, 1906, declared. "Two millions of children, boys and girls, wend, every working day of the year, to factory, mine and shop, there to yield up their blunted energies and underdeveloped minds to the insatiable demands of industry." Working conditions, particularly for women and children, lay heavy on the conscience of the nation during the early years of the twentieth century. They inspired much labor legislation during the first and second decades, and these in turn inspired plays dealing with the political aspects of the problem. This proved especially true the second decade, when several plays of power and influence were good theatre, for they wedded the natural humanitarian impulses of such legislation with the hard-headed business reasons that used politics to oppose restrictions on working hours and working conditions.

The ground for labor legislation was laid by the periodical writers of the first decade. They pointed out conditions which eventually resulted in legislation changing them. In 1907 a writer noted that shopgirls during the Christmas holiday season worked ten hours a day, six days a week, for an average salary of seven dollars to twelve dollars a week. The girls were at the twin mercies of male customers and floor walkers, the floor walkers being hired to protect the pretty girls from their admirers. "In many cases he [the floor walker] was also unprincipled and designing, and should his advances be repelled by a girl in his department, he has it in his power to ruin her chances for advancement, even to make her lose her position."[2] Of course a

shopgirl's social life was somewhat hindered by living in a furnished room, for which she paid $2.50 a week. The walk-up
unheated room with an iron bed, combination washstand and
dresser, and one chair was not exactly conducive to entertainment, even if she had the money with which to entertain. Some
of the better paid girls could afford rooms with heat and better
furniture for three dollars to four dollars a week, and a very
few earned enough to pay five dollars for a comfortable room.
Fourteen-year-old girls worked in box factories the year round
from seven-thirty in the morning to six in the evening, with a
half-hour off for lunch. During the Christmas rush season, they
increased their income slightly by working Monday, Tuesday,
and Thursday nights until nine o'clock, with five minutes off for
supper. Delivery and messenger boys also worked long days
during the Christmas rush. "I ain't had a decent sleep since
November," one messenger boy mumbled. "Eleven this morning
when I began to work. I won't get done till one tomorrow . . .
these here holidays is hell for us fellers."[3]

"You need not know that your Christmas delight comes out of
thousands of little sorrows," thundered the poet Edwin Markham. "But you will know this by and by; and then you will rise
up in holy anger and sweep away the system that makes these
inhumanities possible."

An early play dealing with these conditions was *The Offenders*
(1908), by Elmer Blaney Harris. Unfortunately, the play is a
confused piece of work. Its main plot concerns the efforts of
Helen Street and Judge Winter to push a child labor bill through
the state legislature. The big corporations and the big political
boss, Helen Street's husband, oppose the measure. Its fate is
never adequately explained as the story goes off on diverse
tangents.

Two arguments against passage of the measure appear, both of
them having some current truth. "Well," one of the mill owners
says gloomily to Mrs. Street, "I've got to compete with Southern
mills—where child labor is a legitimate asset, and I've got to
employ children."

The other comes from Horace Street. "Last night you asked me to support Judge Winter's bill prohibiting child labor," he tells his wife. "If I do, I shall lose the backing of the most influential corporations of this state. I shall jeopardize my own position. I can't afford to do it."

Mrs. Street later declares that the bill has been side-tracked because "My husband is in the clutches of a vicious political system—government by corporations. He has to support the machine and the machine's against Judge Winter." It is interesting to note that this play appeared at the end of the so-called "muckraking period," when attacks on big business manipulation of state and national lawmaking bodies were still popular.

Probably the best of the plays integrating labor legislation and politics was Edward Sheldon's *The High Road* (1912). It opens on an act faintly suggesting Eugene O'Neill's *Beyond the Horizon*. Mary Page, a country girl, longs for the world beyond the small limits of her home. She becomes the mistress of an artist and travels with him to distant lands. Years later she becomes a leader in the fight for labor legislation to better working conditions for children and women. Mary meets and marries the governor of the state, who has ambitions to be president. The governor is ready to sign a labor bill limiting the workday of women to eight hours when interests fighting the measure threaten to bring Mary's past into the open unless the governor vetoes the bill. In an exciting scene Mary denounces the boss and dictates a statement admitting her past and revealing how the opposition was using it for political purposes. She has the statement ready for newspaper publication, but the boss withdraws his opposition and all ends happily.

The pathetic efforts of working girls to better their conditions during the early years of the twentieth century are described by Mary. She tells of a strike of laundry girls:

> When they first began, they had a funny little parade.
> My brougham was held up while they crossed Fifth
> Avenue on Eighteenth Street. All the men were

laughing at them and making jokes—you can imagine. One little girl carried a very home-made banner, with 'Sisters we need you' sewed on in red letters. I was quite close—close enough to see their faces. They were so young—and tired—and brave.

But they were unorganized. And so they lost the strike. However, it was the memory of this scene which inspired Mary to fight successfully for labor legislation years later.

Conditions in the mills of the nation were studied by Bayard Veiller in *Back Home* (1915), a play based on a series of magazine stories by Irvin S. Cobb. Called the "Billy Sunday of the theatre" by many critics, Veiller declared he was "somewhat like a revivalist because I try to reach people through the basic emotions that are the same everywhere and in all persons." The appeal to people on the subject of child-labor abuses in mills was a basic one in 1915. *Back Home* tells how Robert Carter tried to expose working conditions in a mill owned by J. W. Wayne. Intertwined with this theme is the fight of Judge Priest, who backs Carter, to win renomination. During the action Carter kills a thug in a street fight, and the jury trial becomes part of the other two situations. The play is straight melodrama, but its sympathetic approach to the child labor question indicates how the people were thinking during the era.

The Earth (1916), by James B. Fagan, mixes politics, labor bills, and newspaper influence. A labor bill in Parliament appears likely to win, in spite of the opposition of Sir Felix Janion, newspaper publisher. Janion learns of an illicit love affair the backer of the bill is having with the Countess of Kilone and threatens to expose them unless Denzil Trevena withdraws the measure. Trevena agrees, but the Countess defies the publisher and refuses to allow her lover to withdraw the bill. Janion bows to defeat and surrenders the incriminating documents to the lovers. The similarity to *The High Road* is immediately apparent. The play not only focused attention upon the labor situation but also brought into prominence the question of a monopolistic press controlling public opinion. Janion tells Trevena at one point, "The circulation of my morning papers alone is close to 4,000,000 a day, and it's going to be more. I disapprove of your bill. I'll smash it if I can."

"In London," a critic said, "the play created a small sensation for in the character of Sir Felix Janion everyone quickly recognized a forceful portrait of Lord Northcliffe, the directing mind of the Harmsworth Press, which practically controlled the destiny of England and her policies."[4] With Grace George, Clarence Derwent, and Louis Calvert in the leading roles, the play proved a "hit." In the cast was another young actor destined for later fame, particularly as a director—Guthrie McClintic.

*   *   *   *   *   *   *

Before 1910 women had voting privileges only in Wyoming, Colorado, Utah, and Idaho. In 1910 the State of Washington granted suffrage to women, and the following year California followed suit. From then on the movement gained adherents in many states. Declarations favoring woman's suffrage by both major parties in 1916 virtually assured the vote for women in the near future. President Wilson himself wrote the plank for the Democratic platform that year, "We recommend the extension of the franchise to the women of this country, state by state, on the same terms as to the men." For the Republican Party the plank drafted by Senators Lodge, Borah, and Wadsworth said, "We favor the extension of suffrage to women, but recognize the right of each state to settle this question for itself." On May 21, 1919, the House voted approval of the Nineteenth Amendment, giving suffrage to women. On June 4 the Senate followed suit, and by August 25, 1920, the necessary thirty-six states had ratified the amendment, and it became officially effective August 27, 1920. Women had won the long hard fight for voting and holding office.

Despite these stirring events only two trivial plays treating the part women were playing in politics reached the Broadway stage.

The dramatization of this problem, then, was essentially what it had been in the 1890's. One was *The Fight* (1913), and the other *Her Honor, the Mayor* (1918). *The Fight,* by Bayard Veiller, was a lurid melodrama about the efforts of local politicians to force Jane Thomas' withdrawal as candidate for mayor. The plot includes a run on the bank, which had been left to Jane by her father, adventures in a house of ill-fame, and a corrupt senator. *Her Honor, the Mayor,* by Arline Van Ness Hines, is an amusing play about a spinster who is elected Mayor and cleans out the corrupt politicians in her household-approach to running the city. The play ends with the Mayor turning down the nomination for governor in order to marry the District Attorney.

* * * * * * *

The crusading spirit of second decade plays hitting the evils of boss rule and bad working conditions for women and children was lost in the carefree and irresponsible atmosphere of the 1920's. These themes were overshadowed by prohibition and attendant problems revolving around "the noble experiment." Innocuous plays about woman's suffrage and the Washington scene also continued into the next decade, indicating that the good times of this lush era had turned the political playwright away from serious themes. It was not until the depression and the 1930's that the political dramatist, with some rare exceptions, returned to a thoughtful examination of the world about him.

The Twenties was the fabulous era. It was an era of marathon dances, English channel swimmers, and flag-pole sitters. Night club patrons grinned happily when "Texas" Guinan greeted them with "Hello, sucker," and waxed sentimental when Helen Morgan, sitting atop a piano, sang lachrymose ballads. The nation became hot with Teapot Dome and kept cool with Coolidge; held Disarmament Conferences that did not disarm, and made the great American withdrawal into its own backyard. It was also an era of zooming stock markets and large dividends. "Big business is very happy," according to the *Nation,* September

7, 1927. "If anybody questions it, let him look at the continued boom in the stock market, the unprecedented speculation which is filling the pockets of bankers, brokers, and the general public in a way even to alarm Wall Street." And the *Outlook* for July 25, 1928 echoed the *Nation's* sentiments in a cheerful article entitled, "Nearly Every Prospect Pleases." The article lived up to its title:

> the output of steel set new records for all time (in the first half of 1928); auto production was well ahead of 1925 and 1927 and not far behind 1926, the industry's best year; and new construction contracted for in the 37 states east of the Rocky Mountains during the first five months was the largest ever.

It was further an era of woman's suffrage, talking moving pictures, and prohibition. But above all it was an era of "the noble experiment." Few facts in American life hit so closely home, to drinker and non-drinker alike, as the Eighteenth Amendment. "Bathtub gin" was a slap-happy phrase of the period, and respectable citizens gloried in the way they evaded the law. With prohibition came speakeasies which closed one day and opened the next. On their heels rode gangsters and gang rides, law enforcement and graft. Prohibition and politics and gangland became mixed up more and more as the decade advanced. "The underworld organization is interrelated with and is a phase of political control," a report on the period concluded.

> The relative immunity to punishment of gangsters encouraged in organized crime has its counterpart in the huge amounts of graft received for protection by police and politicians. This is a form of crime on which there are few or no available statistics, but the individual cases that have been uncovered in many of our cities indicate its wide prevalence.[5]

Americans like to put into personalities facts that appeal to them. It personified itself as lean-faced, long-legged, and goatee-bearded Uncle Sam. Theodore Roosevelt's trust-busting tactics inspired cartoons showing him speaking softly but carrying a "big stick." Dry advocates were pictured as blue-nosed, gloomy-faced, and black-dressed men. The country needed a symbol for the excesses of prohibition, and Al "Scarface" Capone became its symbol. He more than satisfied the nation's morbid curiosity about gangsters and gang leaders. He wore two hundred and fifty dollar suits, thirty dollar monogrammed shirts, forty dollar shoes, twelve dollar silk underwear, and stayed in lavish hotel suites.[6] The Chicago gangster intrigued the country by his ability to stay out of jail. It was not until the government convicted him of income tax evasion that Capone was put behind bars. Only in his funeral did Capone fail to fulfill the nation's conception of a gang leader, and by that time the lush period had long passed. Instead of the customary $50,000 silver-and-bronze coffin, flowers filling several autos, and thousands of mourners milling around a chapel to hear services, Capone was buried in January, 1947, in a $2,000 coffin, without bands, with few flowers, and fewer mourners.

There were surprisingly few plays on prohibition and politics. But one of them, *The Racket* (1927), by Bartlett Cormack, fully caught the spirit of the Chicago picture. It did so, so faithfully that the author wrote a sharp preface to the printed work declaring:

> The names, the characters themselves, and the story of *The Racket* are imaginary. The author is thrilled with satisfaction at having worked so well that his characters and story are believed, of course. But he is, also, annoyed, and when the protestors are mighty in authority and means, as those who have been so falsely identified with *The Racket* are, he is annoyed in no uncertain terms. For the sake of his character as, if I may say so, a creative artist, and for the sake of the actual persons he is reported to have skinned alive and penned, hurt, and embarrassed in their nakedness, against his scene, the playwright consequently denies that he is a combination photographer, stenographer, phonograph and dictaphone, and asks to be regarded instead as a play-

wright, to whom unrelated facts, people and experiences are the raw material from which he distils, as
perfectly and significantly as he is able, a play.[7]

The story is comparatively simple. Nick Scarsi, a leading
gangster with a strong political pull, and Captain McQuigg, an
honest policeman, are feuding. Captain McQuigg has been
shunted into a desolate section of the city, apparently through
Scarsi's political influence. Joe, Scarsi's young brother, is
brought into McQuigg's station for stealing a car. McQuigg sees
his chance to get at Scarsi and manages to keep Joe in jail
despite political pressure. Scarsi, failing in his efforts to release
Joe, tries to bribe the policeman who made the arrest. Scarsi
fails here, too. Angry and worried by how much the policeman
knows, he shoots the officer as Ames, a new reporter on the
police beat, walks into the station house. Tricked by the girl
who was with Joe at the time of the arrest, Scarsi later blurts out
that he shot the policeman. With Ames' identification of Scarsi
as the murderer to complete the case, McQuigg slaps the gang
leader into jail. Scarsi tries to escape and is shot in the attempt.

Within the limits of the fast-moving play, Cormack shows how
the police, newspapers, party nominations for office, orders for
city jobs, campaign donations by gangsters, and influence were
integral parts of the prohibition picture. The last was carefully
developed through a series of ascending steps. At the start of
the play Scarsi is credited with getting McQuigg transferred to
his present isolated post. His political influence rests upon
Scarsi's control of foreign voters in an important area of the city.
"How does Scarsi control voters?" Ames asks.

"He gives them their daily beer," Pratt answers, "so hallowed
be his name. Anyway, weren't you always fascinated by pirates
rather than saints?"

Assistant State's Attorney Welch tries to get Scarsi out,
and is accused by McQuigg of sticking by the gangster. Welch
cries:

I'm not sticking to Scarsi. I'm sticking to the Old Man. *(His voice rising)* Why shouldn't I? He's helped me— put me on the ticket for County Judge. This is for him. And the quieter things are till after Tuesday— Nick's too influential to fuss with, that's all.

The scale of influence rapidly goes up and up, until it finally reaches the unidentified "Old Man." Scarsi, angry because McQuigg is foiling every effort to free him, threatens Welch that he will make public all he knows. He yells:

I got it on paper. Yeh, I got everythin' up my sleeve—ready for a double-cross by you. How you made that special investigatin' grand jury o' prom- inent high-hats fold up last month by condemnin' the elevators in a couple o' million dollar department stores. Yeh. And by reminding some o' our leading citizens o' the extra apartments they keep . . . how you framed the Civic Board, to get your own hogs in there, because that Board's got 75 million to spend next year. . . . I won't stop blown' up this town. I'll talk some o' your State politicians into court— making me pay ten grand a head for pardons and paroles. I'll talk some o' your Republicans in the Federal Building into committin' suicide over the liquor dope I got. Who do you suppose I pay for the breweries I own? Who do you suppose I pay for the alcohol I get? I'll knock your whole organization cuckoo.

When Scarsi makes his break for an escape, it is with the con- nivance of Welch. The Attorney knows Scarsi's gun is without bullets, but that the state policeman is carrying a loaded gun. The official explanation, McQuigg tells the reporters, is "Mr. Scarsi tried a getaway. Sergeant Turck o' the State's Attorney office got him."

To which one of the reporters say, "So that government o' the professionals, by the professionals and for the professionals, shall not perish from the earth." Ironically, among those taking a minor role in the play was Edward G. Robinson, who later became famous in moving pictures as the portrayer of gangland leader roles. Here Robinson was merely "an unidentified man."

Prohibition was more than an era of gangland atrocities. It had its genteel side, the side of men in public office who voted dry and drank wet. On March 1, 1926, Augustus Thomas' *Still Waters* brought this side of prohibition to the stage. It was written, Thomas said, "with the purpose of presenting in the theatre some of the objections to national prohibition in America."

In the play Senator Clayborn votes dry, but drinks wet. He comes out for modification of the Volstead Act in the race for renomination, and, by compromising with both politicians and bootleggers, wins. He is cynical about prohibition and his own role in relation to the Act. "Some men achieve dryness, some have dryness thrust upon them," he tells his bootlegger. "Only a political dry could get the camp meeting vote in our state, you know that, and the real people'd rather have a liar than a fanatic." The strongest supporters of prohibition were the bootleggers. The Senator's bootlegger gets excited when Clayborn tells him he is in favor of having the Volstead Act modified.

"Then where's my business gone," the bootlegger cries. Asked by Clayborn if that is why he is against him, the man says, "Do you want any better reason?"

Oh, Henry, by Bide Dudley, was a 1920 satire on prohibition. It told how a correct family met the problem when a drunken stranger is put into the master's bedroom by the new butler, with anti-drink and wealthy Aunt Annabelle arriving soon after. All turns out well when the stranger proves to be Aunt Annabelle's recently acquired husband. Chief value of the play today lies in the way it made use of jokes current in its own period. Lizzie tells Boswell she only drinks "when I'm sick," and then adds, "I'm a good deal of a weaklin'—sick about half my time."

A play that started out with the effect prohibition had upon politicians and politics and ended with the influence politics had on women in their home life was William Hodge's *The Judge's Husband* (1926). Signs of the times are evident when a young man is arrested because he has liquor in his car. It is later learned that the liquor had been given by the city's solid citizens to the judge, who placed it in the car.

Another play of gangsters and politics was *Merry-Go-Round* (1932), by Albert Malz and George Sklar. A bellboy in a hotel sees gangster leader, Jig Zelli, shoot a rival who is trying to muscle into his territory. Police force the bellboy to identify Zelli as the man who shot Stransky, and praise the boy for his courage. But Zelli exerts strong political influence by threatening to give the newspapers information involving political leaders in the liquor racket. Desperate, the politicians decide to make bellboy Martin the goat. Martin is beaten badly at police headquarters and taken to the hospital. A doctor becomes interested in the situation, and through him a smart lawyer builds up an airtight case against the machine. Faced with an election, the political leaders decide the murder trial must not take place. Martin is hanged in his cell, and the verdict is suicide. The play is fast moving and exciting. Some of the major characters achieve individuality, and the impact of prohibition days is felt by the reader.

* * * * * * *

By 1924, women had been able to vote and hold office for four years. But the debate hadn't died down. If anything, it was more virulent. Proponents and opponents of woman's suffrage marshalled their figures in neat battalions and marched them to battle. "Lost, 14,000,000 Women Voters" one magazine article said. Other articles read, "Did They Know What They Wanted?," "What Have Women Done With The Vote?," "Are Women a

Failure in Politics?," and "Are Women Making Good in Politics?"

These articles had something to debate. In 1920, one tendency was to view with alarm the "Awful Dangers of Woman Suffrage"— a serious discussion of America's ratification of the Nineteenth Amendment by a British publication. Another tendency was to make fun of the new privileges, such articles as "How Is Your Cook Going to Vote?" being popular. More serious students, intent on analyzing the historical background leading up to the winning of the ballot for women, wrote essays on "The American Woman Gets the Vote." By the end of the decade, however, the controversy had died down. In contrast with the Eighteenth Amendment, the Nineteenth Amendment had comparatively easy sailing into the harbor of public acceptance. After the 1928 election, there was no question but that woman suffrage had come to stay. The fight that began with the first woman's rights convention at Seneca, New York, in 1848, and had been carried on by Lucretia Mott, Elizabeth Cady Stanton, Susan B. Anthony, and others, had been largely won.

Probably the easy acceptance of woman's suffrage had something to do with the frothy plays on the topic. The earliest still regarded it as something in the nature of a joke. *Immodest Violet* (1920), by David Carb, combined woman's suffrage with the Twenties' penchant for putting ladies on stage in night clothes. Violet wants to attend a woman's suffrage convention in Texas. She borrows the ten dollars she needs for fare from a young man rooming in the home of her aunt, where Violet is staying. But Violet was indiscreet, for she went to the man's room at midnight, in her nightie, to borrow the money. Caught, the two young people run away, are captured, and escape going to jail by getting married.

Everyday (1921), by Rachel Crothers, was a better play. Nineteen-year-old Phyllis Nolan returns home from Europe to learn that her father has arranged for her marriage to the political boss of the state. In return, Nolan was to receive the nomination for governor. Phyllis rebels and marries a World War I veteran who has promise as a painter.

So This Is Politics, originally *The Clean-Up* (1924), by Barry Connors, indicates the more serious part women were taking in political campaigns. By 1924 women weren't satisfied merely to sit back and listen to what their husbands and others told them; they wanted to find out for themselves. They also wanted to hold office and to be in on the party counsels. Nina Buckmaster is nominated for mayor of a mid-western town, and accepts the support of its political boss to win. Butch McKenna, the boss, teaches Nina the tricks of the trade, and by the end of the play she is holding her own in the hard-boiled game of politics. She wins the election. Butch McKenna's advice has three points. Don't have a slogan of economy, he warns. "It would lose votes, ma'am," he advises. "The people are sick of economical administrations. They always cost too much." Platforms, he continues "are a good deal like street car platforms; they're not to stand on—they're to get in on." Finally, fight fire with fire. Nina's husband and brothers lose their jobs, the mortgage on the house is suddenly called in, and the finance company wants its payments on the car at once. McKenna meets these tactics by employing similar ones on the ladies in Nina's club. He lets one lady know her husband may lose his job with a firm McKenna has an interest in unless he stops making trouble for Nina. He tells another lady her son wouldn't get the appointment to West Point unless she takes a more active interest in furthering Nina's campaign.

The Judge's Husband (1926), by William Hodge, illustrated the "awful dangers of woman's suffrage." Judge Kirby has become so interested in politics that her home life suffers. Mr. Kirby disappears, and their daughter gets into a scrape. The Judge is finally shocked into realizing that politics and home life do not mix. She decides to devote her full time to the home and resigns from the bench.

Love and politics is the theme of *Skidding* (1928), by Aurania Rouverol. Mary, Judge Hardy's daughter, pitches into the campaign for his renomination against the political bosses with such skill and vigor that she is also nominated for office. But her fiance doesn't like the idea, and gives Mary an ultimatum of "When you marry me you promise to love, honor and stay out of politics." She marries the man.

*   *   *   *   *   *   *

Plays revolving around elections reflected the irresponsible spirit of the Twenties. They embodied the feelings of an elderly lady who during the depression somewhat wistfully said, "It would be nice to be able to afford Jimmy Walker as mayor of New York again."

Loud Speaker (1927), by John Howard Lawson, was in this spirit. It is a farce about a candidate for governor who gets full of synthetic gin just before he delivers a radio speech. Unrestrained by inhibitions, the candidate tells his invisible audience, "I've done a lot of crooked things and I've enjoyed them. I'm too good to be governor; I get more satisfaction out of telling the American public to go to hell." The result was a landslide victory for him.

The disappointing part of *Make Me Know It* (1929), by D. Frank Marcus, was its failure to develop an interesting theme. The colored boss of a colored neighborhood decides to run a colored candidate for alderman against the white incumbent. "Boss" Bannon's motive is to forestall the reform movement that threatens to cut into his rackets. The play unfortunately does not pursue its theme, but instead is sidetracked into an unbelievable triangle involving Bannon, his adopted daughter, Mona, and the colored candidate for office. Bannon proves himself so noble that the adopted daughter marries him.

Seed of the Brute (1926), by Knowles Entrikin, has several exciting scenes and strong characters. It is the story of an uneducated man who has become a political power in a small town. His son refuses to follow Calvin Roberts' footsteps, but an illegitimate son does. This son buys the town newspaper and defeats Roberts and the political machine in an ensuing struggle.

*   *   *   *   *   *   *

The dramatist who was concerned with political themes made definite progress during the first thirty years of this century. During the 1890's playwrights used political situations chiefly for the local color they brought to a plot or for the emotional responses they evoked. There was little effort, save in a few cases, to make the political situation an integral part of the play. The dramatist followed this path because that was what audiences wanted. The success of *The Senator, The Last Stroke,* and *A Contented Woman* indicates the political immaturity of the audiences.

With the turn of the century, the public's response to the burgeoning sources of information in the daily press and the weekly and monthly magazines became apparent in the plays on the Broadway stage. Specific abuses in American political life began to appear in plays because there was a large enough public now to see them. *The Sultan of Sulu, The Lion and the Mouse, The Man of the Hour, The Undertow, The High Road, The Governor's Boss,* and *The Racket* each attacked definite abuses in American politics. That they could have appeared with anything like equal success before 1900 is extremely doubtful, for the man in the street then had neither the sources of information nor the consequent awareness of political tides to appreciate their messages. Yet these plays had a limitation those following sought to correct. By attacking a particular abuse the playwright implied it should be abolished. But he did not go beyond that, except possibly in *The Undertow.* He did not point towards a philosophy of government that each citizen should have. This concept was to be the contribution of plays written since 1930.

7

TWO TRIALS THAT
SHOOK THE WORLD

THE EYES of the world were on Boston the night of August 22, 1927. In Paris crowds gathered before the bulletin boards of the city's newspapers, waiting tensely for news from Massachusetts. Demonstrators crowded London's Hyde Park and marched past Buckingham Palace singing the "Red Flag" and shouting "Sacco and Vanzetti must not die." Work came to a complete stop in Buenos Aires. Berlin mobs cheered speeches urging that American goods be boycotted if the two Italians died, and in Tokyo the United States embassy was guarded following the receipt of bombing threats.

In Boston 800 police stood guard before Charlestown Prison. They weren't needed. At the governor's mansion, Governor Alvan T. Fuller heard last minute appeals from Sacco's wife and Vanzetti's sister. "I am sorry," he told them. "My duties are . outlined by law."

At 11:45 P.M. William G. Thompson, chief counsel for the prisoners, left the governor's mansion and told waiting reporters, "I was trying to do my full duty by my former clients whom I believe to be innocent and who have not had a fair trial. If I had not believed it, I would not have been here tonight."

As the minute hand of the clock crept towards the twelve mark, preparations within the prison for the executions went on. First to go was Celestino Madeiros, admitted criminal who confessed he had been at the shooting of the Slater & Morrill Co. paymaster and guard on April 15, 1920, in South Braintree, Massachusetts. His statement absolving Sacco and Vanzetti from participating in the murders was not believed. He died for another murder.

Next to go was Nicola Sacco, shoemaker, draft evader, and anarchist. As the guards adjusted the straps,

> Sacco sat bolt upright in the chair of death. Casting about wildly with his eyes, he cried in Italian 'long live anarchy.' Then he calmed himself, and in a quieter tone in English added, 'farewell, my wife and child and all my friends.' His last was 'farewell, my mother.' The farewell was in English, the rest 'mia matre' in his native tongue.[1]

Last to go was Bartolomeo Vanzetti, fish-peddler, natural poet, anarchist. He went calmly, quietly. Perhaps as he walked the final few steps he thought of the letter he wrote, in poor grammar but of noble thought, to a well-wisher:

> If it had not been for these thing, I might have live out my life talking at street corners to scorning men. I might have die, unmarked, unknown, a failure. Now we are not a failure. This is our career and our triumph. Never in our full life could we hope to do such work for tolerance, for joostice, for man's onderstanding of man as now we do by accident. Our words— our lives—lives of a good shoemaker and a poor fish-peddler—all. That last moment belongs to us—that agony is our triumph.[2]

He died a few minutes before 12:30 A.M. So came to an end the fight to save Sacco and Vanzetti. They were convicted in 1921 of shooting paymaster Frank Parmenter and guard

Alexander Berardelli as the two carried the payroll from their automobile to the shoe factory. The escape, with the more than $15,000 payroll, was made in a waiting automobile.

From the opening of the trial in Dedham, Massachusetts, on May 31, 1921, until Sacco and Vanzetti met their deaths in 1927, the case became a *cause célèbre*. It quickly gained the ears of people beyond the city, state, and country. "Not since the time of the Dreyfus affair has international feeling risen to so high a peak as it did in the case of Sacco and Vanzetti," a scholarly observer later said. "Throughout Europe and America radical and conservative opinion locked horns over this conviction and the proceedings which followed it."[3]

The case broke when feelings were high against the "Red menace" in America, and the raids instigated by Attorney General A. Mitchell Palmer were still fresh in the public's mind. Defenders of the two men charged that the trial was unfairly conducted and the defendants were "convicted by atmosphere, not evidence." The political battle-lines were quickly drawn, with extremists on one side demanding "electrocute them even if they're innocent" and extremists on the other side demanding "release them even if they're guilty." Judge Webster Thayer was accused by some of "extreme bias" in conducting the case and defended by others as having been "eminently fair." The point of view depended on your political beliefs.

Gods of the Lightning (1928), came to the Broadway stage when the echoes of the case had not yet died down. One critic pointed out that it was "interesting throughout though it is difficult to judge how much of the dramatic is injected by the reaction of the audience. Mr. Anderson knows the value of touching a chord that is still vibrating."[4] Writing after the first performance on October 24, 1928, Brooks Atkinson observed that Maxwell Anderson and Harold Hickerson had fashioned "a strong, harrowing drama" whose chief characters are presented "as innocent of the crime of which they stand accused."

Gods of the Lightning was obviously based on the Sacco and Vanzetti case. The action is placed in a restaurant and a courtroom, and the emphasis is upon the atmosphere that went into making the trial one of political beliefs rather than of criminal prosecution. Sacco and Vanzetti are easily recognized as Macready, labor leader, and Capraro, dreamy anarchist. Judge Webster Thayer bears many resemblances to Judge Vail, and the same is true of many of the other characters to those in the real life drama.

The play early brings up the "red scare" of the period. Gluckstein, lawyer for the defense, visits District Attorney Salter to tell him:

> I know you haven't any evidence. I know the boys aren't guilty. I know the case looks as if it were going against you. But if you keep on playing up the Bolshevik business to that jury—why it's plain murder. You tell that jury a man's a radical and the whole twelve will vote to hang him.

Foreman of the jury in real life was Walter R. Ripley. One of the defense lawyers for Sacco and Vanzetti, later a Pennsylvania judge declared:

> [Ripley] was not only prejudiced against Italians in general, but he had a special and specific prejudice against Sacco and Vanzetti. On May 31, 1921, while on his way to the courthouse, before the taking of testimony began, he met an old friend, William H. Daly. Daly expressed doubt as to the guilt of the defendents. Ripley was incensed, and replied, 'Damn them, they ought to hang anyway.'[5]

In the play the foreman rises in the jury box, points a finger at Macready and asks, "There was a bomb set off under my house last night. Now I don't want to do anybody an injustice, but I was under the impression Mr. Macready believed in violence. If he don't I'd like to know where that bomb came from."

The other charges aired during the long battle for a new
trial are brought out in the play—the Judge's alleged unfair-
ness, the lack of credibility of the witnesses, the confession of
Madeiros. Most effective is the final scene, where those in the
restaurant waiting word of the executions parallel the tense-
ness of the people who kept the death watch the night of
August 22, 1927. "The final act represents the night of execution, with its wild rumors and horrific emotions," *New York
Times* critic Atkinson said. "As Macready's fiancee, Sylvia
Sidney, resolves all the human agony of the execution in her
own playing . . . she acts this searing episode with an unadorned
poignancy that recapitulates and compresses all the emotions of
the *Gods of the Lightning* into one living moment."[6]

Gods of the Lightning was an angry play, a play that came
searing hot from an event whose shadow was still present.
Winterset (1935), is the companion piece of *Gods of the
Lightning*. It represents a change from high to low tempo, from
rapid and tense action to action subordinated to philosophical
speculation, from characters swirling along the stream of events
to those questing the meaning of those happenings. The lyric
mood of *Winterset* fits its atmosphere as the incisive dialogue
suits *Gods of the Lightning*. "Some years ago Mr. Anderson
wrote a stirring play in defense of Sacco and Vanzetti,"
Atkinson observed. "The bitterness that lies deep in the souls of
everyone who believed in their innocence had shot *Winterset*
through with ferocity against injustice."[7]

Winterset is more general than *Gods of the Lightning*, but
there are too many connections between the play and the Sacco-
Vanzetti case not to draw comparisons. *Winterset* is the story
of a youth who wanders into the slum section beneath the
Brooklyn Bridge in New York on a quest to prove his dead
father innocent of a murder charge. Here in the gloomy atmosphere of a dreary tenement house he meets those who were
involved—the trial judge, the dying leader of the gang that

committed the murder, a member of the gang hiding from the police.

Sacco and Vanzetti apparently are merged in the dead Bartolomeo Romagna—Vanzetti's first name was Bartolomeo. Mio, the youth seeking to vindicate his father, tells how "When I was four years old we climbed through an iron gate, my mother and I, to see my father in prison. He stood in the death-cell and put his hand through the bars and said, 'My Mio, I have only this to leave you, that I love you, and will love you after I die.'" The incident had a parallel in real life, Mrs. Sacco taking six-year-old son Ines to look up at his father in prison from the courtyard below. And the thoughts are similar to those Sacco expressed in a letter to his son.

Mio came East because articles written by Professor Hobhouse hint at Romagna's innocence. These suggest the many articles and books written on the real subject, particularly *The Case of Sacco and Vanzetti,* by Supreme Court Justice Felix Frankfurter, then a professor at Harvard Law School.

Much was made of Massachusetts justice in the long controversy during the efforts to gain a re-trial for Sacco and Vanzetti. Massachusetts justice was the pride of the people, and defenders were vigorous in upholding its integrity. "Sacco and Vanzetti," the *Springfield Union* declared, "have been given legal advantages that some men accused of crime did not have, and the case against them has withstood every attack of any kind."[8] Another student of the case said local patriotism aroused by criticism of Massachusetts courts, "long a source of pride to that community, rushed to the defense of these courts without too careful a scrutiny of the particular case which called it forth."[9]

In the play, Judge Gaunt, pressed by the avenging Mio, haltingly says:

> Justice once rendered in a clear burst of anger, righteously, upon a very common laborer, confessed an anarchist, the verdict found and the precise machinery of law invoked to show him guilty—think what furor

would rock the stage if the court then flatly said all this was lies—must be reversed. It's better . . . to let the record stand, let one man die. For justice, in the main, is governed by opinion. Communities will have what they will have, and it's quite as well, after all, to be rid of anarchists.

According to one source, if the Morelli gang of Providence was proven guilty of the Braintree murders, the Massachusetts authorities would have to admit a "ghastly error in convicting Sacco and Vanzetti. . . . they did not propose to allow the state of Massachusetts to be disgraced (as they viewed it) because of two radical labor leaders."[10]

Judge Gaunt is the chief connecting link between the two plays. He is Judge Vail, older, careworn, and broken over the murder trial. He is constantly stopping passersby to convince them his actions were right. The Morelli gang of real life and the Estrella gang of the play bear the same general relationship to the murders, with Trock Estrella as a possible counterpart of Joe Morelli, leader of the Providence group.

The last scene holds two great lessons. One is a note of forgiveness that "such things could be." Mio, coming to the end of the trail, asks Miriamne to "teach me how to live and forget to hate."

And the girl answers simply, "He would have forgiven."

Mio slowly says, "Yes . . . He'd have forgiven."

Nearly the last words uttered by Vanzetti as he sat in the electric chair were, "I am an innocent person. I wish to forgive some people for what they are now doing to me."

The other is the expression of the liberal's creed, uttered by Esdras over the dead bodies of Mio and Miriamne, "This is the glory of earth-born men and women, not to cringe, never to yield, but standing, take defeat implacable and defiant, die unsubmitting."

*   *   *   *   *   *   *

America's distrust of Russia after the March, 1917 Bolshevist Revolution had ripened by 1920 into fear. The "Red raids" of 1919 and 1920 increased this fear until many viewed Bolshevism as a definite threat to our country's security. Attorney General Palmer upheld his "Red raids" and mass deportations by claiming, "The plans for fomenting a nation-wide revolution in this country, prepared by Leon Trotsky in Moscow, are in the files of the Attorney General's office." Senator King of Utah called for a Senate investigation of the "Reds," declaring, "The overthrow of existing governments, everywhere is the aim of Soviet Russia."[11] A Georgia newspaper felt "a sense of impending calamity at evidence of the spread of Bolshevism in the United States."[12]

"A Bostonian I know was stopped the other day because he happened to have a black beard and a red necktie placed, as it were, in juxtaposition," Sidney Howard wrote in 1920. "The sensitive officer of the law (also a Bostonian) could not let that pass. However, Boston demands more than a necktie, and some whiskers of a Bolshevist, and my friend escaped."[13] Mr. Howard added that his friend had trimmed his beard and was now wearing a blue tie instead of a red one.

It is not astonishing that plays depicting communism as a menace to the United States appeared on the New York stage. What is astonishing was the poor quality of the plays. None of them came close to equalling even the ordinary run-of-the-mill anti-Nazi plays performed in Broadway theatres during the 1930's.

The Challenge (1919), by Eugene Walter tells the story of a returned soldier whose idealism extends to revolutionizing the universe for communism. The brother of his fiancee, however, proves to the soldier that the people are untrustworthy when he bribes a Bolshevist governor. The veteran then renounces Bolshevism and decides to marry his girl.

George Arliss had the title role in Booth Tarkington's *Poldekin* (1920). Poldekin is a student and a printer sent by the Bol-

shevists to the United States to spread Soviet propaganda. He
is so favorably impressed by opportunities here that he puts
extracts from the Declaration of Independence into the revolu-
tionary tracts he prints. After Poldekin is wounded in a fight
ending in the arrest of the conspirators, he becomes a good
American.

Another play exploited the conception Americans had of
Russia and Russians soon after the turn of the century. They
thought of the peasant as a black-bearded, wild-eyed little man
dancing around with a lighted bomb in one hand and a tract
called "Workers of the World, Unite" in the other. When an
American did think of Russia, it was as a mysterious land of
Czars and splendor, and of peasants and revolution. *On the
Eve* (1907), by Leopold Kampf, combined these two elements.
A Nihilist is chosen by lot to assassinate the governor of a small
Russian town as he leaves the opera house. He does so and is
killed when the bomb goes off. The play, supposed to represent
contemporary conditions in Russia, was barred in that country.
To present readers the talky play doesn't appear to be much of a
menace, and its talk of "the cause" and "the bell of blood" seems
childish. A contemporary critic's verdict that the "drama is
brutal and terrifying" appears far-fetched today. The assassination in the play was based on the murder of Alexander II in
St. Petersburg on March 13, 1881. As the Emperor rode through
the city, a bomb thrown at him exploded, and he died from the
resulting wounds.

Later plays inspired by Communist activities were scant improvement over the preceding ones. *The International* (1928),
Destruction (1932), and *Picnic* (1934), were all of the same
fluffy mold. *The International* by John Howard Lawson was a
musical play of revolt against capitalism. Two Wall Street
millionaires start a revolt in Tibet. The workers' revolution
spreads to Moscow, Paris, and New York, but it is put down by
capitalist machine-guns. In *Destruction,* by Bertha Wiernik, the
son of a minister renounces his belief in God and a capitalistic

world, but is saved by his father, who brings him home from a Communist meeting. Gretchen Damrosch's *Picnic* solves the threat by love. Vera, the pretty soap-box orator, converts aristocratic Philip to communism. He takes her to his beautiful home in Westchester, where she falls in love with his uncle. They go on a picnic, love comes in, and communism goes out.

*   *   *   *   *   *   *

On March 25, 1931, a freight train was stopped at Paint Rock, Alabama, not far from Sand Mountain, where a sign warned, "Nigger, don't let the sun set on you here." Nine colored boys, two white girls, and a white man were taken off the train and brought to Scottsboro.

So started the Scottsboro case, which in the tensions it aroused and the political repercussions it produced wore a similar path to the more famous Sacco-Vanzetti case. Here, as in the preceding case, the question of atmosphere was held to be an important factor in bringing the "guilty" verdicts by Alabama juries. "It is perfectly apparent that the proceedings, from beginning to end, took place in an atmosphere of tense, hostile and excited public sentiment," the United States Supreme Court later said. "During the entire time, the defendants were closely confined or were under military guard."[14] An observer wrote:

> One thing about the whole elaborate show remained real and that was the poisonous feeling of hate and race prejudice in the court room . . . the feeling rose to its highest pitch on Friday when Solicitor Wade Wright made his summation to the jury . . . as he shouted and ranted, the feeling which had been hidden, kept down by a fair and humane judge, came out like a punctured bell. As he shouted that 'no Alabama jury would listen to witnesses brought with Jew money from New York', you could hear murmurs of approval in the courtroom . . . Wright was speaking the language of prejudice and hate which everyone wanted, and everyone understood.[15]

The Scottsboro case grew out of charges that two white girls on a freight train had been raped by seven colored boys. The colored youths were brought to Scottsboro for trial. It began on April 6, six days after the indictment had been handed in. Basis of the protest against the convictions was that the defendants did not have a fair trial, either in securing counsel of their own choice or of having men of their own race on the jury. Of the first the Supreme Court, in reversing the convictions and ordering a new trial said, "We think the failure of the trial court to give them reasonable time and opportunity to secure counsel was a clear denial of due process."[16]

The long fight to free the colored youths became a sensitive political issue in the South, until the factual issue of the case became subordinate to the passions aroused. "One reporter," said Attorney General Tom Knight, who conducted the prosecution, "has since been elected lieutenant governor, largely as a result of prestige won in opposing 'Communists and New Yorkers' allied against him in the case. Detailed as special prosecutor for the new trials, he is said to have gubernatorial ambitions which new triumphs in the Scottsboro case would serve him handsomely."[17]

Two plays were produced on Broadway during the height of the agitation over the trials. One was *Legal Murder* (1934), by Dennis Donoghue. It was very bad. The other was *They Shall Not Die* by John Wexley. It opened, with Ruth Gordon, Linda Watkins, and Claude Rains in the cast on February 21, 1934, at the Royale Theatre. The story takes the case from the initial arrest of the defendants and accusers through the court room convictions. The race issue aspect is developed throughout the play to simulate the atmosphere charged against the real life trials. Samuel Leibowitz, the New York lawyer brought to defend the colored youths, is the prototype for the defense attorney in the play, as the judge is for Judge James E. Horton, who was praised by both sides for the fairness with which he conducted the trial. Solicitor Wade Wright was probably the prototype for

Solicitor Slade, while Attorney General Knight probably served as the model for the play's Attorney General Dade.

The drama ends on a note of challenge, despite the verdict of "guilty" which was contrary to the real-life facts. The defense attorney, incredulous at the "sound of loud laughter, raucous and derisive" that came from the jury room after his summation, declares in a passionate speech:

> No, we're not finished. We're only beginning. I don't care how many times you try to kill this Negro boy . . . I'll go with Joe Rokoff to the Supreme Court up in Washington and back here again, and Washington and back again . . . if I do nothing else in my life, I'll make the fair name of this state stink to high heaven with its lynch justice . . . these boys, they shall not die.

They did not die. The final proceedings freed four of the nine boys outright, convicted four of criminal assault and gave them prison terms. The ninth boy was jailed for assaulting a deputy sheriff in an escape attempt after the rape charge had been dropped. By September, 1946 all except one were free on parole, and he was later paroled. A footnote to the printed play *They Shall Not Die* said, "All characters, locales and names of organizations in this play are fictitious."

8

THE DEPRESSION, CONGRESS, AND THE NEW DEAL

CHRISTMAS week 1931 was not a merry one. The depression had settled over the nation burying beneath it the traditional buoyant spirit of the season. Rich and poor feared unemployment and bad business, while those who still had jobs were feeling the pinch in wage cuts. Arthur Krock observed, "The depression has now reached all the social and economic strata of the people. Even those with steady jobs who had first suffered losses in capital account, have inevitably seen a shrinkage of their earnings."[1] In Chicago school teachers who hadn't been paid in months were given two weeks of their back pay as part of the Christmas observance. Apartments were going begging for tenants—one owner offered his tenants ten shares of well-known securities as an inducement to sign a lease. "If you are a lucky picker," the advertisement said, "your rent won't cost you anything."[2] In New York State the city of Rochester was boasting how its "scientific spending campaign" had restored much of the community's purchasing power. The campaign consisted of 1,500 volunteers going from door to door urging house-holders, businessmen, and factory owners to spend money on repairs, expansion of facilities, and retail goods they ordinarily would buy at a future date. In Massachusetts the papers were proclaiming that only one bank, a small one, had failed during 1930 throughout all New England. In Washington, Republican leaders held their gloomiest session in years as reports drifted in that things did not look good for 1932.

New York was feeling the pinch along with the rest of the nation, and Broadway was a much subdued, "Great White Way." There were only twenty-one plays and seven musical comedies on the stage, a disheartening contrast to the nearly three times that total in 1928. Ethel Merman in *George White's Scandals* was doing her best to build up the nation's morale by singing "Life is just a bowl of cherries, So live and laugh at all." But another popular song expressed more accurately public sentiment: "Brother, Can You Spare a Dime?"

Into this atmosphere came *Of Thee I Sing* on December 26 at the Music Box. George S. Kaufman, the "gloomy dean of Broadway wits," and Morrie Ryskind wrote the book, George Gershwin composed the music, and Ira Gershwin wrote the lyrics. The play, an immediate hit, is an angry satire. It is angry at the men who run for office and at the platforms on which they run; it is angry at the nation's indifference to its own welfare; it is angry at the superficial thinking people were doing, and at the depression which was a result of that thinking. The authors point sharp, cold fingers at the American dream. There is not, with the possible exception of Alexander Throttlebottom, a truly warm person in the whole show. Nor is there a tender moment. Even the lovers satirize romance: Wintergreen and Mary Turner keep one eye on their public as they go through the motions of making love.

Throttlebottom alone draws the sympathy of the audience. And perhaps for the reason that every one in the 1931 audience felt himself something of a Throttlebottom—confused, lost, and uncertain. With Victor Moore bumbling hesitantly about, hat balancing precariously upon his large head and speech apologetic and halting, the character drew instinctive recognition and sympathy. He was John Q. Citizen trying to do his inadequate best in a cynical world that only wanted him when it could use him. Throttlebottom became the personification of a long line of jokes about the Vice President of the United States. Only a short two years later Vice President John Nance Garner told a newspaper reporter, "There isn't much to do now, but I guess I cannot repudiate this job. It wouldn't look right."[3]

The authors are sharpest in their depiction of how vice-presidential nominees are chosen. The behind-the-scenes operators— Gilhooley, Fulton, and Lippman—in a strategy conference cannot remember the name of their party's candidate for vice president. "Well, think a minute," Gilhooley asks. "How did you come to nominate him?"

Fulton thinks. "I picked his name out of a hat and this fellow lost."

The analogy to real life politics is not too farfetched. Mark Sullivan recounts how little thought was given to the vice presidential nomination at the 1920 Republican convention. "It was a sign of the tautness of the convention that little thought had been given to the nomination for Vice President," . . . the famous newspaper columnist recounted in his classic *Our Times* history . . . "thus it was not until midway of the tenth and final ballot, when for the first time it was certain that Harding would win, and *within an hour* of his nomination, that several of the party's elders bethought of the vice presidential nomination."

Of Thee I Sing is critical of the sham reluctance presidential candidates have to admit their candidacies, and of their real reluctance to discuss campaign issues. In the play the party bigwigs are puzzled about how Wintergreen got the nomination. Fulton wants to know who was calling for "Wintergreen" during the convention. "That was me," Wintergreen explains. "Most spontaneous thing you ever saw. So here I am gentlemen—

nominated by the people, absolutely my own master, and ready to do any dirty work the committee suggests."

Campaign issues, "something that everybody is interested in, and that doesn't matter a damn," also draw fire in the play as do the meaningless slogans so frequently associated with presidential campaigns. "A Vote for Wintergreen is a Vote for Wintergreen," "Vote for Prosperity and See What You Get," and "The Full Dinner Jacket" have the same relationship to the stage campaign as "Tippecanoe and Tyler Too," "Keep Cool with Coolidge," and "The Full Dinner Pail" had in real life races.

John Q. Citizen receives his share of criticism. He looks for things far removed from the essential qualities when voting for candidates. Seth Low was not an attractive person, and he was defeated in 1904 by Tammany's candidate despite giving New York the best administration it had had in years. The late Senator Robert Taft of Ohio, acknowledged to have been one of the ablest members of the Senate, suffered from this lack of "color" in his fruitless efforts to gain the Republican presidential nomination. Wintergreen's sole qualification for president was pointed out by one of his followers, "For President, John P. Wintergreen. He even sounds like a president."

Of Thee I Sing was a sharp examination of American politics, institutions, and people. It was received with glee because it put into concrete terms the critical feelings people had but could not so well express. It was a play attuned to the depression; in better days many of the barbs lose their satirical effectiveness. The musical comedy, which includes some of George Gershwin's most entertaining melodies, had William Gaxton, George Murphy, Lois Moran, and Florenz Ames in its fine cast. Gaxton's take off of New York Mayor, James J. Walker proved dynamic, engaging, and amusing—even to Walker.

By the time *Let 'Em Eat Cake* was produced in October, 1933, an election had been won and lost, and hope for better things was in the offing. But businessmen were still casting anxious backward glances over their shoulders at the depression shadow even as they counted their profits. One typewriter firm announced with something of an air of bravado that it had moved from the two-to-three day work week to a forty-hour full-time work week on the basis of new orders. Henry H. Harriman, President of the U. S. Chamber of Commerce, added another optimistic note by predicting that business looked good for 1934.

Overseas events produced two headlines foreshadowing the world crisis to come: REICH IS THINKING OF WAR DESPITE ITS TALK OF PEACE and GERMAN PLANS TO REARM BRINGING CRISIS IN EUROPE. Inside the United States the New Deal was setting off its own repercussions, with General Hugh S. Johnson, Director of the National Industrial Recovery Act, trading vitriolic statements with Senator Huey Long of Louisiana.

But *Let 'Em Eat Cake* was still thinking in terms of the depression. Its mood continued the critical examination of American life that *Of Thee I Sing* had started. Brooks Atkinson called it "a low-comedy sequel to the low-comedy satire that won the Pulitzer Prize a year ago . . . but in this column's opinion it is not the hearty, guffawing burlesque that began the legend."[4] Many devices used in *Of Thee I Sing* were used again, but they lost effectiveness in repetition. Even Throttlebottom seems a little rundown at the heels, though he was the best character in the play.

The 1932 presidential election is in the minds of Kaufman and Moss Hart in *Let 'Em Eat Cake*. The still grim feeling of the country about the depression and the indifference charged against those in office, appears in Wintergreen's sudden realization that maybe after all conditions did have something to do with his defeat. "Twelve million people are out of work," he tells the newly jobless members of his party. "Factories are shut down. Banks closed. The farmer can't sell his product. *(Suddenly it begins to dawn on him)* Say, I wonder if that had anything to do with the election."

The Nazi menace overseas hadn't reached world proportions yet, but both Kaufman and Hart sensed enough of its future threat to use the trappings in their comedy. Wintergreen and party stage a successful revolution, and the newspaper publisher Fulton shortly after tells the new dictator, "I don't know if it's just a coincidence, Jack, but since you suppressed all the other papers, our circulation has gone 'way up."

To which Wintergreen replies, "I didn't suppress any papers. You know I believe in free speech. I just merged them all into one." On October 5, 1933, Hitler had a national press law passed which "now literally commits the entire press in Germany into the keeping of the Government." Newspapers, and the men serving them are now "servants of the state," the new law asserted.

The Italian Fascist blackshirts and the Nazi brownshirts naturally entered the musical comedy picture. Their shirts inspire Wintergreen and friends to make blue shirts for the revolution they plan to start. But after the counter counter-revolution had restored Wintergreen to the presidency, he announces his withdrawal from politics: "No more revolutions for me. I've learned my lesson," and goes into the shirt and dress business with the perennial radical Kruger and the politician Lippman under the firm name of "Kruger, Lippman and Wintergreen."

The hit song of the comedy expressed the view of many Americans concerning the failure of nations overseas to pay their war debts. The opening line, sung after the Finnish representative pays his country's annual installment and is then booted out of the room, is "No Comprenez, no capish, no versteh." It is the stock answer the statesmen have to inquiries about when they will pay their debts.

Maxwell Anderson's Pulitzer Prize winner, *Both Your Houses,* appeared between *Of Thee I Sing* and *Let 'Em Eat Cake.* It opened on one of the nation's critical dates, the start of the four-day bank holiday proclaimed by President Roosevelt. The curtain went up as New York and the nation, "bewildered but cheerful," tried to go about their business in the normal way. Show business did, accepting checks in lieu of cash for theater seats.

"The only thing we have to fear is fear itself" echoed throughout the country as the key-note statement from President Roosevelt's inaugural speech caught America's imagination. The words gave hope to the nation, hope that both the new President and the new Congress would change things for the better. Percy Hammond's criticism of *Both Your Houses* suggested this view: "It may be hoped Mr. Anderson was thinking of past Congresses when he composed his protest, not the patriots now preparing to assemble in Washington, there to right our wrong."[5] *Both Your Houses* was perfectly timed, for Congress opened a few days later with 127 new members in the House. The play's exposure of corruption and "pork barrelling" in appropriation bills came when the nation was looking to Congress to lead it out of the depression. The idealism of newly elected Representative Alan McLean was obviously an appeal to the new members of Congress to alter some of the evil practices of their predecessors.

Anderson is an artist as well as a man of intense feeling. "Of all the theatrical attacks upon the depravity of representative government, Anderson's *Both Your Houses* is the most stirring and direct," Brooks Atkinson asserted. "It is not only an angry crying of names and cases but an excellent play that will interest those whom it is convincing."[6]

Perhaps the most effective point in the play is McLean's defeat by hardened House members when the appropriations bill is made up. For in defeat McLean illustrates more effectively than he could in victory what must be done if Congress is to live up to its high duties. The plot is comparatively simple. McLean comes to Congress determined to keep his election promises. Put on the Appropriations Committee, he soon learns the bill is loaded with "pork barrel" provisions. Despite his inexperience, McLean decides to fight the bill. He seeks to outmaneuver the committee by so overloading the measure with obviously unessential items that it will fall of its own weight. But McLean hadn't foreseen the cynical attitude of those supporting him because they wanted something, and he is shocked to find that the bill is passed with all the "pork barrel" items in it. In the last scene he leave the committee room, where the others are celebrating their victory, with a declaration to continue the fight against graft despite his defeat.

Anderson wasn't the first playwright to sharpen his knife for this kind of Congressional dishonestly. In 1908 Harrison Rhodes and Thomas A. Wise wrote *A Gentleman from Mississippi*. It dealt with the loading of an appropriation bill in Congress with land graft. Newly elected Senator Langdon comes to Washington and hires Bud Haines as his secretary. Haines learns Langdon's children have invested money in a scheme to secure possession of land in a Mississippi gulf town. In order to capitalize on their investment, the Senator's children try to plant a provision in the Naval Appropriations Bill establishing a naval station in the area. Haines, played by the elder Douglas Fairbanks, exposes the plot and with the aid of Senator Langdon defeats the bill.

The nation was feeling much better economically by the time *I'd Rather Be Right* checked in at the Alvin Theatre on November 2, 1937. The cynical note of *Of Thee I Sing* and *Let 'Em Eat Cake* was replaced by one of genuine optimism. The future, despite the uncertainties of the present, looked hopeful, and in a dream President Franklin D. Roosevelt expressed that thought to the lovers, Phil and Peggy. "Phil, Peggy—you want my advice?" Roosevelt tells Phil in the latter's dream:

> Get married. Take your life and live it. You'll manage.
> People have done it before. You'll get through some-
> how. Listen—suppose I don't balance the budget?
> There'll be a baby born every minute, just the same.
> But I'll balance it. I'm not through trying—not by a
> darned sight.

Phil awakes from his dream and embraces Peggy. "Come on," he tells her, "let's get married—tomorrow." Peggy agrees and they embrace again.

"Hey, where do you think you are, Russia?" a policeman calls.

"No, officer," Phil replies, light of heart, "we're in America, and doing very nicely, thank you."

Those lines would have sounded satirical in 1931; by 1937 they fitted comfortably into the American picture. The big issue then was no longer that of recovery; it was social reform. Balancing the budget and the Supreme Court fight were integral parts of the larger issue. The 1936 presidential campaign had rather thoroughly aired the "balance the budget" fight. It hadn't, however, completely extinguished the controversy. Such headlines as GOVERNMENT TO PAY FARMERS $1,500,000 TO FEED SURPLUS POTATOES TO LIVESTOCK set conservatives tingling with anger.

But it was the Supreme Court fight which drew the headlines and set the battle lines during 1937. On February 7 of that year President Roosevelt, apparently with little or no warning to his closest legislative advisors, sent a message to Congress urging court reform. His principal demand was to increase the number of Supreme Court justices from nine to a maximum of fifteen depending upon the number of justices reaching seventy-five years of age who did not retire. The series of judicial setbacks to New Deal measures seeking social welfare reforms inspired the bill. On such fundamental issues as the National Recovery Act, the Agricultural Adjustment Administration Act, and the Guffey Coal Law, the Supreme Court, by five to four decisions, turned back the New Deal. Regulations on manufacturing, agriculture, and mining contained in the bills were beyond federal regulation, the court decided.

After first calling the Supreme Court justices "nine old men" living back in the "horse and buggy days," Roosevelt cast around for a way to circumscribe the court. The so-called court reform bill was the answer. Quickly the defenders of the court rallied. Among them were many former loyal supporters of the President. Included among those who followed FDR, though doubtful of his wisdom in setting this course of action, was Senator Robinson. When he died at the height of the fight, the plan was defeated.

The battle lasted 168 days. During those hectic weeks, the argument between New Deal supporters and the opposition increased in bitterness. Organizations to defend the Supreme Court sprung into being; among them were the "League Opposed to Remaking the Supreme Court," and the "Citizens Supreme Court Protective Committee." On July 22, 1937, the Senate by a vote of seventy to twenty-one recommitted the bill to the Judiciary Committee. In effect, the vote killed the measure. Claims and counter-claims of victory came pell-mell from each side. Opponents of the measure pointed to its final defeat, and claimed the victory. Roosevelt and his supporters pointed to the many favorable decisions delivered by the Supreme Court during the fight, decisions which otherwise might have been reversed. On this basis, they insisted the fight had been won even though the individual battle was lost.

In *I'd Rather Be Right,* Kaufman and Hart took full advantage of the nation's familiarity with the men who led the opposing forces. And in engaging George M. Cohan to turn his "song and dance" personality into an impersonation of Roosevelt, the producers hit upon the perfect combination. Never has a president been so felicitously portrayed on the stage, and never was an actor more in sympathy with the part he was playing.

Even Mr. Landon appeared in the play, and for once he came off topside against Roosevelt. The President, worried about cutting the budget, calls on Landon to tell him how he balanced the budget in Kansas. "Not a chance, Mr. Roosevelt, not a chance," Landon replies.

"Oh, come now, Mr. Landon," the President urged, "I didn't mean the things I said about you."

"Perhaps not, Mr. Roosevelt," the Kansan answered, "but this makes up for a good deal. It's true I didn't photograph well, nor did I have that smile. And I will frankly admit that I was lousy on the radio. But Mr. Roosevelt, I balanced my budget. So as we say in Kansas, Mr. Roosevelt—try that on your ukulele."

Throughout the show the justices, all wearing long grey beards like that of Chief Justice Hughes, pop in and out from behind the rocks in Central Park. Roosevelt, hurt, tells Phil and Peggy he wants to be friends but the justices won't play. Hughes, popping out again from a rock, voices the justices' feelings. " 'Horse and buggy days,' eh?" he says, " 'old fogies,' eh? Well, that's how much you know." He whistles, and the other justices and nine scantily clad girls appear from behind the rocks and all eighteen go into their dance.

Mr. Roosevelt had no sooner arrived in Washington following his 1936 victory than rumors of third term ambitions swept the country. By 1937 the thought had gone well beyond the whispering stage as evidenced in *I'd Rather Be Right*. Even Arthur Krock in a fantasy dream column for the *New York Times* has Roosevelt and La Guardia talk about the coming elections. "Jim wants to be Governor and there's 1938 to remember," the President says—"and 1940."

"Hum. Yes. There's certainly 1940," the New York Mayor reflects. "I wonder where we'll both be then, Mr. President."

"Why," Roosevelt answers grandly, "helping to nourish the undernourished third, helping to house the ill-housed third, helping to get jobs for the unemployed third, Fiorello, as we are doing now."[7]

There are other political echoes of the 1930's in *I'd Rather Be Right*. There is the search for new taxes, the handing out of jobs to the Democratic faithful by Jim Farley, the intricacies of the Wagner Act, and the many colorful personalities of the period: Vincent Astor and his yacht; Sistie and Buzzie Dall (grandchildren of President Roosevelt), the White House favorites; John

L. Lewis and the newly created CIO; Walter Winchell's newcasts; Bing Crosby's crooning and Walter Lippman's columns.

The play ends on a note of optimism as Roosevelt, delivering a fireside chat with all the trimmings of a commercial radio broadcast, tells the people:

> There are things to worry about, but I do know that this is too big and too fine a country to let anything lick it . . . we fought for our freedom, we fought among ourselves, we've had bad presidents and good presidents; we've had panics and depressions and floods and strikes and wars. But it seems there's something in this country that always sees us through. And we musn't ever lose that.

While *I'd Rather Be Right* centered around Roosevelt and the accomplishments of his administration, *Washington Jitters* was a sharp dramatic criticism of the New Deal. It was written by John Boruff and Walter Hart and produced May 2, 1938, by the Theatre Guild on its twentieth anniversary.

By May, 1938, Roosevelt's popularity was nose diving toward its lowest point. In the two months from March to May, the Gallup Poll recorded a drop in the President's public rating to fifty-eight and a half per cent. As Roosevelt's popularity decreased, criticism of him and of the New Deal increased. It was to continue to do so through the election of 1938, which resulted in substantial gains for the Republicans in both the Senate and the House.

Chief target of the opposition was a charge of inefficiency and loose administration in various New Deal governmental agencies. On May 15, 1938, a lady co-organizer of a group calling itself "Women's Rebellion," charged that people on relief refused to take jobs offered them. Her particular grievance was that she could not get a man to "Mow my lawn for $2 or $3 a day. It seems to me," she continued before a sympathetic group at Suffern, New York, "that people ought to be made to take jobs or starve. If the jobs do not pay enough, they can get supplementary relief."⁸ The same day George Letterhouse, trust officer of the Commercial Trust Company of New Jersey, told a meeting of bankers at Atlantic City that "Since 1930 a balanced budget has been unknown. Deficits have been growing bigger and better. Government borrowings have been staggering, and a heavy mortgage has been placed on the future of this country."⁹

Washington Jitters attacks these grievances. Henry Hogg, a young sign painter who carried a small plaque with his name on it, sits down in the executive's office of a new agency. A well-known radio commentator enters the office, sees the plaque, assumes Hogg is head of the agency, interviews him, and promptly broadcasts the sign painter's grandiose schemes for solving the nation's problems. Henry overnight becomes a national figure, sought by political leaders for advice and by society matrons for their parties. The administration eventually decides Hogg must go, but to their consternation, the leaders learn he has never been appointed to the position they think he holds. They fear to do anything, but Henry saves them by voluntarily retiring to the peace of sign painting.

Washington Jitters satirizes how Congress passed New Deal "must" legislation, how the "gobbledegook" of governmental jargon grew, and how people were hired for jobs. Eula explains how she got her position to a friend:

> Well, you see, my aunt's sister-in-law has a cousin whose brother lives in New York. The New York brother is married to a woman who has a sister living in Washington. The sister knows a friend whose uncle is closely connected with Congressman Dinwitty. So I got the job.

Roosevelt's "Cummings, take a law" command in *I'd Rather Be Right* is further mocked in *Washington Jitters*. Mehafferty, a close political adviser to the president, upon being asked about a certain new bill declares, "It's a great hunk of statesmanship. It's the damndest, finest piece of legislation that's come out of our administration, that's how good it is."

"What's the bill about?" a friend asks.

"Damned if I know," Mehafferty replies. "I haven't read it yet. I'll let you know tomorrow."

As for the conglomeration of letters making up the numberless New Deal agencies, truth here is stranger than fiction. Some of the agencies whose full names may be unscrambled by the curious are the FDIC, RFC, FFMC, HOLC, SEC, WPA, CCC, PERA, NYA, PWA, AAA, REA, NRA, and NLRB. The government employees in *Washington Jitters* talk of these agencies by their capital letters, and so did the workers in the Nation's Capital. *Washington Jitters* did not have the appeal of the Kaufman comedies. It received half-hearted reviews and closed after a brief run.

On February 4, 1946, *Born Yesterday* by Garson Kanin opened at the Lyceum Theatre. It, too, struck at the seamy side of graft and political fixing in Washington. But whereas Anderson's *Both Your Houses* was an angry play and the Kaufman comedies satirical ones, *Born Yesterday* combined low comedy humor with high moral purpose. The play instantly caught the fancy of the public, made Judy Holliday a full-fledged star overnight, and set a record for long runs on Broadway. It ran for 1,642 performances, the seventh longest run in the history of the New York stage. The play, later made into an equally successful moving picture, has become since 1946 a perennial attraction on the summer stock and little theatre circuit.

Born Yesterday centers around the efforts of a big business man to manipulate, by bribing a Senator, legislation in Congress so he could extend his unsavory tactics internationally. Harry Brock is a millionaire junk dealer who comes to Washington with his mistress, chorus girl Billie Dawn, to push his project. Billie, whose knowledge of life begins and ends with show business, obviously would hinder Brock in his scheme unless she learns how to act properly in Washington society. Brock turns to Paul Verrall, a journalist living at the hotel, for help. Against the advice of his lawyer, Ed Devery, the junkman hires Verrall to teach Billie the proper social graces. Billie in turn offers to instruct Paul in the facts of life as she knows them. The two fall in love. But what is even more important, the chorus girl develops a strong sense of social responsibility. This proves the key around which the action revolves.

One of the incidents to awaken Billie's latent social consciousness is Brock's habit of keeping her up most of the night boasting what a big man he is. She complains to Devery, adding that the junkman has predicted he will one day run everything, including the United States government.

> DEVERY: He may at that.
> BILLIE: Personally, I don't care one way or the other.
> DEVERY: Very few people do, that's why he may get to do it. The curse of civilization. Don't-care-ism. Satan's key to success.

Verrall points out the dangers of this attitude to Billie, who gradually sees there is more to life than owning two mink coats. Once she realizes Brock has been shoving people around for his own selfish ends, she rebels. The first to feel her ire is the junkman's brother, Eddie Brock. He had been given an unmerciful tongue lashing by Harry without fighting back. When Eddie and Billie are finally left alone, she tells the little man she is angry at him.

> EDDIE: What'd I do? What'd I do?
> BILLIE: It's a new thing with me, Eddie. I'm going to be sore at anybody who just takes it. From now on.

In his crude selfishness, Harry Brock pushes around everyone who stands in his way. This even includes Senator Hodges, whom he has bribed to maneuver the desired bill through Congress. When the Senate does not act quickly enough to please him, Brock tells Devery, "I could get a better Senator out of Lindy's."

> DEVERY: Best I could do.
> BROCK: I'd like to trade him in, no kidding.
> DEVERY: They're not all for sale, Harry. That's the trouble with this town—too many honest men in it.

Verrall meanwhile has stumbled upon papers revealing that Brock's international combine and Senator Hodges' amendment have more than coincidence in common. Through Billie, who has been made owner of his junkyards by Brock as a means of getting around the law, Paul stops Harry's scheme for international power. When Brock asks what Verrall wants, Billie jumps in and tells him, "To try and stop you from buying and selling legislation as though it was junk." She adds that since she is his partner in 126 junk yards and that he cannot act without her consent, she will return the yards to Brock "one a year, if you behave." The couple leave the room then with Brock fuming helplessly at the situation he had himself contrived. Devery, the once brilliant, but now rum-sodden lawyer, ends the play by raising his glass

> With a toast to all the dumb chumps and all the crazy broads—past, present and future—who thirst for knowledge and search for truth—who fight for justice—and civilize each other—and make it tough for sons of bitches like you *(to Hodges)*—and you *(to Brock)* and me. *(He drinks toast.)*

Emmet Lavery's *The Gentleman from Athens* turns on the theme that each citizen must see that his government is properly run. Here the roles of hero and heroine are reversed from *Born Yesterday*. Steve Christopher is a wealthy Californian who runs for Congress and beats the incumbent who had refused to take orders from him. Christopher comes to Washington and rents the famous home of Lee Kilpatrick, spoiled daughter of a late senator. She has become cynical about the inevitability of another world war, and decides to rent her house in order to run away from civilization.

Christopher is impressed by Lee's knowledge of political and social Washington and asks her to become his secretary. She first laughs at the offer, but when the Greek Congressman expresses his reverance for that governing body and reveals he wishes to do the right thing in office, her interest is awakened.

LEE *(incredulous)*: You mean you intend to be absolutely on the level in your dealings in Congress.
CHRISTOPHER: Easy—not so loud. I wouldn't want a thing like that to get around.
LEE: Oh, I see. You mean this government thing is rather sacred to you, is that it?
CHRISTOPHER: Yeh, that it is—sacred—kinda sacred —that is the way my old man brought me up.

Miss Kilpatrick decides to accept Christopher's job offer, a move that arouses her old time admirer, Congressman Ed Lawrence, a power in Washington politics.

ED: At the moment, I am interested in something else. For example, your sudden change in plans. Can it be that the world is not really doomed? That rigor mortis has not set in?
LEE: It's true. I said I was running away, that the world was going to hell and what could I do about it. Then, suddenly, Steve made it all quite clear—the world still has a chance as long as people are willing to fight for the right to be part of it.

Christopher, imbued by his enthusiasm to do something big, introduces a bill in the House that would make the United States part of a world government. He tells his mentor, Lawrence, about the measure. "You get it, Ed?" Steve explains. "United States of America—United States of the World —Say, *(softly)* that was the thing Willkie was always talking about. He wrote a book about it—hey, this is a pretty big idea."

But the freshman Representative offends the leaders by his crude and unorthodox methods. When he gets the bill to the House floor by a ruse, the leaders determine to bring Steve's career to a quick end. They demand that he resign on a charge that he bought his own election. Christopher has obtained, through the efforts of a follower, information of a nature that could be used to blackmail the chairman of the committee and force withdrawal of the expulsion move. After a struggle with himself, the Californian decides not to use the potent informa-

tion but rather to resign from Congress. Lee, who appealed to
Steve's better side in this crisis, admires his decision and decides
to marry him. She tells the somewhat confused Christopher to
return to California, and run for Congress, and win the election
without buying it.

Three major themes appear in most plays about Washington.
The first is an accusation that people don't care what happens
in their government. Whether Congress is run honestly or
crookedly, whether the other branches have efficient officeholders or political hangers-on is of no interest to the people. All
the latter want is to be left alone. This is the charge in *Born
Yesterday, The Gang's All Here, State of the Union, The
Gentleman from Athens,* and *Both Your Houses,* among other
plays.

But the second theme presents a more encouraging side.
This asserts that there are those who do care and who will fight
to see that our country is properly run. Matthews in *State of
the Union* tells newspaperman Spike MacManus that while he
isn't running for president that doesn't mean he is going to keep
quiet. "No, Spike," he declares, "it's all over but the shouting—
but, oh, boy, am I going to shout. Sam and his type are dead.
They want to go back to something they've had. We've got to
move on to something we've never had before . . . Thank God,
I can speak my mind now. I don't have to worry about being
a candidate."

When Rafferty caustically accuses Bruce Bellingham in
The Gang's All Here of being a smart boy by the questions
the latter asks, Bruce feelingly replies, "No, I'm not. Some
one has to give a damn and I give a damn." Once chorus girl
Billie Dawn has been awakened to the need for action against
politicians and others who shove people around, she blazes
her determination to fight back in *Born Yesterday.* Despite
the severe beating his bill has taken in committee, Alan McLean
raises his banner of defiance against graft in *Both Your Houses.*

A less serious, though still important theme, is the advice several plays give to budding politicians—be married and be sure your married life is a happy one, at least so far as the electorate is concerned. The strained relationships of husband and wife in *State of the Union, The Gang's All Here,* and *First Lady* are hurriedly glossed over for the public as soon as there is a chance that the husband might run for high political office. Such a slight play as *Affairs of State,* by Louis Verneuil, turns on this issue. Senator Philip Russell advises ambitious George Henderson, who wishes to run for the Senate in another state, to get married if he wants to succeed in politics. The latter, clandestinely in love with Russell's much younger wife, weds the older Senator's niece, Irene Russell, on a purely business basis and as a cover for the real love affair. Henderson is offered the post of Undersecretary of State and Constance Russell, recognizing that a scandal would ruin her lover's promising career, gives him up and cancels her demands for a divorce from Senator Russell.

Despite their frequently critical nature the plays on Washington express confidence in the inherent good of our country and of its government. The searching playwright lays bare the imperfections of our political figures, but he also points out the unsung heroes who fight the evil, and who, in the end, win. That is the encouraging conclusion to be drawn from these plays.

SUNRISE AT CAMPOBELLO

A SHORT FERRY ride from a small village at the northeast tip of Maine, called Lubec Narrows, brings one to Campobello Island. The island, on Canadian territory, lives up to its Italian meaning of "beautiful meadow," and adds to this beauty excellent fishing and a panoramic view of the sea and the rugged Maine coastline.

Through the years Franklin Delano Roosevelt eagerly looked forward to summers on the small island his father James had bought in 1883. Here in the large red house, Roosevelt could relax and enjoy the smell and the sound of the sea. In 1921 he came to Campobello with his wife Eleanor and their children. The summer started in routine fashion, with the family enjoying the place as in the past. Then suddenly infantile paralysis struck the thirty-nine-year-old Roosevelt. With its dread appearance FDR's once promising political career seemed destined to end at mid-beginning. Only a year earlier his aspirations had been dealt a severe setback. He had run for vice president on the Democratic ticket headed by James W. Cox, and the crushing

121

defeat of 1920 was a body blow to future hopes of political office.

This disheartening period in Roosevelt's career is brilliantly developed in *Sunrise at Campobello* by Dore Schary. In the play Schary takes FDR from the day he was stricken with infantile paralysis to the moment he ascends the rostrum at the old Madison Square Garden in 1924 to nominate New York Governor Alfred E. Smith for president on the Democratic Party ticket. The play opened January 30, 1958 in the Cort Theatre, with Ralph Bellamy giving an unforgettable performance in the title role.

Audiences were momentarily shocked at the new insight they were receiving about the World War II President. Few remembered Roosevelt moving about without crutches. The world accepted his leaning upon son James as the natural order of things. The nation had forgotten the months and years Roosevelt fought against becoming a bedridden invalid for life.

"Those first few days at Campobello when this started, I had despair—deep, sick despair," he explains in the play:

> It wasn't the pain—there was much more than that later on when they straightened the tendons in my legs. No, not the pain—it was the sense that perhaps I'd never get up again. Like a crab lying on its back. I'd look down at my fingers and exert every thought to get them to move. I'd send orders to my legs and my toes—they didn't obey me.

One thing sustained him, FDR tells Eleanor in the play:

> I turned to my faith, Babs—for strength to endure. I feel I have to go through this fire for some reason. Eleanor, it's a hard way to learn humility—but I've been learning by crawling. I know what is meant—you must learn to crawl before you can walk.

Roosevelt had this religious nature before he was stricken. While Assistant Secretary of the Navy in Washington, he served as a vestryman at St. Thomas Episcopal Church. After his election as president, FDR went to St. John's Episcopal Church on Lafayette Square opposite the White House and prayed before going to the Capitol to take the oath of office.

From the depths of physical and mental despair, Roosevelt fought upwards to the point where Smith asked him to make the nominating speech placing the New York Governor as a presidential candidate before the Democratic convention. The opportunity was a golden one, but the hazards were equally great. If he faltered on the way to the rostrum, if he fell, if he even hesitated, the world would say, "Too bad, but Roosevelt simply is not physically able to handle the responsibilities of political office."

In *Sunrise at Campobello* Roosevelt turned to his loyal friend Louis McHenry Howe after Smith had left the stage and asked how far it would be from his seat on the platform to the lectern.

> HOWE: About ten steps, I'd say, not more.
> FDR *(Thinking)*: Ten steps. I can do that. I'll take Jimmy with me—he's the biggest. *(Rolls his chair and seems to be measuring.)* Ten steps—about twenty feet?
> HOWE: About.
> FDR: I'll work on that. We have got to get the exact measurement.
> HOWE: Work hard, Franklin. *(A pause)* They are liable to be the ten biggest steps you ever took in your life.

Those ten steps were the natural climax of the play. They represented the challenge of Roosevelt's physical victory as well as the hope for future political success. *Sunrise at Campobello* is more than the story of a great man overcoming crippling odds. It is the larger story of all men who refuse to admit defeat despite apparently insurmountable obstacles. This is the essence of the play, and the fact that a great president is its symbol adds, rather than detracts, from the universal lesson it presents.

In his uphill battle, Roosevelt had two staunch allies—his friend Howe and his wife Eleanor. The Damon and Pythias relationship of Howe and Roosevelt is one of opposites attracting each other. No two men could be less alike in appearance, in background, in personality. FDR was handsome, rich, charming, self-assured, athletic, gay, outgoing. In addition, he bore a great name. The small Indianapolis-born newspaperman had none of these qualities.

A noted radio commentator once called Howe "a medieval gnome," and the name stuck. He was indeed "small, gnarled, gnome-like, brown eyes, bushy brows, large ears, wore high white collars, hermitlike." A Sweet Caporal cigarette was constantly between his lips. He dressed carelessly and his brusque manner hid a pungent and keen sense of humor reserved for the few who knew him well.

Howe was covering the New York State legislature at Albany for the *New York Herald* when he met Roosevelt in 1911. He had grown up in nearby Saratoga, where his father owned a newspaper. At seventeen Howe was serving as local correspondent for the large New York paper. The next step, reflecting his early interest in politics, was an assignment for the *Herald* at the state capital.

Here he was first attracted to FDR when the latter, a freshman Democratic senator from a previously rock-ribbed Republican district, opposed Tammany Hall's nominee for United States Senator. Those were the days when state legislatures, rather than the public, elected United States Senators. The New York political machine had chosen one of its old wheelhorses, "Blue-eyed" Billy Sheehan, for the position. The young Senator from Hyde Park rebelled, and despite threats and pressures gathered enough fellow legislators around him to defeat Sheehan and to earn the undying enmity of Tammany.

Roosevelt's single-handed fight against the country's most powerful political machine captured the imagination of Howe. He went to see FDR, quickly became his friend and was early convinced the youthful legislator had a great political future. From then on Howe's loyalty knew no bounds, and until his death in Washington on April 18, 1936, he dedicated his life to advancing FDR's political career.

When his friend was stricken with infantile paralysis, Howe gave up a good job and rushed at once to Campobello. Here he proved invaluable in the crisis, and many believe that without his insight and devotion, Roosevelt might not have won his fight. A magazine writer summed this up by remarking upon Howe's death, "The picture of a little 'gnome' of a man clinging tenaciously to his hero down with infantile paralysis is bound to be part of the folk-lore of the future."[1]

So close was Howe to Roosevelt that when the family wanted to ask Dr. Robert W. Lovett of Boston what chance FDR had to regain his health, they called on the newspaperman to question the noted specialist. Said the physician:

> His improvement will be very slight unless he has the most extraordinary will and patience. It will mean hours, days, weeks, months and years of constant effort to bring the muscles back, efforts which must not be relaxed for a single day. My experience has been very few people possess the courage and determination to make this fight.[2]

Howe reported the analysis to Roosevelt, who said, "Very well. When do the treatments begin and what do I have to do?" The question was not an academic one for FDR. He was courageous and determined, and in addition, had a sense of humor that helped him over the most discouraging periods. Months later Howe came upon Roosevelt "early one morning moving his foot up and down and from side to side, and heard him exclaim with an almost boyish enthusiasm, 'You people don't realize what fun it is just to wiggle your foot.'"[3]

The newspaperman also studied how to keep Roosevelt's spirit from faltering. He knew the game of politics and the business of government most engrossed the mind of his stricken friend, and he was certain that the greatest lure to live Roosevelt could have was to be convinced that a political future was still possible despite his illness. This knowledge and Howe's efforts to keep it alive played an important, perhaps an all-important, part in carrying Roosevelt triumphantly through that crisis in his own mind and in sending him onward ignoring every physical handicap.

This understanding is a key theme of *Sunrise at Campobello,* for Howe and Eleanor were fighting for this side of FDR against an aristocratic and strong-willed mother who regarded politics as "one step above garbage collecting."

Eleanor proved a powerful, though at first, shy ally. She came from a family as highly placed and patrician as that of her husband. Her uncle was Theodore Roosevelt, President of the United States. Her mother was Anna Hall, a direct descendant of Philip Livingstone, a signer of the Declaration of Independence. Eleanor was also ninth in direct line from Claes Martenzen Van Rosenvelt, who migrated from Holland to found the Roosevelt clan in America.

Orphaned when only nine years old, Eleanor was brought up by her strict and aristocratic grandmother, Mrs. Valentine G. Hall. The young girl was educated in private schools and was introduced to society in New York when nineteen years old. Two years later she married her fifth cousin in the most brilliant social wedding of the 1905 season. Among the guests was President Theodore Roosevelt, who made a special trip from Washington to attend the affair.

With her early life dominated by two such rigidly strong personalities as Mrs. Hall and Mrs. Sara Delano Roosevelt, Eleanor needed the shock of FDR's grave illness to transform her from a retiring young wife into the active crusader for justice our present day world knows.

In Mrs. Sara Delano Roosevelt, Howe and Eleanor faced a formidable opponent. Franklin was an only child, and the widowed mother was determined to order his life in accordance with her ideas. These concepts came out of the patrician background in which she was raised. Her father, Warren Delano,

traced his lineage to Philippe de La Noye. The latter and his
wife were the last surviving man and woman who came to
America on the Mayflower. Warren was a tea merchant in the
China trade who sailed to the then mysterious land on the clipper
"Surprise" to recoup his fallen fortunes. He took his family of
eleven, including seven-year-old Sara, with him.

After living a year in Hong Kong and spending the intervening
years attending private schools in Berlin and Paris, the beautiful
and vivacious Sara returned to Newburgh, New York. She
quickly bcame the belle of the Hudson River Valley, and her
marriage to James Roosevelt, then a widower with a son Sara's
age, was the social event of 1880. Sara moved across the Hudson
River to Hyde Park, where she lived happily with James until his
death at the start of the new century. He left the forty-six-year-
old widow the Hyde Park estate, to be passed on to their son
upon her death. This was not her only source of wealth, for
when her father died he willed Sara $1,000,000.

Mrs. Sara Delano Roosevelt was one of the most cultured
women of her day, and her manner always proclaimed her
upbringing. At all times she was head of the household. Even
when FDR was President and came to Hyde Park for dinner,
she sat at the head of the table with the Nation's Chief Executive
beside her.

Her innate independent nature, reinforced by the factors of
birth, upbringing, and wealth, resulted in set ideas about how
things should be done. They were especially strong concerning
Franklin, whom she hoped "would grow up to be a fine, upright
man, respected in his community—I hoped he would be like his
father."[4] This ruled out a political career. She once remarked
after meeting some of his political associates, "The reason why
I did not want Franklin to go into politics was because he meets
such terrible persons."[5]

The struggle between Howe and Eleanor on one side and Mrs.
Sara Roosevelt on the other over the course of FDR's future was
another major theme in *Sunrise at Campobello*. Roosevelt not

only had to fight infantile paralysis but also a strong-willed mother who was not above using his crippling illness as a means of diverting him from the career he loved.

When Smith appeared on the stage, the play entered its third and most dramatic phase. In the noted New York Governor Roosevelt was dealing with one of the truly great figures of American life. Smith achieved fame and position by a route neither Roosevelt nor Howe had taken. Born December 30, 1873, in a tenement on New York's East Side, he was only thirteen years old when his father died. Alfred assumed the task of supporting his mother and sister by selling newspapers and later clerking at Fulton Fish Market. In more prosperous years when other candidates flaunted their college degrees, Smith tacked the letters "F. F. M." after his name—"Fulton Fish Market."

Smith added the letters during a debate in 1911 in the New York State Assembly. One of the members, Assemblyman Wender, interrupted the debate to announce, "Mr. Speaker, I have just heard that Cornell won the boat race."

"That doesn't mean anything to me, I'm a Yale man," Assemblyman Ed Merritt said.

"I'm a Harvard man," contributed Assemblyman Fred Hammond.

Smith then declared, "It doesn't mean anything to me, either, because I'm an F. F. M. man."

"What's that, Al?" shouted another Assemblyman.

"Fulton Fish Market," Smith answered. "Let's get on with the debate."[6]

The East Sider was first elected to the New York State Assembly in 1903. From then on he lost only one election on his way up the political ladder. The sole defeat came in 1920 when he ran for re-election as governor of New York and lost by a small margin during the national Republican presidential landslide. Smith's terms as governor of New York, 1918-20 and 1924-28, were outstanding administrations.

In 1924 he made his first bid for the presidential nomination on the Democratic Party ticket. This was the first time a Roman Catholic had to be seriously considered as a candidate. The venture was a delicate one, and the New York Governor needed a highly respected, strong man to make the nominating speech. That he came to FDR was a tribute far beyond the value of the Roosevelt name at the convention. Perhaps the honor might be better understood by the numerous references Howe and Smith make in the play to W. Bourke Cockran. The last earned fame in the America of that day by still a different route than those already mentioned. Cockran was born in Sligo, Ireland, and came to the United States as a boy of seventeen. He studied law and soon entered politics, where his quick wit, joyous spirit, and warm friendliness brought him success. He was elected to Congress six times, dying in March, 1923 at Washington.

Cockran was widely known as an orator. One observer declared:

> He was the last of the old school—a fitting successor to Daniel Webster. Bourke Cockran could talk eloquently upon any subject with which he was in sympathy after merely a cursory study of the facts. He could carry a message to the multitudes so that they were moved and convinced. He could sway a crowd and impress an audience. His vitality was second only to his enthusiasm.[7]

When Smith asked Roosevelt to make the nominating speech, he was paying FDR the highest possible compliment. Cockran had always performed that role at state conventions and his speeches had been classic orations of their kind. To be linked with Cockran was indeed a flattering tribute. But the keen Smith had already seen what the world was later to learn so thoroughly—Roosevelt was a great public speaker.

Smith chose well. Although he failed to win the 1924 nomination, Roosevelt's speech included the famous phrase that characterized Smith from then on—"The Happy Warrior." America

forgot that the title had been applied to District Attorney of
New York County William Travers Jerome twenty years earlier,
and they reserved the appellation for the New York Governor.
Four years later Roosevelt again nominated Smith for president,
and this time the Democratic convention at Houston, Texas,
chose the latter on the first ballot. But the speech of FDR had
more importance than bringing the nomination to Smith. He
made a tremendous impression upon the nationally represented
gathering, a factor that helped him immeasureably in later years.

"Here on the stage is Franklin Roosevelt, beyond comparison
the finest type of man that has appeared at either convention,"
the *Literary Digest* of July 21, 1928, declared.

> Beside him the master minds at Kansas City (where
> the Republicans nominated Herbert Hoover for presi-
> dent) were crude bourgeois, porters suddenly struck
> rich. A figure tall and proud, even in suffering; a face
> of classic profile; pale with years of struggle against
> paralysis; a frame nervous yet self-controlled with that
> tense taut unity of spirit which lifts the complex soul
> above those whose calmness is only stolidity; most ob-
> viously a gentleman and a scholar. Nothing better
> could be said for the governor of New York than that
> Franklin Roosevelt loves him.

Unlike Mrs. Sara Roosevelt, who is constantly present in the
play, Smith only appears in one scene. But it is the key scene,
setting up the climax of the story. The New York Governor has
come to ask Roosevelt to put his name in nomination at the 1924
Democratic Party convention. Until this request, FDR's political
future was a thing of dreams, taken seriously only by those close
to him. The offer was a concrete political opportunity, placing
Roosevelt in a position where the limelight could not help but
focus on him. Here was his reward for refusing to admit defeat
during those heartbreaking months of complete invalidism. Here
was the reward Howe and Eleanor had earned by their staunch
and unswerving devotion.

That Smith and Roosevelt later became estranged is one of
the tragedies of American political history. The former had been
raised in a school where club loyalties were all important, and
to ignore them was an unforgiveable sin. Oswald Garrison
Villard in the *American Mercury* of February, 1935 expressed
the view as follows:

> Al Smith had created Franklin D. Roosevelt by pick-
> ing him for the nomination as governor of New York
> (in 1928) and had backed him for two terms. For
> him to reach out deliberately and deprive Al Smith of
> the presidency of the United States (by winning the
> 1932 nomination) could not be characterized in print-
> able language.

In *Sunrise at Campobello* Schary cleverly inserted remarks
and allusions revealing the germs of Roosevelt's ideas that so
fully took bloom during his presidency. FDR's progressive views
are constantly being pushed to the fore. Howe, in an argument
with Roosevelt's mother, declares, "He happens to be the best
damned progressive in the country."

And FDR himself, in denouncing the Teapot Dome scandals
of President Warren G. Harding's administration, insists, "Scandals or no scandals—this country will be enduring Republican
presidents for a long time unless we rip the barnacles off the
Democratic organization and make it a progressive and modern
political party."

People even then had forgotten how Roosevelt as a young
state senator had maneuvered the New York State Legislature
into such a position that it had to pass a fifty-four-hour-work-
week bill. In our day of the forty-hour and five-day work week,
the magnitude of Roosevelt's accomplishment may not be appreciated. But nothing he did later, even his most radical
measures in the White House, produced more bitter opposition
and denouncement.

The fact that a Roman Catholic might be nominated for
president did not disturb Roosevelt. His firm stand for tolerance

appears forcefully in the play. The issue comes to a head when
Mr. Lassiter visits Roosevelt and tells him many people are
alarmed by his close association with Smith. FDR asks the
caller if a statement on his position is wanted. Lassiter, antic-
ipating solid support for his bigoted views, quickly agrees.
Roosevelt then dictates to his secretary:

> I am not worried that the Roosevelt name will be tar-
> nished by any association with Governor Smith. If a
> Catholic who has the ability, broadness of view and
> fine record that entitled him to be considered presi-
> dential timber, cannot be nominated or elected presi-
> dent because of his religion, then we might just as well
> be consistent and say he cannot be governor or Con-
> gressman or mayor or hold any other public office or
> be called upon to serve in the Army or Navy in defense
> of his country in war.

The deep feeling engendered by the latent religious issue was
sharply expressed by Smith in the play. Pointing out that he
early had learned the first objective of a politician was to be
elected, the New York Governor declared, "But in the case of
the Klan. I'm willing to forget an early lesson."

So strongly did he feel that Smith did not conceal his antipathy
for William Gibbs McAdoo. The latter, his chief rival for the
1924 Democratic presidential nomination, had tacitly accepted
support of the Ku Klux Klan, ardent anti-Catholic organization.
"I'll tell you one thing, Frank," Smith bitterly declares in a tense
scene, "If it isn't going to be me, it'll never be McAdoo. I'll fight
him with my last breath. Any man who can take the support of
an organization like the Ku Klux Klan—he's not my kind of
man."

Smith kept his word. He fought McAdoo, Woodrow Wilson's
son-in-law, to the finish. Who then living can forget their epic
battle in New York's old Madison Square Garden, lasting for
103 ballots before the weary and spent delegates compromised
on Wall Street lawyer John W. Davis? Those who then gathered
on street corners before stores to hear the first national convention

broadcasted countrywide will never forget the classic opening of each roll call by the delegate from Alabama, "Alabama casts twenty-four votes for Senator Oscar W. Underwood."

The colloquy between Roosevelt and Smith in *Sunrise at Campobello* revealed the latter's interest and the former's disinterest in foreign affairs. The great East Side figure focused his tremendous understanding and keen mind upon local and domestic questions. Even Woodrow Wilson's idealistic crusade for a world-wide organization aimed at global peace left Smith cold. When Roosevelt suggests that support of the League of Nations be included in the nominating speech, the New York Governor first replies, "Frank, if you're talking about the League of Nations, that's a dead dodo." Upon FDR's insistence he grudgingly submits with an "It's all right with me."

Roosevelt could not help but be imbued with the great vision Wilson had, for during the years he served as Assistant Secretary of the Navy in the latter's little cabinet the two were frequently together. Wilson's letter in Act II thanking FDR for supporting the Wilson Foundation was not merely a polite note of thanks to a friend going through the motions of backing a treasured organization. It was true acknowledgment of the unselfish efforts a stricken idealist had made in forwarding the project of another stricken idealist. To say that the United Nations is an outgrowth of Roosevelt's close association with Wilson would not be doing violence to the truth.

Although *Sunrise at Campobello* came to Broadway twenty-one years after the first play having Roosevelt as a major character was produced—*I'd Rather Be Right*—it should have priority in any dramatic reading about his career. For Schary here catches the essentials of FDR's character and develops them so future generations, whose knowledge of Roosevelt must come from history books and literary works, will have a true understanding of the man. Within the confines of an evening at the theatre, the author has written a memorable play about one of our country's greatest presidents.

10

NAZIISM
AND FASCISM

THE MORNING of November 7, 1938, opened without incident in Paris. Members of the German Embassy started on their regular duties, and the day had every indication of being another routine twenty-four hours. By nightfall, however, the picture had radically changed, and thousands of cities, towns, and villages many miles from Paris were to be saddened by the unthinking act of a seventeen-year-old Polish boy. During the day Herschel Grynszpan sought entrance and was admitted to the German Embassy. He asked to see the secretary of the embassy, Ernest von Rath. The Nazi official met the youthful Polish refugee, who had been temporarily deranged by the persecution of his Jewish kinfolk in Poland. Grynszpan pulled out a hidden pistol, quickly levelled it at von Rath, and squeezed the trigger. The Nazi sank to the floor, mortally wounded.

Within a few hours news of the assassination swept throughout the world. Even those who hated the Nazis deplored the act. In Germany the killing let loose another vicious wave of anti-

Semitic rioting. Synagogues were burned and looted; Jews were beaten in their homes and on the streets. The Nazi government within a matter of days announced that the Jews of Germany were to pay $400,000,000 in fines for the thoughtless deed of a foreign youth.

In New York members of the German consulate became alarmed at the reaction of citizens to the huge fine. If the deed had been reprehensible, the fine on innocent persons was even more so. Crowds gathered before the consulate and booed its staff members. The consul appealed to Mayor LaGuardia for protection, and the diminutive mayor with a sardonic sense of humor detailed three Jewish policemen, among others, to guard the building and its inhabitants. This situation formed the basis for Clare Booth Luce's *Margin for Error,* which opened November 3, 1939 at the Plymouth Theatre.

Political repercussions soon followed presentation of Miss Booth's anti-Nazi murder mystery play. Herr Herbert von Strempel, first secretary of the German Embassy in Washington, registered a vigorous protest with the State Department following the play's Washington tryout, claiming it "was in bad taste." Miss Booth replied that *Margin for Error* was not written with any political purpose in mind. "The play was not intended as a compliment to the Nazis," she said, "but neither is it supposed to be a blast . . . the political setting is simply the background for a murder mystery."[1]

Whether that was true or not, *Margin for Error* proved to be the first popular anti-Nazi play to reach the Broadway stage. In the characters of Karl Baumer, German consul in New York, and his associates, Miss Booth brought out the reprehensible qualities of naziism. In Police Officer Finkelstein, sent to guard Baumer and his staff, she developed many fine qualities associated with the democratic way of life. The author wrote the play in two weeks, turning the last page on the day before the European war began. Two days after it was completed, the mystery drama was accepted for production. The plot was a simple one. Karl Baumer, hated by six people, each with a good motive for killing him, is murdered in the office of the consulate while he and his enemies are listening to a Hitler speech on the radio. Officer Finkelstein, in the room and mindful of the punishment innocent people underwent because Grynszpan killed von Rath, sets about solving the murder to save himself and thousands of Jews in Germany.

"I ain't worried much about myself," he tells Baron Max von Alvenstor of the Embassy staff, "but there's still a lot of people with noses like mine in Germany."

Max replies, "I remember what happened in Berlin when Grynszpan shot the secretary of our Paris Embassy."

Miss Booth uses the different motives the six persons had to murder Baumer as a means of bringing out the vicious aspects of the Nazi system. Dr. Jennings has bankrupted himself giving money to Baumer on the latter's promise to get his daughter and her husband out of Germany. The doctor only a short while before has learned that the couple are dead and that Baumer has been taking the money without any possibility of helping them to escape. Baron Max and Baumer have fallen out, and the latter has been employing spies to track down the fact that Max's English grandmother was a full-blooded Jewess. Otto Horst, whose characteristics suggested the would-be American Fuehrer Fritz Kuhn, has been told by the consul that he has served his purpose and now must die. Sophie Baumer hates her husband for his brutality and lack of moral scruples, and the American newspaperman Thomas Denny despises Baumer for himself and the things for which he stands.

Finkelstein, big-hearted, keen and good humored, is the major achievement of the play. His outlook and way of doing things stand in sharp contrast to those of Baumer, whom the reader dislikes for himself as well as for the arrogant, brutal, and selfish traits associated with the Nazis of 1939. In a conversation with Baumer the policeman vindicates the democratic way of life.

"I take it you don't like being my personal bodyguard," Baumer asks.

"Well," Finkelstein replies, "my mother doesn't like it. But momma's sentimental. I say, it's got its merits. Imagine me being responsible for your health. Now, where could a cockeyed thing like this happen, except in a Democracy?"

"Nowhere," the consul answers.

And the Jewish officer continues, "Yeah, ain't it swell? I mean—this is the kind of a country where you gotta defend the other guy's life and liberty with your own life, even though you know he ain't feeling so sweet toward your person."

Finkelstein solves the murder, and the Jews in Germany can rest peacefully for a little while longer. Baumer had neither been shot by Dr. Jennings nor stabbed by his wife. He had died before either took place by drinking whiskey he had poisoned for Baron Max von Alvenstor to take.

In the preface to the printed version of *Margin for Error,* Henry Luce wrote:

> Thomas Denny is not a believable democrat . . . I am still waiting hungrily for the theatre to give me a believable, disinterested democrat. In the face of a world-wide challenge to all that we have ever felt about Liberty and Justice and Truth, let us see a man, without any particular axe to grind, who will throw back in the face of that challenge an enthusiastic love of Freedom, championing of Truth and defense of Justice.[2]

Superintendent of Schools Riggs in *Decision* by Edward Chodorov was that man. Without anything to gain and with everything to lose, he stands up for his belief in goodness and truth and against intolerance and reaction. He dies in the effort, but in doing so proves more convincingly than ever that the democratic way of life is worthwhile.

"Edward Chodorov has written a sincere study of the fight against fascism in this country," Lewis Nichols wrote in his

New York Times review of February 3, 1944, "and his players
act it to the hilt . . . Mr. Chodorov is writing in praise of the
man behind the man with the gun, the one who fights fascism in
the United States . . . after waltzing through half the season,
the theatre with *Decision* has become aware that not all of the
war is taking place on distant fields."

Superintendent Riggs is asked by fellow citizens to ferret out
the true reason behind a race riot at a local plant. He suspects
United States Senator Dufresne is responsible. Masters, owner
of the local paper and a henchman of the Senator, threatens
to break Riggs when he refuses to call off the investigation.
The next day Riggs is accused of raping a fifteen-year-old student and is put into jail. He is refused bail, and during the night
is strangled. In the meantime, Riggs' soldier son, wearing the
Purple Heart and refusing to believe democracy is in trouble at
home, has returned. Masters tries to squelch the investigation by
besmirching the dead man's character, and the younger Riggs
vacillates between running away and bringing the criminals to
justice. He finally decides to stay and fight the home front
menace as he had the enemy overseas.

There are many unbelievable moments in the play, and
too many polemical speeches halt the action and weaken the
drama. But the story deals with events recognized by its audiences. Senator Dufresne was representative of those public
figures who in their desire for power were willing to accept
Fascist philosophy. Masters was suggestive of those newspaper
publishers who under the guise of patriotism were preaching
race hatred and Nazi doctrines.

The desertion of Riggs by the very men who asked him to
undertake the investigation recalls the earlier experience of Dick
Wells in *The Undertow*. Pressed by the ruthless Dufresne and the
opportunistic Masters, the citizens supporting the Superintendent
drop silently away when their own welfare is menaced. Once
again the question whether an honest man of ordinary means can
afford to stand firm for the ideals of justice, fairness, and toler-

ance comes up. The willingness of Virgie, colored servant who has been in the Riggs family for years, to believe the rape charge against her boss without waiting for convincing evidence is a disheartening example of how quickly honest people will turn against those fighting for them. Howard Barnes' observation in the *New York Herald Tribune* of February 4, 1944 that "even though it does not completely come off, *Decision* is not to be dismissed lightly" stands up today as a sound appraisal of a play about the fight for democracy at home.

*   *   *   *   *   *   *

Other dramas dealing with fascism in America during these years were *It Can't Happen Here* (1936), *American Landscape* and *Knickerbocker Holiday* (1938), *The American Way* (1939), and *The Searching Wind* (1944).

Sinclair Lewis, whose play *Jayhawker* (1934), dealt with politics during the Civil War, turned to the problem of dictatorship in America by dramatizing, with John C. Moffitt, his novel *It Can't Happen Here*. The play had probably the largest mass opening in the theatre's history, first nights being held October 26, 1936, at the Adelphi Theatre in New York, and, under the auspices of the WPA Federal Theatre, in eighteen other cities. Before the play was withdrawn, it had been presented in Spanish at Tampa, Florida; in Yiddish in New York; in Italian at Newark, New Jersey, and in other languages throughout the country. The Adelphi opening was also probably the first and only time speculators sold tickets to a Federal Theatre production. A newspaperman for the *New York Times* reported "a number of them were hawking their wares in front of the Adelphi before project officials managed to get the tickets back; no one knew how the speculators got the tickets."[3]

Lewis was inspired to write anti-Nazi novels and plays through personal experience as well as political convictions. In 1934, Dorothy Thompson, then his wife, ran into trouble with the

Nazis in Germany and was ordered out of the country. One result was the novel *It Can't Happen Here,* published in October, 1935. It was promptly banned in Italy and Germany. Lewis later charged that Will Hays prevented the book from becoming a moving picture because of possible international complications. The writer's agent flatly declared that the picture, for which Sidney Howard had prepared the script and Lionel Barrymore had been chosen to play the part of Doremus Jessup, was shelved by Metro-Goldwyn-Mayer "in fear of international politics and threat of boycott abroad."[4]

"Insistence upon isolation was at its peak between 1935 and 1939," historian Nichols observed in *Twentieth Century United States.*[5] Both the novel and the play *It Can't Happen Here* were attempts by Lewis to awaken the American people to the international danger of naziism. The heated discussion each aroused served his purpose. "Mr. Lewis has a story to tell that is calculated to make the blood of a liberal run cold," Brooks Atkinson wrote after witnessing the play's premiere performance. *"It Can't Happen Here* ought to scare the daylights out of the heedless American who believes, as this column does, that it can't happen here as long as Mr. Lewis keeps his health."[6]

The play omits many sidelights of the novel, but retains the main theme. Doremus Jessup, editor of a small town Vermont newspaper, refuses to believe "Buzz" Windrip and his "Corpo" guards will take over the country following Windrip's election as president. But Jessup changes his mind when the Corpo guards beat his anti-totalitarian grocer friend to death and then shoot down Doremus' son-in-law. The editor, vainly trying to stem the tide of fascism, is thrown by the Corpo guards into a concentration camp. He is brutally beaten and is only saved from death by escaping to Canada, from where he continues his fight for democracy.

Many contemporary "cure-alls" advocated by politicians of the period appear in *It Can't Happen Here.* The Townsend

Old Age pension plan is suggested by Mrs. Veeder's statement, "My, we certainly would like this fifty dollars a week they say Mr. Windrip is going to give all the old folks, if he's elected President. We could use it, with another winter coming." And the promises made to the people in Germany have their American counterparts in the Corpo promises.

"The Corpos intend everything," Lorinda exclaims. "They tell the industrialists, they'll stop all strikes. They tell the workers, unions will be sacred. They tell the well-to-do they'll lower taxes. They tell the poor they'll have $2,500 a year."

But what brought reality to the situation was the shadow of the depression, still strong in American minds in 1935 and 1938. "We need a miracle," Doremus gloomily says. "Unemployment up another two million, stock market way down, everybody scared of war—the world is filled with trouble." And the fodder for the Mussolini Black Shirts and the Hitler Storm Troopers and Windrip's Corpos was expressed by Julian, "I'm not asking for an inch, or looking for glory. I'm yelling for a job." When the jobs were not forthcoming in Italy and Germany, fascism and naziism were.

Maxwell Anderson's *Knickerbocker Holiday* was a musical comedy commentary on contemporary conditions under the transparent disguise of early New York history. Peter Stuyvesant arrives from Holland to take over the corrupt government of New Amsterdam, and to set himself up as a dictator. "The dialogue and the lyrics are rich with satiric implications in language the no less telling, for being, as they usually are, both broad and funny," Joseph Wood Krutch said in the November 5, 1938, *Nation*. "Under the circumstances one need not worry if Peter Stuyvesant's conception of the totalitarian state seems suspiciously modern or if the unhappy political choice with which the burghers are faced bears a striking resemblance to our own."[7] The choice, in the arguments of the day, is between an efficient totalitarian state which runs everybody's lives and an inefficient democracy in which men are free. The Dutch burghers in the musical decided a little inefficiency and freedom were preferable to perfection and servitude.

Mr. Krutch had high praise for the play, its "literate lyrics and coherent plot with robust music and honest low comedy was to make *Knickerbocker Holiday* the first musical show of several years in the middle of which no one went to sleep."[8] Richard Watts, Jr., the *New York Herald Tribune* critic in his October 20, 1938, review called the comedy "both ponderous and heavy-handed," but praised Walter Huston, as did all the critics, for his superb performance and his personal qualifications "as a skillful and winning actor."

In a more serious vein, two plays in which the German-American Bund figured were *American Landscape* by Elmer Rice and *The American Way* by George S. Kaufman and Moss Hart. The Bund was an imported version of the Nazi Storm Trooper organization. It set up camps in New Jersey and Long Island where the members gathered on weekends and holidays to put on uniforms, march in troop formation, and sing Nazi songs. In *American Landscape,* a Bund leader tries to buy the Dale estate in Connecticut for a Bund camp. In one of the poorest plays Rice has written, he brings the living and dead relatives of Captain Frank Dale to the family home in order to stop the sale. The Captain dies before making a decision, but his heirs turn the Bund leader down. *The American Way* is an episodic play that follows the life of German emigrant Martin Gunther from the day he arrives in America to his death in 1933. Gunther, who first becomes wealthy and then loses everything in the depression, is killed when he tries to prevent his grandson from joining the Bund.

Lillian Hellman's *The Searching Wind* has two centers around which the plot revolves. One is the willingness of American businessmen to do business with Hitler and Mussolini; the other is the pent-up feelings of returned soldiers towards those who brought on the war by closing their eyes to what was going

on. Through a series of episodes, starting with Mussolini directing the Fascist march on Rome in October, 1922, the three-
cornered love affair of Alexander Hazen, his wife Emily, and her
one-time best friend Catherine Bowman is told. Catherine and
Alexander, an American diplomat, broke off their engagement
in 1922 when he refused to view Mussolini's march on Rome
seriously.

"You have to work with what there is to work with," he
later tells Emily's father, Moses Taney. "You accept the people
you have to accept, and that doesn't mean you always like them
or always trust them."

To which Taney replies, "A very dangerous game. Mr.
Wilson played it. It goes on the assumption that bad men are
stupid and good men are smart, and all diplomats are both good
and smart. Well, the last time, Mr. Clemenceau was both very
bad and very smart."

During the period immediately preceding the Munich conference, speculation of a German-Russian war was rife in England,
France, and the United States. Hitler used this illusory hope by
holding out promises to be satisfied if the conference ceded the
Sudetenland to him. In the United States his emissaries spread
the propaganda, making it more palatable through such arguments as Count Max von Stammer used with Hazen. "I speak
unofficially, of course," the count told the American, "but if
we are given the proper freedom and cooperation we might be
prepared, in time, to turn East. To rid Europe of the menace of
Russia. We realize you would wish such a promise to come from
men more highly placed than I. So I have been instructed to
suggest to you. . . ."

By April, 1944, many wounded American soldiers were back
from their overseas battles. Samuel Hazen, son of Alexander and
Emily was one of them. He was back, in order to have his leg
amputated. But he was also back to voice the thoughts of many
American servicemen whose lives had been uprooted because a
war was on. They were particularly bitter about the businessmen

who had played ball with Hitler. One day, Samuel told his parents, a buddy on the battlefield in France handed him a newspaper clipping. It came from the society column of an American newspaper. The writer, after remarking how handsome Mrs. Alexander Hazen looked at the affair, said, "I looked around the table and thought Europe isn't dead. These people will go home some day and once more make it the charming, careless, carefree place I knew so well."

Samuel bitterly tells Alexander and Emily that the soldier then commented, "Glad to be sitting in the mud here, Sam, if it helps to make a carefree world for your folks."

Another buddy, he adds, told him:

> Sam, that banker the piece talked about, he used to deal with the Germans before it got too hot. He's a no good guy. And the rest of those people; they're all old tripe who just live in our country now and pretend they are on the right side. When the trouble came in their countries they sold out their people and beat it quick, and now they make believe they're all for everything good.

The play ends with Samuel denouncing his parents and their generation for bringing on the war by closing their eyes to what was happening and for feeling ashamed to express their love of country at a time when such an expression was necessary. These sentiments have been repeated many times in postwar books and magazine articles by American servicemen.

*   *   *   *   *   *   *

Kaj Munk was the pastor of a small Lutheran church at Bedersee, Denmark, when the Nazis came in 1941. But he was more than merely the pastor of a tiny fishing village-church. He was Denmark's leading contemporary dramatist, a playwright whose works had been produced in the three Scandinavian capitals and whose dramatic stature leading critics had compared to that of Ibsen and Strindberg. In 1938 Munk wrote *He Sits at the Crucible*. It dealt with a scientist, Professor Mensch, who believed in his science and in his country. Mensch discovers an original portrait of Christ and presents it to the Fuehrer of his country. But the picture shows Christ no Aryan but a Jew, and for the first time Mensch is faced with the conflict between his honesty as a scientist and his devotion to the Vaterland.

One character in the play was Bishop Beugel. In him Munk personified the fight of the German clergy against the Nazis. The play was not forgotten by the invaders when they came to Denmark. During the early months of the occupation Kaj Munk was left alone. Then as he spoke out against Hitler and the Nazis, threats against his life were made. This failed to stop him. In August, 1943, a revolt against the Nazis failed, and Munk was thrown into a concentration camp as one of the leaders. Two months later he was freed, and he immediately resumed preaching against the Germans, not inside the church but outside. On the Sunday following New Year's Day, 1944, Kaj Munk denounced the Nazis from the steps of the church. The next day a wave of strikes broke out. Later in the week Storm Troopers called at the parsonage and took Kaj Munk to Gestapo headquarters in the forest of Silkeborg. He was never seen alive again. The next morning a passerby observed a badly beaten and bullet-riddled body in a ditch. It was the beloved and heroic dramatist-parson, Kaj Munk.

When the history of resistance to the Nazis in Germany and occupied countries is written, the church will be found to have played a mighty role. "In actual fact, the Christian Church ran true to its highest traditions as the Church Militant," one church writer wrote. "Ministers, priests and laymen abounded in the German underground."[9]

Glorious Morning (1938), and *The Seventh Trumpet* (1941), were dramatic expressions of religion's fight against naziism. The former, by Norman Macowan deals with the resistance of religious people to orders that God does not exist. The daughter

of a family living in the hinterlands of a dictator state has a
vision in her university class that God exists and that it is her
destiny to bring this message to the people. "Her message is in
direct opposition to what the people are commanded by the
Supreme Council to believe," the worried professor tells her
parents. "To put it shortly as I can, her message is that God does
exist, and that a people who do not know Him are utterly lost."

Leda, a kind of hopeless Joan of Arc, carries the message to
her people despite threats from a member of the state's Supreme
Council. "Put me in prison and I will still have God," she tells
Gurgani. "I will not fear what man can do to me." Leda is
put in prison, and on a "glorious morning" she and those who
accept her message are hanged.

But as she is led away the professor whispers to her, "I want
you to know that I shall use all the power I have in Zagnira to
make certain that your sacrifice is not in vain—here or in the
world outside."

By the time *The Seventh Trumpet* opened on November 21,
1941, at the Mansfield Theater, England had taken a good share
of its bombings, and clergymen and others saw with outraged
feelings the gaping ruins of cathedrals and churches. The play,
written by Charles Rann Kennedy, was one of a cycle of seven
plays on contemporary problems, all religious in tone and subject.
The cycle was begun in 1905 with *The Winterfeast* and completed with *The Seventh Trumpet* thirty-six years later. Best
known plays are *The Servant in the House* and *The Terrible
Meek*.

In *The Seventh Trumpet,* Percival, a London bobby whose
body is shattered when he throws a time bomb off Ludgate Hill,
arrives at Glastonbury the morning after the monastery of St.
Lazarus has been blown to bits. There he meets other sincere
believers, who discuss what the Christian should do in the war.
They agree that the peaceful believer and the instinctive pacifist
are justified in taking up arms against evil. In this respect at

least they undergo the same struggle the liberal experienced during the years between World War I and World War II.

"I'm with you, Sam," Father Bede says, "in most of your jeremaid. This war is different. Pacifist though I've always been, still am, I'm forced to confess Hitler has used my pacifism as his cat's paw . . . if it [war] isn't Armaggeddon, it jolly well ought to be." He adds that church people changed their concepts with Dunkirk. "The moment Dunkirk happened the stupendous miracle of national repentance began," Bede asserts. "Then they stampeded to a man. Some to the ambulance corps and chaplaincies, some to the potato field and cow-barns. They looked swagger, marching off in their monk's toggery."

The fear that naziism could spread, expressed by Sinclair Lewis and others, is felt by the girl Madeline. "Hitlerism, if we don't take care," she says, "is possible in every land, every heart. It symbolizes, precisely, the Liar, the Satanic, the Rebel against God, in all of us. Until we are delivered from that evil, perfect forgiveness is not ours to grant." Here was Hitlerism carried back to the personal equation of the Puritan tradition in English life, of Milton's *Paradise Lost* and Bunyan's *Pilgrim's Progress*.

* * * * * * *

With the rise of the Nazis to power, the position of the Jew in Germany underwent a radical change. Laws were passed prohibiting him from holding certain positions, barring him from hitherto open professions, from sitting on any except designated park benches, from marrying German Aryans. The change soon furnished American playwrights with dramatic themes. The subjects, unfortunately, proved superior to the plays, but the latter serve as a reminder of a grim period in a persecuted race's history.

Birthright (1933), by Richard Maibaum depicted the difficult position of the Jew shortly after Hitler came to power.

One of the claims on which the Nazis rose was that World War I had been lost because of the Jews. They used this specious excuse to justify their harsh treatment of fellow countrymen. In the play, Kurt comes to the home of the Eisners and tells the family, "All of you are responsible for what happened to us. You think Germany lost the war? The German army was never conquered. It was unconquerable. It was knifed in the back by pacifists, the socialists, and profiteers—by Jews."

Friedrich is a Gentile. He and Clara Eisner were engaged, but Nazi pressure forces him to give her up and join the party. It was a common occurrence in Germany those days. Even Captain Hugo Eisner, who had turned Protestant years before, learned that his war record and change of faith did not help. The Nazis considered him a Jew, and as a Jew he was condemned.

The Shatter'd Lamp (1934), was an appropriate title for the broken lives caused by Nazi laws. The play, originally called *Derelict,* was written by Leslie Reade. It deals with university life in old Germany, which was kindly, romantic, and placid. To be an "Herr Professor" was a great title, and a mark of distinction. Fritz Opal is a professor, but when the Nazis come to power his close friends begin to avoid him, and the happy life soon disappears. Professor Opal had married a Jewess. A few years earlier it didn't matter. Now it makes a great deal of difference. Louise Muller breaks her engagement to Karl Opal when she learns his mother was a Jewess. Sophie Opal kills herself, and Professor Opal is shot down by storm troopers.

Dorothy Thompson and Fritz Kortner in *Another Sun* (1940), dramatized still another phase of the Nazi racial laws. By 1940 the Nazis had decreed that plays written by Jews could not be performed in Germany. In *Another Sun,* George and Marie Berndt, famous stage stars, leave the country when Hitler refuses to permit Berndt to produce a play written by a Jew. The couple go to America, but are invited to return to Germany by Hitler following the fall of Austria in 1938. Marie goes back, but George decides to stay in America.

The American attitude toward the racial question is treated in
Edward Chodorov's *Common Ground* (1945). A USO troupe,
composed of Americans with Jewish, German, Irish, and Italian
ancestry, is shot down inside Italy. The actors are taken to
prison by the Germans and given the opportunity of saving
themselves by performing for the Nazi and Italian soldiers.
One exception is made. Buzz Bernard, the Jew, is automatically
condemned to a concentration camp. A renegade American
newspaperman visits the troupe in prison. His sneers help
the actors make up their minds to stick together and defy the
Nazis, even if it means death. But the Americans escape when
the Italian commandant of the prison turns out to be an anti-Nazi
professor whose family has been murdered by the Germans.

Clifford Odets' *Till the Day I Die* (1935), is a wartime
version of *The Undertow* theme that people will turn on
those who fight for them. Ernest Taussig, worker for the underground, is captured by the Nazis. They arrange his public
appearances so that his comrades believe he has turned traitor.
Even his wife and brother finally turn against him. The underground brands Ernest a traitor, and he becomes an outcast.
In the final scene he escapes and, broken and ill, appeals to his
wife and brother to believe in him. They turn him down, and he
goes into the next room and takes his life.

Odets' characterizations are sharp and his handling of the
scenes skillful, but the play is unconvincing. It is inconceivable
that the underground, so well informed in so many things, could
be almost naively unfamiliar with Nazi methods not to recognize the tactics used on Ernest. The play is a severe, if un-
intended, indictment of the underground in its willingness to
believe a comrade has turned traitor. The situation is similar to
the one Dick Wells encountered in the Committee of Seventy
meeting in *The Undertow* and that Superintendent Riggs met
from his servant in *Decision*. Such things may be, but they do
not speak well either for man's head or heart.

During a critical period in the rise of Fascist power, Giacomo

Matteotti was a feared foe of Mussolini. On June 1, 1924, Matteotti, a member of the Italian Chamber of Deputies, disappeared. Several weeks later his mutilated body was found. A shocked world, not yet inured to Fascist tactics, charged Mussolini with the crime. The Duce never stood trial for the murder, though several who participated in the crime were convicted by Italian courts and sentenced to prison after the fall of the Fascist government. *Tell My Story* (1939), by Richard Rohman was a dramatization of the rivalry between Matteotti and Mussolini, and of the former's murder by hired gunmen.

The plays on naziism and fascism performed a function of the utmost importance to the America of the nineteen-thirties. They made a reluctant nation aware there was a demonic force loose in the world and impressed upon audiences that this satanic power was not content to remain overseas but would eventually extend its tentacles to all lands. Newspaper and magazine accounts, scenes in newsreels, and even the hourly radio reports failed to bring home the menace facing the world in these twin ideologies. It remained for an evening in the theatre, with the immediacy of footlight impact, to awaken a somnolent America to the danger. *Margin for Error, Decision, It Can't Happen Here, Knickerbocker Holiday,* and *The Searching Wind* startled as well as entertained audiences. They helped pave the way for a better understanding of the political hazards abroad during the decade.

11

EVOLUTION
OF A LIBERAL

A SHORT TIME after World War I ended an unusually tall, rather shy, and somewhat thoughtful appearing young man came to New York. He had been away for several years, fighting the Germans as a kilted soldier in the Black Watch Regiment of the Canadian Army. He had been gassed at Vimy Ridge in France and wounded in both legs on returning to action after several months in the hospital. The soldier, who had left Harvard to enlist in the "war to end all wars," brought back with him a desire to write and a burning hatred of war.

Following a period as a reporter on the old *New York Herald,* Robert Emmett Sherwood became a staff writer for *Life* when that publication was a humor magazine. In 1924 he became its editor and held the post until 1928. During this period Sherwood's militant liberalism, aimed fundamentally at achieving a warless world, gradually coalesced with his writing ambitions. The first important result of this combination was *The Road to Rome,* which opened January 31, 1928, in the Playhouse Theatre.

151

Placing his characters in the pre-Christian Rome of Fabius Maximus, Sherwood has them talk in twentieth century language bearing the stamp of twentieth century attitudes about life and war. Even the sophisticated plot bears a contemporary trade mark. Hannibal, general of the Carthaginian army, is about to attack a panicky Rome. He is visited the night before the assault by Amytis, Greek-born wife of Rome's dictator, Fabius Maximus. The two talk about the impending battle, with Amytis persistently asking Hannibal: if you take Rome, so what?

Hannibal, unable to answer the question, finally cries out, "If I recognize your truths, I'll have to believe that all my life has been wasted, that all those men who have fallen along the road to Rome have died for nothing. Do you want me to believe that?"

To which Amytis replies, "I do. I do. I want you to believe that every sacrifice made in the name of war is wasted."

Amytis and Hannibal spend the night together. The next morning she returns to Rome, and Hannibal and his troops leave without attacking the Imperial City.

Here was one of the keys to Sherwood's early thinking, and of much of America's thinking in the 1920's. Amytis expressed another popular view when she exclaimed:

> I may be a traitor to Rome, but I am not a traitor to my own convictions. I didn't start this war. I've never given it my support or encouragement. I have no axe to grind with Hannibal. Why should I sacrifice my life merely because the Roman army has failed to subdue a weaker enemy?

To this she adds a statement concerning the causes of war that was to find its ultimate expression by Sherwood in *Idiot's Delight* eight years later. "That wasn't the voice of a Ba-al, Hannibal," Amytis answers his assertion that the god called him to war.

> That was the voice of the shopkeepers in Carthage, who are afraid that Rome will interfere with their trade . . . hatred, greed, envy and the passionate desire for

revenge . . . those are the high ideals that inspire you soldiers . . . and when you realize the shameful futility of your great conquests, you turn around and attribute it to all the Gods . . . the Gods are always convenient in an emergency.

Between *The Road to Rome* and *Idiot's Delight* Sherwood wrote two other plays expressing his attitude towards war. The unproduced *Marching As To War* centers around a conscientious objector who refuses to follow Richard the Lion-Hearted on his crusades. *Waterloo Bridge,* written in 1929 and made into a successful moving picture the same year, has a convalescent Canadian soldier tell his girl, "It's that guy up there in his aeroplane. What do I care about him and his bombs? What do I care who he is, or what he does, or what happens to him? That war's over for me. What I've got to fight is the whole dirty world. That's the enemy that's against you and me. . . ."

Sherwood's anti-war bias reached its peak in *Idiot's Delight.* From there he went to the next stage, one of uncertainty, in *Abe Lincoln in Illinois.* This was followed by *There Shall Be No Night,* with its decision that there are some wars that must be fought. Then came *The Rugged Path,* with its conviction that the liberal must not wait but must act affirmatively in the face of evil.

In *Idiot's Delight,* with Alfred Lunt and Lynn Fontanne in the leading roles, Sherwood reached the height of his anti-war dramas. In a postscript to the printed play he declares:

Those who shrug and say "war is inevitable" are false prophets. I believe that the world is populated largely by decent people, and decent people don't want war. Nor do they make war. They fight and die, to be sure —but that is because they have been deluded by their exploiters, who are members of the indecent minority.

Achille Weber was one of the "indecent minority." Quillery, the Italian worker at the inn where the characters in the play are detained pending news of the war, excitedly declares that

> [Weber] can give you all the war news. Because he
> made it. . . . He has been organizing the arms industry.
> . . . In every part of the world, the good desire of men
> for peace and decency is undermined by the dynamite
> of jingoism. And it needs only one spark, set off
> anywhere by one egomaniac, to send it all up in one
> final, fatal explosion.

Here, also for the first time in plays about war, appears the
scientist who wants to be above and out of politics. Dr. Walder-
see, trapped in the hotel with Weber and his mistress, Irene, and
Harry Van and his six American dancing girls, fumes at the
stupidity of man which renders his years of research valueless by
delaying his return to his laboratories. "Fascism," he rages,
"has nothing to do with it. I am a scientist. I am a servant of
the whole damn stupid human race. If you delay me any longer
here, my experiments will be ruined. Can't you appreciate that?
I must get my rats at once to the laboratory in Zurich, or all my
months and years of research will have gone for nothing."

But he is delayed, and his experiments go for nothing while
Harry Van tries to convince Irene she is the girl he spent a night
with in a hotel room in Omaha, Nebraska. Irene is deserted by
Weber after she turns on him and denounces his traffic in human
lives by manipulating wars. And the end comes with Weber and
the others, including the American dancing girls, on their way to
safety while Irene and Harry Van remain in the bombed hotel,
whose crashing walls forecast a world doomed to destruction.

Idiot's Delight was a violently anti-war play, seeing no cause
or reason ever for the liberal to take up arms. *Abe Lincoln in
Illinois* (1938), was the next step in Sherwood's thinking. It
dealt with:

> The story of a man of peace who had to face the issue
> of appeasement or war. He faced it . . . Lincoln, on
> his own authority, ordered the relief to be sent to Fort
> Sumter. It did mean war—and for Lincoln it meant
> four years of anguish and then violent death. But it
> saved the Union.[1]

The play was written in the shadow of the Munich Conference, September 29, 1937. Prime Minister Neville Chamberlain of England and Prime Minister Eduardo Daladier of France faced the same problem Lincoln faced in the play, that of "resigning their democratic ideals or fighting for them . . . they made their choice. They surrendered without a fight."[2]

By the time *Abe Lincoln in Illinois* opened, Hitler had so strengthened his position in Europe as to settle disputes without heeding the wishes of England, France, or Italy. On October 15, 1938, the day the play opened, Hitler received the envoys of Hungary and Czechoslovakia as the over-all umpire of their boundary disputes. His word was law, and he was rapidly assuming the role of "the peacemaker of Europe, to the exclusion of the three other statesmen in the Munich four-power consortium."[3] Other signs of the coming conflict were preparations in England for an "Army in Overalls," volunteers whose duty was to guard vital factories in case of war; the accusation by the Vatican that Hitler's Nazis had inspired the anti-Catholic riots then raging in Vienna, and a move by President Roosevelt urging Congress to expand the Army and the Navy.

Abe Lincoln in Illinois purports to be biographical, taking its hero in episodic scenes from his early years in New Salem, Illinois, to the day he left Springfield for Washington as president-elect. He, too, faced the problem of appeasement, and earlier seeking to avoid running for Congress said:

> One day I might have to cast my vote on the terrible
> issue of war or peace . . . what attitude would I take
> in deciding which way to vote? "The liberal attitude,"
> of course. And what is the liberal attitude? To go to
> war for a tract of land, or a moral principle? Or to
> avoid war at all costs?

When a friend exults at Lincoln's election to the presidency, the issues facing the nation nearly eighty years later are mirrored in Billy Herndon's remark, "Would you want to become President of the United States at this time? Haven't you been reading the newspapers lately?"

Then came *There Shall Be No Night* (1940). The play
brought down on Sherwood's head the wrath of the Communist
paper *The Daily Worker,* and the anger of Father Coughlin's
Christian Front. Sherwood had been inspired to write it by
Russia's invasion of Finland earlier that year. With *There Shall
Be No Night,* Sherwood made the step from uncertainty to certainty that so many liberals of the period eventually took:

> With the outbreak of the second World War in 1939 I
> was in a frenzy of uncertainty. . . . Being confused I
> couldn't speak up with any positive conviction . . . but
> my mind was settled principally by two events: the
> first was a speech in October by Col. Charles A. Lind-
> bergh, which proved that Hitlerism was already power-
> fully and persuasively represented in our own midst;
> the second was the invasion of Finland.[4]

So he wrote *There Shall Be No Night* and was denounced as
a warmonger by Communists and Fascists. During the period of
writing from January 15 to February 10, the playwright rarely
left his New York apartment except for some exercise. On
occasions he worked twenty hours a day. "I turned out the first
handwritten draft in two weeks, although I doubt if I could turn
out a play in that brief space of time," he said in an interview.
"But I was feeling at a white heat when I was writing this play."[5]

Sherwood was in tune with the country when he wrote the
drama. As a critic pointed out, "Mr. Sherwood has not been
a leader of thought, nor has he gone off on tangents of his own.
His plays are popular. Their meaning is accepted by large
audiences. He has been neither ahead, nor behind, nor away
from the life with which he has been surrounded."[6]

There Shall Be No Night has as its central figure Dr. Kaarlo
Valkonen, a Nobel Prize winner living in Finland with his
American wife, and their son. As the play opens Dr. Valkonen
believes that the Munich conference will prevent war. But war
does come, and his son Erik marches off to die. Beaten back
gradually but steadily by the pressure of events, Dr. Valkonen

finally rejects an offer of safety in America with his wife in order
to leave for the front as a doctor:

> I have suddenly realized what and where I am. I am
> trying to defeat insanity . . . degeneration of the human
> race. And then a band of pyromaniacs enters the
> building in which I work. And that building is the
> world—the whole planet—not just Finland. They set
> fire to it . . . this a war for everybody—yes—even
> scientists who thought themselves immune behind their
> test tubes.

Dr. Valkonen, however, is not the intellectual who, dragged
from his "ivory tower," succumbs to despair. "We have within
ourselves the power to conquer bestiality," he declares, "not with
our muscles and our swords but with the power of the light that
is in our minds. What a thrilling challenge this is to all science."

Two men in the play, Frank Olmstead and Sergeant Gosden,
mirror the liberal whose beliefs came full turn by 1940. Cynical
and frank, Olmstead answers a question about his conscience on
going to war:

> What the hell do you think it says? How could I ever
> live with myself again if I didn't go? That's what
> happens when you expose yourself to this. Oh, God—
> how many times have I taken an oath that if the United
> States were ever again duped into going to war, I'd be a
> conscientious objector . . . but—here's the choice—
> given to me now—and I haven't the guts to say, "No,
> I won't fight."

And Gosden, agreeing with him, says, "Every one of us can
find plenty of reasons for not fighting, and they're the best reasons
in the world. But—the time comes when you've bloody well
got to fight—and you might just as well go cheerfully."

This was the attitude of the liberal who, forced into fighting
against his convictions, does so without changing those convictions. The situation of Morey Vinion, the newspaper editor in
The Rugged Path (1945), was different. He had already arrived
at the decision America must fight naziism to survive. But he

had not yet settled his thinking on where he fitted into the picture. Wrestling with his problem of a liberal editor on a conservative paper—whose business manager's views were, "we may sympathize with the British—we may hope they'll pull through—but, if they don't—if the Germans win—okay, we do business with them"—Vinion finally came to his decision. He enlisted in the Navy.

"Maybe going into the Navy is the craziest, silliest thing I could have done," he tells his wife, "but I'm tired of being merely someone who stands by and watches. I want to be part of something. You said I have demons in me—and maybe you're right. They're demons of doubt. I want to dispel them. I want to find out whether there really is anything in this world worth fighting for and dying for."

He finds his answer in the second half of the play, when he is thrown on a small Philippine Island and joins a guerrilla band. Volunteering for an action that results in his death, Vinion tells his Filipino comrades as they prepare for the foray:

> There's one piece of equipment we've got for this fight, and it wasn't manufactured yesterday and it won't be destroyed tomorrow, and that one piece of equipment is faith. . . . You people on this island—you have proved the power of that weapon and that hope. You may not seem to have much to fight with, but you know what you've got to fight for, and that gives you dignity. It makes you unconquerable.

The Rugged Path, with Spencer Tracy as Vinion, received mixed reviews. Lewis Nichols in the *New York Times* probably hit the chief defect of the play by pointing out it "often seems to be two separate plays," adding "the approach to the first is intellectual; the second is more active."[7]   As a matter of fact, the drama was first thought of by Sherwood as two plays. One was to be concerned directly with editorial actions and reactions of newspaper publishers during the war, and the other with the feelings of an intelligent serviceman towards the conflict. Burns

Mantle said, "Despite its unhappy adventures, it seems to this editor that *The Rugged Path* is an interesting, frequently eloquent and always honest report on several vitally important aspects of a democracy at war."[8]

One point Sherwood does make in this play is the need of the liberal to act in the face of evil, even to the extent of taking up arms. But it is action bolstered by faith in the right—"the faith of the people—the devotion of the people to the God who created man in His own image—reached through experience even more than reason."

* * * * * * *

The evolution of Sherwood's thinking reflected in microcosm that of most liberals during the same period. His plays expressed their original militant pacifism, later heart-searching uncertainty, and final firm decision.

In the theatre the first phase was dominant through 1936. Such plays as *Men Must Fight* (1932), *If This Be Treason* (1935), and *A Woman of Destiny* (1936), adequately reflected the liberal's ideas. Two events outside the show houses pointed up the motives that impelled playwrights to write in the vein they did.

First of these was the Senatorial investigations of munitions graft, bankers' profiteering, and propaganda aspects of war conducted by Senator Gerald P. Nye, Republican of North Dakota. From 1934 to 1936 Senator Nye laid bare the sordid details of profiteering by those interests during the "war to save democracy." His grim revelations turned a country already strongly opposed to war to a cynicism about all wars. Playwrights of the Twenties like R. C. Sheriff in *Journey's End* and Maxwell Anderson and Lawrence Stallings in *What Price Glory?* had reinforced novelists and other writers in debunking war of its glamour and romance. They had brought readers to a conviction that America must stay out of future wars.

Hard upon Senator Nye's iconoclastic investigation followed an episode whose humor did not hide the serious feelings beneath it. On March 16, 1936, *The Daily Princetonian* spread across its front page an announcement that the "Veterans of Future Wars" had been founded. The demands of the newly formed organization were simple and direct. Since there will be a war within the next thirty years, the future veterans called for a $1,000 bonus to every male between the ages of eighteen and thirty-six, retroactive, with three per cent interest compounded annually, from June 1, 1935. As Thomas Riggs, Jr., one of the originators of the group, explained in a magazine article, these men will be killed and wounded in the coming conflict and "they, the most deserving, will not get the full benefit of their country's gratitude."[9]   Other demands included preference for government jobs, exemption from federal, state, and local taxes, and a refund on all interest paid for future loans. The movement rapidly spread. By June that year the sponsors claimed 500 posts having 28,000 members. Representative Maverick, Democrat, of Texas came to Princeton to address a meeting. Riggs and others challenged the veterans' organizations of World War I to debate, and hostile Congressmen denounced the youths. Riggs even came to Washington to call on Representative O'Connor, chairman of the House Rules Committee, with regard to introducing a $2,500,000,000 bonus bill. The Congressman, red-faced and angry, had a sharp exchange of words with the Princeton students. The movement gradually died a natural death, but its existence makes more understandable how Sherwood in *Idiot's Delight* and Dr. John Haynes Holmes, co-author with Reginald Lawrence, in *If This Be Treason* reflected the spirit of the times.

Dr. Holmes had for many years been one of America's great liberal voices in the pulpit. A native of Philadelphia and a graduate of Harvard, he founded the Community Church of New York in 1907. Ten years later the Unitarian minister became a director in the American Civil Liberties Union. Two years later, in 1919, he left the Unitarian Association to become an independent minister. During World War I, Dr. Holmes offered his resignation as pastor of the church he founded because he could not support the war. In December, 1941, shortly after Pearl Harbor, he repeated his earlier move, again offering to resign "at such time in the uncertain future as my retirement may preserve this beloved church from embarrassment, odium or peril."[10] The offer on both occasions was rejected.

If This Be Treason was produced September 23, 1935, at the Music Box. From today's vantage point, the plot was incredibly naive. John Gordon, elected President of the United States on a pacifist platform, is faced with war when Japan seizes Manila without warning. The pressure to build up his defenses and man America's forces for an all-out conflict with Japan are resisted by Gordon. Instead, he recalls the Navy, holds the Army at home, and goes personally to Japan to talk over the situation with the premier of that country. The war lords in Japan have the upper hand when Gordon first arrives. But he meets a crusading pacifist, Koye, who supports the American's plea for peace. Koye arouses the people to action. They overthrow the military clique, establish a new regime, and bring peace to both nations.

The attack on Manila suggests Japan's onslaught on Pearl Harbor six years later. The excuse, too, has a prophetic ring, for here also the Japanese claim Manila was taken to forestall American aggression. Gordon's quixotic trip to Japan has its parallel in Wilson's effort to write a League of Nations for the prevention of war by travelling to the Versailles Peace Conference.

In the play the authors emphasize the current charge that munitions makers are behind all wars. Koye declares, "I say to you that wars are made like market goods. And it is governments that do this business—kings and premiers, bankers and munitions-makers. The people are innocent." The profits which Senator Nye exposed the munitions makers as having made in

World War I have their parallel in the play. Here Turner remarks to Senator Wilmot, "That was a nice jump Jennings steel
took this morning. Broke the amateur record, the boys tell me."

An amazing similarity is at once apparent between *A Woman
of Destiny,* by Samuel J. Warshawsky, which opened March 2,
1936, at the Willis Theatre, and *If This Be Treason.* Mrs. Constance Goodwin, who receives the nomination for vice-president
by forcing the National Republican Convention to write an
anti-war plank into its party platform, becomes President when
the chief executive dies of a heart attack. The President's sudden
death is caused by the assassination of the American ambassador
to Japan and the consequent necessity of declaring war on that
country. Deserted by her cabinet members and hounded by the
opposition, Mrs. Goodwin meets with the Emperor of Japan.
She appeals to his reason and personal desire for peace, and between them they withdraw the armed forces of both nations and
stop the war. The concept in each instance confirms the remarks
of Amytis to Drusus, a Roman leader in *The Road to Rome,*
"Why don't you get out, under a flag of truce, meet Hannibal
and talk the thing over in a civilized manner? He sounds to
me like the type of man who might listen to reason."

The munitions makers are represented in *A Woman of Destiny*
by Roger Harmon, opposition leader to Mrs. Goodwin's party.
A senator in the play declares war has been "forced on us by the
Harmon-Hoyt bloc. You know what they're after, oil and mining
concessions for Harmon, graft for Hoyt."

Perhaps the most interesting forecast is Mrs. Goodwin's anti-
war plank specifically stating that "war shall be a matter of
personal guilt; that any individual or group of individuals guilty
of acts tending to force us into aggression shall be tried for
attempted murder and imprisoned like common criminals." The
statement fits in perfectly with one of the basic justifications
for the Nurenburg trials following World War II.

Men Must Fight (1932), by Reginald Lawrence and S. K.
Lauren, expresses the pacifist attitude towards any war. The

assassination of an American ambassador to an unnamed South American country catapults America into war with all the nations in that hemisphere. Secretary of State Edwin Seward abandons his traditional pacifist stand and insists that the United States must declare war. His wife, whose first husband was an English flier who was killed in action during World War I, bitterly opposes Seward's new views. The two clash, and she taunts him on his failure to believe any longer in his oft-expressed peace-at-any-price conviction. "I know," Seward tells her, "I still do—abstractly. Unfortunately, war is no longer an abstraction. It's a grim reality that we've got to go through with. I am committed to this war in all sincerity. If I were young enough, I'd resign my position and fight."

Seward here was voicing thoughts liberals some years later held. He is probably the first liberal in the political drama to wrestle with the dilemma that a repugnant but necessary choice forces on him. Robert, their son, at first stands with his mother. He turns Seward's earlier arguments against his father, declaring, "You are thinking of that mob that was out there a minute ago. I'm trying to look ahead to the future—to a civilization that will really consider war the greatest of all crimes."

So firm was Robert that his fiancee, Peggy, finally blazes at him, "I despise the man who thinks his own ideas are worth more to him than his country's honor or safety."

America's unpreparedness for war, so apparent in the dark days following Pearl Harbor, is expressed in the play. "We've let them get ahead of us, that's all," Seward explains. "All these years while we've sat back and waited—dismissed war from our minds—all our talk of peace and disarmament—it's all resulted in this; death to thousands of our boys. We weren't prepared for war like this."

At the end Robert unconvincingly decides to do an about face upon learning his real father was the English aviator and not Seward. Robert enlists and leaves Peggy, who fiercely turns to Laura as the play ends, to echo the same words Mrs. Seward had uttered years earlier, "If I ever have a child—he won't go through this. I won't let him."

* * * * * * *

In Elmer Rice's *Flight to the West* (1940), the author in the drama, Howard Ingraham, tries to explain the dilemma of the liberal during the late Thirties:

> Well, a man doesn't readily throw overboard the convictions of a lifetime. For twenty years, I've devoted myself to decrying war and the war makers, agitating for disarmament, for a world commonwealth. But more and more, I began discovering to my horror that my facts and my arguments were being used in ways that I had certainly never intended, by the rabid isolationists, by the critics of democracy, even by the Nazi propagandists. And I tell you, its knocked the props from under me. I've been deluding myself with the belief that I was a clear thinker with a constructive liberal program but now as I look at myself, all I see is another confused liberal.

Sidney Howard, whose untimely death in 1939 robbed America of an outstanding playwright, as early as November 22, 1937, tried to assess the role of the liberal in world politics. In the *Ghost of Yankee Doodle* Howard plumbed the thinking of liberals and in prophetic words declared, "Our kind can't stand in the middle of the road much longer. Sooner or later we'll have to choose one of the sidewalks." But the choosing was not easy. For liberal-minded factory owner John Garrison it was a difficult decision. Confronted by the choice of closing his factory or taking war profits from orders of the Italian government, he takes the orders. "Well, I'll be god-damned," his friend Rudi bursts out. "You, chasing war profits. You, with your convictions."

"What else can I do with no orders at home?" Garrison asks. "Shut down? Throw the men out of work? When you've got a business to run, you can't let go your hold on it. It won't let go its hold on you." And later he adds, "I've learned an important lesson these last four days; that we liberals have to live in two opposite worlds. Our beliefs in one, our experience in the other."

Some segments of the so-called isolationist press sought to discredit liberals by connecting them with communism. Liberal professors in universities were frequent targets, especially those teachers who advocated firm steps against Nazi and Fascist nations. In *Ghost of Yankee Doodle* the newspaper owner intent only on his own gains has forced the fiance of the daughter whose family he is visiting to be discharged from the university as a Communist.

Martin tries to explain the situation to the family. "It's so hard to say without being solemn," Martin says, "but I just don't know how to teach present-day economics without some mention of the late Karl Marx. So I came right out and spoke that four-letter word to a lot of our American boys and girls."

Newspaper publisher Clevenger replies:

> Well, after all, Communism's only a kind of trade name for all kinds of thinking one doesn't happen to relish. Unless of course one happens to be a Communist. In which case the term Fascism may be employed for the same purpose and with the same poetic disregard for making sense. . . . And a Red raid, particularly on a university faculty, can be made to provide all the gladiatorial action the modern taxpayer seems to require before he'll read the paper I want him to read. And the worst that can possibly be said against me is that I interpret our civil liberties in the classic American way; that is, to my own private advantage as a conservative member of a conservative society.

What might have happened to the liberal hedged in by doubts and rendered impotent by inaction because of these doubts was studied by Sinclair Lewis in *It Can't Happen Here* previously discussed. In the play Doremus Jessup, editor of the *Fort Beulah* [Vermont] *Informer* regards lightly the threat of a Nazi-model dictatorship in the United States. By the time he awakens it is too late, and he becomes a victim of his earlier indecision.

Perhaps the best thing about S. N. Behrman's *No Time for Comedy* is its title and the unwritten play the author in it planned to do. *No Time for Comedy* should have been that play, and it is the theatre's loss that it wasn't. The title comes from Gaylord Esterbrook's belief that 1939 was not a year for gay and witty comedies. The play Esterbrook was going to write would have combined his talent for witty conversations and the troubles of the world. "I see refracted through it [the play about two women and an artist] the disturbance and the agony of the times," he explains to his wife, Linda. "The whole thing formed in my mind—in there—just now—while I was looking for a shoe." And, he adds a little later, "I've got a hell of a title for it . . . No Time for Comedy."

Unfortunately, *No Time for Comedy* was chiefly concerned with the attempt of Amanda Smith to take Gaylord away from his wife by inspiring him with the "serious" play he wanted to write. But Linda, in the person of Katherine Cornell, was more than a match for Amanda, played by Margalo Gillmore. Gaylord, played by Laurence Olivier, finally decided to remain with Linda and to use his natural talent for writing drawing room conversation plays to advantage by linking them with problems of world importance.

Five years earlier Behrman had toyed with a serious subject in *Rain from Heaven* (1934). Its central theme was the effort of the artist to find his place in a Nazi-controlled world. Jurin says in the play:

> These days it would seem nothing eludes political dictatorship. Not even music. To hear people talk you might think music is a form of political pamphleteering. Hindemith is Bolshevik. Strauss is reactionary. Shostakovich is the orchestrator of the Five-Year Plan. Even dead composers are pulled out of their graves to hang in effigy.

The liberal who thinks she is going somewhere, but who is actually shadow boxing with world problems is Lady Wyngate. She is the cultured person who thinks in liberal terms but never

acts, mainly because she cannot decide what to do. Her break
with her lover, Rand Eldridge, because of political differences
lacks conviction since Rand doesn't seem much concerned about
politics in the first place. Lady Wyngate's sudden love affair
with the Jewish refugee, Hugo Willens, is more intellectual than
emotional, and the clever talk each indulges in heightens that
feeling.

Perhaps the most interesting incident in *Rain from Heaven* is
its account of the break between the German critic Alfred Kerr
and Gerhardt Hauptmann, author of *The Weavers*. Hauptmann,
a great liberal in his youth, was the only top German writer to
embrace wholeheartedly the Nazi movement. In doing so he
turned his back upon the Jew Kerr, to whose championship Hauptmann owed his early recognition as a dramatist of great power.
Kerr, thinly disguised as Willens, recounts an imaginary interview
with the dramatist.

"This is a new day," Willens tells the others the writer told
him:

> "There is no place in it for Oriental decadence."
> Oriental. My family had lived in Germany for hun-
> dreds of years. I sat there staring at him. In his eyes,
> already glazed with mortality, I saw something im-
> penetrable, incurably hostile, I saw something that no
> appeal to the heart could soften. That look did for me.
> I'd never had such a sense of helplessness. For in his
> youth this man had been the voice of the submerged—
> he had written the saga of the oppressed and the poor;
> he had been a living instrument of justice.

But the liberal did not long remain in doubt concerning his
stand in the conflict between democracy and totalitarianism.
During the late Thirties he may have been uncertain and weak
as John Garrison in *Ghost of Yankee Doodle,* confused as
Howard Ingraham in *Flight to the West,* futilely seeking to place
his abilities as Gaylord Esterbrook in *No Time for Comedy.* He
wasn't, however, as indecisive as Doremus Jessup in *It Can't Happen Here.* By 1940 he had made up his mind, and from then on

the artist, scientist, writer, and just plain liberal were in the forefront of the battle on the side of democracy. The liberal had
chosen "the sidewalk" on which he was going to walk, and had
set out to do a job for victory.

*   *   *   *   *   *   *

Flight to the West (1940), *Watch on the Rhine* (1941), and
Candle in the Wind (1941), followed *There Shall Be No Night*
in rapid succession. Each play was a declaration of the liberal's
decision in the conflict between democracy and naziism. The
decision may be summarized in Madeline's defiance of Nazi
Colonel Erfurt in Maxwell Anderson's *Candle in the Wind*.

"I came into this fight tardily and by chance and unwilling,"
she says. "I never thought to die young, or for a cause. But now
that I've seen you close, now that I know you, I'd give my life
gladly to gain one-half inch against you."

Flight to the West, by Elmer Rice, employs an airplane trip
from Europe to America as the setting for the liberal to resolve
his dilemma. Two liberals, author Howard Ingraham and
newly-wed Charles Nathan, start the trip uncertain and per-
plexed. They end it, after close contact with the Nazis Dr. Walther
and Count Paul Vronoff, decided and determined. Early in the
flight Charles tells Ingraham that his books had influenced the
thinking of college students in the Twenties until their present
confusion was reached. "But I don't exaggerate when I say that
your books were a sort of Bible to my generation," he explains.

> We read them and mulled over them and discussed
> them—especially *The Betrayal of Democracy*. You
> taught us how some old men in Paris made America
> trade away the Fourteen Points to get the League of
> Nations, and then how some old men in Washington
> shut us out of the League—and then what happened
> afterwards. So we joined up with something called the
> youth movement. We had the Red tag pinned on us,
> though most of us weren't Red at all, but just young
> people who wanted the right to lead lives in which
> going to war had no part.

Ingraham admits that he himself is now confused and uncertain, that his arguments are being turned against their intended aims by clever isolationists and Nazi propagandists.
"I've been deluding myself with the belief that I was a clear
thinker with a constructive program," he admits. "But now as
I look at myself, all I see is another confused liberal."

On the plane the close contact with Dr. Walther and Count
Vronoff, who is coming to America as a Nazi spy though carrying a Russian passport, results in arguments between these
two and Ingraham, Nathan, his bride Hope, and Louise Frayne,
a newspaper correspondent. Vronoff, exposed, is taken off the
plane by the British at Bermuda. Nearing New York, Dr.
Walther and Ingraham get into a violent argument. Marie
Dickensen, a refugee whose family has suffered greatly from the
Nazis, shoots at the German. But Nathan instinctively steps
in the way, and the bullet hits him instead. It is the resulting
action which resolves the dilemma in Ingraham's mind. As
Charles lays seriously wounded from his unselfish act, Dr.
Walther coldly refuses to express gratitude for what Nathan had
done. "Surely," he asks Ingraham, "you don't really believe that
there is anything admirable in risking one's life to save an
enemy?"

Ingraham is at first amazed. Then, recognizing in Dr.
Walther's actions the microcosm of the Nazi philosophy, he
bursts out:

> When I came aboard this plane, I was in a state of
> confusion and bewilderment—filled with a sense of
> defeat and frustration. But now my faith and my
> sense of values have been restored—by what Charles
> did and by a very illuminating talk I've just had with
> Dr. Walther. I see clearly now something that I only
> sensed before. It's just this: that rationality carried
> to its ruthless logical extreme becomes madness, be-
> cause man is a living and growing organism and not a
> machine, and in all the important things of life, a sane
> man is irrational.

Charles had come to his decision before the shooting. Hope asks him, "Why have you changed? You've always hated war. We've discussed it a thousand times—it's one of the things we've always had in common."

Charles replies:

> Yes, that's all true. I have changed my point of view— but not suddenly. I've just been telling you how I felt when Paris was bombed. And now I see the danger being carried to America—this insidious invasion of the Walthers and the Vronoffs. And our own Colonel Gages, quite prepared in the interests of their pocket- books to do business with our enemies. That's why I feel it's my duty to do what I can to try to stop it.

Kurt Muller in Lillian Hellman's *Watch on the Rhine* was the liberal who had already found his place and was acting on his decision. As portrayed by Paul Lukas, he was an appealing and sympathetic character. How he made his decision is told simply and feelingly to his wife's mother, Sara:

> I will try to find a way to tell you with quickness. Yes, I was born in a town called Furth. *(Pauses. Looks up. Smiles.)* There is a holiday in my town. We call it Kirchweih. It was a gay holiday with games and music and a hot white sausage to eat with the wine. I grow up, I move away—to school, to work—but always I come back for Kirchweih. It is for me the great day of the year. *(Slowly)* But after the war, that day be- gins to change. The sausage is made from bad stuff, the peasants come in without shoes, the children are too sick—*(Carefully)*. It is bad for my people those years, but always I have hope. In the festival of August 1931, more than a year before the storm, I give up that hope. In that day, I see twenty-seven men murdered in a Nazi street fight. I cannot stay by now and watch. My time has come to move. I say with Luther, "Here I stand." I can do nothing else. God help me. Amen.

So Kurt and his wife and their three children become under- ground fighters against the Nazis. They flee to America. Here they can be safe, in the home of Sara's mother. But word comes that the key underground leader has been taken prisoner. Kurt has the money to bribe the leader's way to freedom. He kills the impoverished Count Teck de Brancovis, who tries to blackmail Kurt by threatening to expose him. Then, bidding his family a tender farewell, Kurt leaves for Mexico—and Germany.

He now stands at the far extreme from the liberal who swore undying resistance to any cause involving war. He is a step beyond Ingraham and Charles and the others who finally made their decision. He is even beyond Dr. Valkonen, marching off to fight the enemy as a doctor in the Army ranks. Kurt is the liberal driven to the extremity of committing an act inherently repulsive to him so freedom can live. He even commits murder.

He explains in his farewell talk with his son Bodo:

> The world is out of shape, we said, when there are hungry men, and until it gets in shape, men will steal and lie and *(a little more slowly)* kill. But for whatever reason it is done, and whoever does it—you understand me—it is all bad. . . . But you will live to see the day when it will not have to be. . . . In every town and every village and every mud hut in the world, there is always a man who loves children and who will fight to make a good world for them. And now good-bye. Wait for me. I shall try to come back to you.

And he leaves, the man of peace goaded into murder so a better world than the one he lives in may be possible for his children. It is here that Sherwood and the other liberal thinkers coalesce. They arrive at two fundamental points. One is that the liberal must come out of his ivory tower and act. If he wants a better world, he must do something more than talk about it. The second is that he must have faith that the better world will come. Morey Vinion on his squalid Philippine Island and Kurt Muller leaving safe Washington for a rendezvous with death in Nazi Germany both face the infinite, firmly believing right will eventually triumph over might.

12
COMMUNISM

SHORTLY AFTER the Russian revolution of 1917 had overthrown the ~~old and tired~~ Czarist regime, Americans began to look with growing uneasiness at the new Communist government. The increasing ruthless ~~and despotic~~ actions of the Bolshevist leaders soon aroused horror and fear in people everywhere. Newspaper stories, magazine articles, books, and plays expressing this uneasiness appeared first in trickles and then in avalanches as the world watched the Russian experiment.

The early plays dealing with the goings on beyond what has now become known as the Iron Curtain were emotional, but ineffectual pieces of drama. Thirty-four years were to pass before a production, *Darkness at Noon,* possessing dramatic stature as well as political depth, came to the Broadway stage. *Darkness at Noon* by Sidney Kingsley had its opening night at the Alvin Theatre on January 13, 1951. It was a dramatic presentation of Arthur Koestler's novel of the same name. Both dealt with the methods used by the Communists to wring a confession from a former top leader, N. S. Rubashov, and to justify the court's sentencing him to death.

The novel, and subsequently the play, was inspired by the
mass trials of 1937 and 1946 in which prisoners grovelled
before their judges and denounced themselves for treason to
their country, the Communist Party, and Stalin. These "blood
purges," violating all established court procedure of a civilized
world, shocked people everywhere. Those being tried were
obviously prejudged guilty before even entering the courtroom.
But what amazed Americans looking on was the abject manner
in which prisoners admitted their guilt. They not only confessed; they literally shouted their duplicities and called for the
death penalty on themselves. Such actions did not make sense
to a more balanced civilization.

An example of this tragi-comedy procedure was the trial of
eight top Russian generals in the summer of 1937. Among
them was Marshal Mikhail Nikolaevich Tukhachevsky, a former
vice commissar for defense. They were tried in a small bare
courtroom for treason, the charge being that they sold secrets
to a foreign power. The generals loudly pleaded guilty. They
were immediately stripped of the insignia of their rank, taken
out, and shot. "Dogs die like dogs," Pravda icily commented.
"There is no place for such murderers in the Soviet scheme of
things."[1]

Nearly a year later, in March, 1938, twenty-one prisoners
were brought to trial in Moscow charged with plotting to kill
Stalin. *Time* of March 14, 1938, reported that:

> As at previous Moscow trials, the prisoners, drawn
> into elaborations of their confessions by Public Prose-
> cutor Andrei Vishinsky, gave the now familiar signals
> that everyone in court saw repeating a rehearsed
> drama. They chuckled and even laughed aloud be-
> tween phrases of their most damaging admissions.
> As Vishinsky would get half through a sentence, the
> prisoner he was supposed to be grilling would snatch
> the words out of his mouth and finish the sentence
> before the prosecutor—and since it was the agreed
> sentence, Vishinsky would let it go at that.

Time, a week later, March 21, 1938, noted that one prisoner, after his confession, shouted, "Millions of Soviet children, including my own, sing 'There is no other land in this world where one breathes with such freedom.' I say farewell. Long live the Bolshevist Party under the leadership of Stalin. Long live Communism."

Harold Denny of the *New York Times* in reporting the trials gave a searing description of Genrikh Grigorevich Yagoda, head of Stalin's Secret Political Police from 1920 to 1936. Yagoda could easily have served as the prototype of Rubashov in both the novel and the play.

> This man, once so agile and fox-faced, smartly uniformed and loudly sinister in manner, sat as if in a daze. In appearance he is the most crushed of all the defendants. He has lain for at least ten months in the same prison walls to which he has consigned so many others. He sits lackadaisically in a rear seat of the courtroom. He is dressed in a dark suit. He is only 47 but his hair is whitened in the past year and his face is lined with despair.[2]

What puzzled the world was how these prisoners, without physical punishment, had been so beaten down mentally as to call for their own annihilation. That was the question both the novel and play, *Darkness at Noon,* sought to answer. In the stage version Rubashov, ex-Commissar of the People, ex-member of the Central Committee, ex-general of the Red Army, appears in his underground cell shortly after his arrest. The cell is without windows and has only an iron bed and a straw mattress. The playwright observes, "There is no day here, no night; it is a timeless dank grave for the living corpse."

At this point Rubashov is still strong in mind and body, firm of purpose, and determined not to confess. This he tells the prisoner in the next cell by means of taps on the wall. How he is broken without physical torture furnishes the conflict of the play. Two men do the job. First an old comrade Rubashov had befriended, Ivanoff, head of the prison, and then Gletkin, second in command, set themselves to the task. The latter is anxious to use physical force as well as mental stress, but Ivanoff sternly warns him, "As for Rubashov, my instructions remain. He is to have time for reflection. He is to be left alone, and he will become his own torturer."

How was this done? Rubashov, as played by Claude Rains, appears unbreakable at first. One important instrument was the cell, with its cramped quarters, its lack of fresh air, and its perpetual semi-darkness making the passage of time meaningless. As he sits in this gloomy vault, ghosts of the past rise to plague him. The faces of those Rubashov had ordered killed appear until he shrieks, "The waking, walking dreams. . . . My debts will be paid—my debts will be paid."

The debt haunting him most grew out of a love affair with his worshipping young secretary, Luba Loshenko. One of the original fighters in the 1917 uprising against the Czar, Rubashov had later been imprisoned by the Germans and tortured. But he refused to yield despite the physical beatings he underwent, and he finally was released and returned to Communist Russia a national hero. The idealistic Luba is overwhelmed by his deeds and gives herself to him as only a spirited young girl could.

One day Luba is taken away and finally shot. Later Ivanoff, seeking to save Rubashov, charges that a bourgeois conscience prevents him from grovelling before a public court. This conscience developed, the prison head declares, "Nine months, two weeks ago—at 3:10 A.M.—when your little secretary, Luba Loshenko, was shot." Ivanoff intimates that Rubashov in seeking his own advancement had not done all he could to save the girl who loved him. Gletkin later uses the same haunting episode to break the prisoner.

Added to these ever present memories is the sight of prisoners, some of them one-time intimate friends, being dragged from their cells to execution. One day Rubashov looks out of his little cell opening to see

two dimly lit figures, both in uniforms, drag between
them a third whom they hold in their arms. The
middle figure hangs slack and yet with doll-like stiff-
ness in their grasp, stretched at its full length, face
turned to the ground, belly arched downwards, the
legs trailing after, the shoes scraping on the toes.
Whitish strands of hair hang over the face; the mouth
is open. As they turn the corner of the corridor and
open the trap-door to the cellar we see this tortured,
mangled face is Bograv's.

The contempt of his fellow prisoners plays a part in Rubashov's
final breakdown. By the grapevine system of tapping on the
walls, word of the former Commissar of the People's presence
sweeps through the prison. Even here Rubashov's past catches
up with him. His ruthlessness while in power had been known
throughout Russia. Now the hatred of those who were his
fellow inmates penetrates the solid walls of the jail.

It remains for the cold, robot-like Gletkin to achieve the
complete dissolution of Rubashov's will. The former had engi-
neered the removal and death of Ivanoff on false charges of
treason. Gletkin, aroused by the certain accolades he would
obtain if Rubashov should confess in open court, brings the
prisoner in for grilling. A bright, harsh light shines directly
into the victim's face as the questioning begins. After hours
without rest, with Rubashov muddled and exhausted from lack
of sleep, Gletkin breaks off the inquisition and returns the
prisoner to his cell. The commander tells his subordinate, "In
exactly twenty minutes wake him up and bring him back here.
I will interrogate him until midnight. You take him till 5 A.M.,
and I will take him again at 5."

On resumption of the ordeal, Gletkin cleverly appeals to
Rubashov's loyalty to the Communist Party for the final blow.
The inquisitor cites passages from the latter's writings to drive
his point home. Insisting that the one-time hero now is worn out
and useless, Gletkin storms:

> You are going to die. The only question is whether you
> will die uselessly, or whether you will confess and per-
> form the last service for the Party. But die you will,
> you understand? . . . There is only one way you can
> serve it (the Party) now. A full confession in open
> court. A voluntary confession of these crimes.

Mentally tired, physically exhausted, spiritually void,
Rubashov succumbs. He tells the court:

> Covered with shame, trampled in the dust, about to
> die—let me serve my final purpose. Let my horrible
> story demonstrate how the slightest deviation from
> the Party line must inevitably drag one down into
> counter-revolutionary banditry. . . . I am confronted
> by my absolute nothingness. Therefore, on the thresh-
> old of my final hour, I bend my knees to my country
> and to my people. The political masquerade is over.
> We were dead long before the Public Prosecutor de-
> manded our heads. With this my task is ended. I
> have paid my debt. To ask for mercy would be de-
> rision. You must hate me, and you must kill me.
> I have nothing more to say.

So ends this dreary and frightening play. There is not a light
moment in it. The portrayal of a national hero brought to
disgrace and self-immolation gives the audience a ghoulish
picture of the enemy that other efforts could not equal. After
viewing *Darkness at Noon* people of free countries left the
theatre with a better understanding of why prisoners at the
Moscow and other purge trials made their abject confessions.

*   *   *   *   *   *   *

On the morning of March 11, 1948, a crumpled body was
found in an apartment house courtyard at Prague, Czechoslovakia. It was the body of Jan Garrigue Masaryk, son of Thomas
G. Masaryk, first president of Czechoslovakia, and at the time of
his death, foreign minister in the cabinet of President Eduard
Benes.

Six hours later the Communist-dominated government issued
a statement, "In consequence of his illness, combined with in-
somnia, he [Masaryk] resolved, probably in a moment of
nervous disorder, to finish his life." Soon after the Prague radio
broadcast that "Mr. Masaryk was a sensitive man who
suffered under the attacks of the foreign press."[3]

But almost as quickly, rumors spread throughout the city
and country countering these explanations and asserting that the
popular Jan Masaryk had been killed by the Communists and
thrown from his third story apartment to the ground. These
whispered stories pointed to his witty and essentially joyous
personality, his love of life even under the harsh conditions
imposed upon the nation through Communist rule, and his
earlier disdain of a friend who had committed suicide by jumping from a window, to refute the official account.

"Jumping out of a window is what a servant girl would
do," Masaryk had exclaimed when told about the suicide of a
friend earlier that year.

> Anyway, it is a stupid way to go about it. For one
> thing, there is no guarantee of success. Further,
> suicide doesn't absolve one of his responsibilities.
> Really, if a person feels he must do away with him-
> self, he should use a bullet or poison.[4]

Two days later Jan was buried at Lany next to the grave of
his great father. The burial was ordered after a hurried post-
mortem, from which his close friend, Dr. Oskar Klinger, was
kept by a ruse, had been performed. On the day following his
death more than 200,000 persons filed slowly and tearfully
past Jan's bier in the Cernin Palace in Prague. On March 13,
over 400,000 people jammed Wenceslaus Square for the
funeral. Since then the mystery of his death has challenged all
those interested in the man and in the destiny of his country.
Why has so much time and effort been spent by both Communists and Czechoslovakian patriots in pressing their explanation of his death? The answer is a simple one—Jan Masaryk

was a symbol of his country's finest hours, respected and loved by his fellow countrymen and by the western nations, and respected, if not loved, by the Communists.

This point is graphically brought out in *The Great Sebastians* at a midnight dinner party attended by Communist government officials before news of the death is announced.

> NOVOTNY: General, for a little while nothing else must happen. That is why I feel we must keep Masaryk in office. It is important. Don't you think so, Pavlat?
> PAVLAT: Yes, Masaryk is a symbol.
> ZANDEK: You think we need that symbol?
> PAVLAT: At present, yes.
> CERNY: We need prestige abroad. They are bound to respect a regime of which Masaryk is foreign minister.

But General Zandek forecasts the impending tragedy by observing, "I'm still not sure of him. All through the February events, I had him watched."

To which Pavlat rejoins, "He will go along. He has to."

What qualities endeared this genial and cultured man to his people? They rested upon far sounder grounds than the fact that he was the son of the revered Thomas G. Masaryk. Jan's own charming personality, his deep faith in democracy and its eventual triumph, and probably most of all, his willingness to exchange personal security for a dangerous post caught the imagination of fellow Czechoslovakians. Marsaryk was in the safety of America as his country's representative to the United Nations when called to Prague in December, 1947. Asked by friends why he would go back to a Communist-dominated country where his life might well be in danger, Jan explained, "I cannot abandon my people, nor President Benes."[5]

So he returned home, supported by the conviction that democracy must eventually win out. After the diplomatic debacle at Munich, Jan told the noted radio commentator Edward R. Murrow, "Don't worry, Ed. There will be dark days

and many men will die, but there is a God and He will not
let two such men (pointing to pictures of Hitler and Mussolini)
rule Europe." To bolster this fundamental principle, the
younger Masaryk added an urbanity and cultured cosmopoli-
tanism that stayed with him under the most trying conditions.
He was proud of his ability to cook, and once in London after
a bomb had rocked a nearby building, Jan came out of the
kitchen and ruefully remarked to Murrow, "Uncivilized swine,
the Germans. They have ruined my soufflé."[6]

While in Prague his Honza (Little Jan) tales lightened the
dreary days for his unhappy countrymen. The stories were
oblique ways of getting at the Communists without their having
anything tangible to justify retaliation. The foreign minister
even used a Honza to explain how Marshal Stalin turned him
down on a request that Czechoslovakia be allowed to par-
ticipate in the Marshall Plan. Asked how he felt upon being
rebuffed, Little Jan said, "Nothing, except that we did not know
whether we had to sign with Marshall or with the marshal. Now
we know."[7]

Although Jan Masaryk does not appear in *The Great Sebastians* by Russel Crouse and Howard Lindsay, produced January
4, 1956, at the ANTA Theatre, he is the dominating character
of the play. The entire action revolves about Jan's death, with
Sergeant Javorsky, top Russian party leader in the drama, trying
to force Essie and Rudi Sebastian to sign a statement supporting the government's explanation of Masaryk's death. That
the play, superbly acted by Lynn Fontanne and Alfred Lunt in
the title roles, was entertaining even for those whose knowledge
of Masaryk and his death was limited, is a tribute to the play-
writing skill of Lindsay and Crouse. Still, the importance of the
Czech martyr had to come through to all in the audience.

In the play Essie and Rudi Sebastian are a mind reading
vaudeville act playing a theatre in Prague in March, 1948. They
are personal friends of Masaryk, who was the godfather of
their son. On their arrival Jan sends them flowers welcoming

the two to the city, and then invites the couple to have lunch with him. As the plot unfolds it turns out that the Sebastians are the last people to see the statesman alive. This makes their account of Jan's feelings of great importance to Javorsky and the government's attempt to convince the world that Masaryk was a suicide. The sergeant types a statement declaring that the foreign minister had been depressed at lunch and had told his friends this unhappy feeling resulted from his betraying Czechoslovakia by working against its best interests. "It is clear to us now that it was for these reasons Jan Masaryk committed suicide," the statement concludes.

But the Sebastians, prisoners in the home of General Otokar Zandek, refuse to sign the document and defy Javorsky to do his worse. Word meanwhile has gotten through to the British consulate, and Essie, an English subject, has to be released. Rudi, however, is a native of Prague, and Javorsky orders him arrested. The enraged sergeant must leave in order to see that Essie is sent to the border in the custody of Zandek. He handcuffs Rudi to the grill door and goes out with the others.

What Javorsky does not know is that Zandek, trapped earlier by the Sebastians, has confessed that he wants to escape and is using the orders to take Essie to the border as his means. Before the three leave, the carefully built-up-word-device used in the Sebastians' act provides an exciting climax. Rudi had spotted the key to the handcuffs in Javorsky's possession. Using their identification word "quickly," meaning "key" in the act, he relays the information to Essie. She feigns hysteria and beats Javorsky, stealing the key by sleight of hand. Essie then quiets down, asks permission to kiss Rudi for the last time, and in doing so, slips the key from her mouth to his. The play ends with Rudi unlocking the handcuffs and slipping out of the room for a pre-arranged rendezvous with Essie and the general.

While *The Great Sebastians* is essentially a witty and entertaining vehicle showing the virtuosity of Lunt and Fontanne at their best, it is also a commentary on an historical event of more than passing importance. The fact two unimportant people like the Sebastians could have the courage to stand up against evil at its worst provides inspiration that democracy breeds men and women of solid character whose finest moments come when they are confronted by a choice to do the right thing or to live. Self-centered Rudi and cautious Essie induce laughter by their antics early in the play, but they inspire admiration by their actions at the end. Communism cannot win when ordinary people like the Sebastians assume heroic stature at times of crisis.

* * * * * * *

On May 2, 1957, Senator Joseph R. McCarthy of Wisconsin died at the Naval Medical Center in Bethesda, Maryland. So passed at the early age of forty-eight one of the most controversial figures ever to stride across the American political scene. To his friends, the Republican Senator was the leader of a great crusade against communism. To his enemies, he was evil incarnate, ruthlessly sweeping aside those who opposed him whether they were innocent or guilty of the charges against them.

His meteoric rise dated from a speech he made on Lincoln's birthday in 1950 at Wheeling, West Virginia, where he told a large audience that he had in his possession a list of government employees who were members of the Communist Party. Listeners declared that McCarthy said he had two hundred and five names, while he later set the number at fifty-seven. From this point on McCarthy was at sharp odds with the Truman administration, asserting that it was part of a history marked by "twenty years of treason." He attacked Secretary of State Dean Acheson and General George C. Marshall among others, and as the ferocity of his attacks grew, so did his power. *Time* of May 13, 1957, in reviewing the Senator's career, pointed out that from the Wheeling speech on the McCarthy "legend grew, and with it the fear that opposition to McCarthy's crusade would turn him upon them as he turned upon (Senator Millard) Tydings (of Maryland)."

Observers generally agree that the high point of McCarthy's power was reached in 1952 when he won a great primary victory in seeking re-election. His decline dated from the hearings before a special Senate committee in 1954 and his resulting censure by the Senate, sixty-seven to twenty-two on two counts: abusing the subcommittee that investigated him in 1951-52, and attacking the committee headed by Senator Watkins of Utah in a way that impaired the Senate's integrity and dignity.

Out of all the turmoil the word "McCarthyism" was coined to symbolize the views and actions of the Senator. To his adherents "McCarthyism" stood for the fight to save America from communism; to his foes it meant an insidious and dangerous form of slander. At any rate the word has become a part of the language, the meaning depending upon who is interpreting it.

One of the items linked with the over-all picture of "McCarthyism" is the loyalty oaths, which in truth actually preceded the heyday of the Senator. The loyalty oath was part of the Taft-Hartley Law of 1947 and said:

> I am not a member of the Communist Party or affiliated with such Party. I do not believe in, and I am not a member of, nor do I support, any organization that believes in or teaches the overthrow of the United States by force or any illegal or unconstitutional methods.

Opponents of the oath claimed that it was being used to incite "witch hunts" and asserted that McCarthy had a great deal to do with this development. The *Nation* of August 27, 1955, declared that despite the setbacks to McCarthy:

> It is clear that the institutional supports of the witch hunt are still in place unimpaired. . . . The test oath is almost universally accepted as vital to our security. Ralph Brown of the Yale Law School believes that

one-fifth of all employment is now subject to some kind of loyalty screening; the numbers of Americans who have executed the test oath of some kind is set at 12,600,000. If McCarthyism is at an end, therefore, it is only in the sense that loyalty screening and the policing of political activities and associations by agencies of the federal government is so much taken for granted nowadays that we fail to note the loss or curtailment of formerly well established rights and privileges.

At a time when the controversy was at its height, Arthur Miller's *The Crucible* was produced at the Martin Beck Theatre, January 22, 1953. It dealt with an actual witch hunt and trial held at Salem, Massachusetts, in 1692. The author explained, "I was drawn to this subject because the historical moment seemed to give me the poetic right to create people of higher self-awareness than the contemporary scene affords."[8]

The play centers around the false accusation by Abigail Williams that Elizabeth Proctor, wife of John, is a witch. Abigail has been mistress to John and hopes to become his wife if Elizabeth is hanged. But Proctor loves his wife and to save her denounces Abigail as a whore. He is thrown into jail when Elizabeth, seeking to save him but giving the wrong answers to planted questions, denies she has dismissed Abigail for wrongdoing. Seeking to live so he can help his pregnant wife, Proctor decides to confess he has seen the Devil and has been his helper. He signs a confession, but refuses to hand it to the governor deputy upon learning it will be displayed on the church door. Proctor, who had also refused to name others as doing the Devil's work, then repudiates his confession and is sentenced to be hanged.

John is one of many accused by young girls of having commerce with the Devil. Behind their accusations, inspired by villagers having special personal concerns in persecuting different people, are modern parallels. These include groundless charges accepted without examination, the refusal of those accused to name others, insistence that a confession not be used as a public weapon, and a willingness to be judged guilty in the belief one is doing the right thing.

Giles Corey dies in the play because Thomas Putnam wants his land. John Proctor dies because Abigail Williams hopes to become his wife. The Rev. Samuel Parris seeks revenge on those in the community who do not like his narrow preaching. Others have similar reasons for pinning the term "witch" on their victims. And Deputy Governor Danforth sentences people to death to preserve his standing.

The Crucible received a mixed reception by critics and audiences. Miller said several years later:

> I believe that on the night of its opening, the time when the gale from the right was blowing at its fullest fury, it inspired a part of its audience with an unsettling fear and partisanship which deflected the sight of the real and inner theme which was the handing over of conscience to another, be it woman, the state or a terror, and the realization that with conscience goes the person, the soul immortal and the "name."[9]

Two other plays dealing with communism and loyalty oaths were *The Traitor,* by Herman Wouk, and *The Egghead,* by Molly Kazan. The former, opening March 31, 1949 at the Forty-eighth Street Theatre, deals with a brilliant young atomic scientist, Professor Allen Carr, who gives atomic secrets to a Russian spy on the idealistic premise that Soviet possession would result in world peace. His plan is exposed by Navy Intelligence Officer Lieutenant Henderson, cousin and former lover of Carr's fiancee, June Bailey. Captain Gallagher, played by Lee Tracy, is sent to help Henderson capture the top Russian spy, Baker. This is eventually achieved, but not until Carr is shot. He dies insisting upon his idealistic theory about the bomb and world peace.

Among the issues appearing during the play is the question whether revered Professor Tobias Emanuel, played by Walter

Hampden, should sign a loyalty oath demanded by the university of its faculty members. This also involves the guilt by association theme so much debated at hearings in real life.

In *The Egghead,* which opened October 9, 1957 at the Ethel Barrymore Theatre, two Federal Bureau of Investigation agents come to a college town in New England to check on the loyalty of Perry Hall, a former student of Professor Hank Parson. The latter heatedly denies that Hall, a Negro, is a Communist and impulsively invites Hall to address his class. The invitation results in a sharply divided campus, but Parson stands firm until his wife, Sally, traps Hall into admitting that he has been writing Communist propaganda under the name of Charles Henry. Hank then denounces Hall and tells the FBI agents he will expose his former student at the plant where he is working.

The Crucible is a powerful drama whose literary excellence will survive its day. But *The Crucible,* with *The Traitor* and *The Egghead* will also be read in the future as examples of what people were thinking about in mid-century America.

13

ONE WORLD

TWO MEN died in 1924—one at Cambridge, Massachusetts, and the other at Washington, D. C. In death as in life their fates were unwillingly related, and this unwillingness to be associated in part brought the agony of a global war to the world. One was Senator Henry Cabot Lodge; the other, Woodrow Wilson.

The portrait of Lodge bespeaks the man. It reveals an aristocratic face, a highly cultured, intellectual face. The brow is unusually high; the white hair above is carefully combed; the wide-spread mustache and the closely cropped Van Dyke are fastidiously trimmed. The eyes are those of a patrician and a scholar, deep and thoughtful. The picture is an honest appraisal of the tall and thin gentleman who moved through the halls of Congress like a grandee of old Spain.

The Senator from Massachusetts—he was rather a Massachusetts institution than a senator—came by his position naturally. He was the son of wealth and social position. His father was John Ellerton Lodge, prosperous merchant and owner of China clipper ships. His mother was Anna Cabot, granddaughter of George Cabot, the Federalist sage. Henry Cabot Lodge mar-

187

ried wealth and position; his wife was a cousin, Anna Cabot Davis, daughter of Rear Admiral Charles H. Davis. The Senator was by heritage, tradition, and inclination a "Lodge who spoke only to the Cabots, while the Cabots spoke only to God." Some Senatorial colleagues suggested not too kindly that the faultlessly attired patrician carried his inherent exclusiveness too far. He moved among them with what was described as the "Boston chill," wearing an icy mantle few were able to penetrate. A lawyer who had never practiced, Lodge was charged with eschewing this course so he could avoid "addressing juries, which are most promiscuously made up."

But none denied Lodge his great intellectual attainments. He was a scholar in politics at a time when such a person was an oddity in public life. A graduate of Harvard who had the additional advantage of a year's travel in Europe, Lodge early achieved literary distinction. His thesis on *The Anglo-Saxon Land Law* earned him a doctoral degree in political science in 1876 at Harvard. Throughout his long life he continued to write books on politics, international affairs, and literature.

"Of all living American statesmen," Arthur Fell Low wrote in *Forum* magazine of March, 1921, "one cannot help but feel that Mr. Lodge is the most scholarly, the best read and the ablest." Yet with this he carried a narrowness that did much to vitiate his many gifts. He was, another writer commented, a complete representative of an older New England, of the Boston of 1850 when it was the town of Emerson, Longfellow, and Lowell—"the cultural metropolis and the moral pole of the Northern states." His extensive reading seemed to narrow rather than to expand his view of the world and the part he would play in it.

To these intellectual and social qualities, Lodge brought an uncompromising nature, a confirmed conservatism, and a ruthless attitude towards his enemies. The irony of fate decreed that Lodge, as majority leader of the Senate, should pronounce the eulogy upon the death of Woodrow Wilson. The *Washington*

Evening Star of November 10, 1924, reported he "pronounced a brief eulogy on the intellectual attainments of the departed war president."[1] When someone blundered and named Lodge as one of the members representing the Senate at Wilson's funeral, the same paper recorded "a formal statement from his office announced that a slight illness would prevent his attendance."[2]

Thomas Woodrow Wilson—he early dropped the Thomas—was another scholar in politics. He achieved distinction in the world of letters after returning to academic studies following a fruitless year in an Atlanta, Georgia, law office. The University of Virginia graduate then enrolled at Johns Hopkins University, where he published his first study of American politics, *Congressional Government*. His subsequent studies and writings on government, history, and belles-lettres drew Wilson's path in the opposite direction of that pursued by Lodge. The former became more and more left of center, his domestic and international vision broadening as his reading and practical political experiences increased. Certainly his fight against the club system as president of Princeton—a fight which first brought him to the attention of the general public—and against bossism in New Jersey as governor, strengthened this liberal trend in his make-up.

There was also in Wilson a leavening spirit of kinship with the common man that helped incline his path away from that followed by Lodge. He liked good bourbon; he was an avid vaudeville-goer; even "the statesmen of Europe were charmed by his oratory, his wit, and his personality." There is a picture of Wilson standing in line at a parade in Washington; he is dressed in white trousers and coat, and is wearing a straw hat. He is carrying a small American flag over his shoulder, waiting for the parade to begin. Somehow, it would be difficult to think of Lodge in the same situation. There was, unfortunately, another side of Wilson. The statesmen of Europe were charmed with Wilson "until they bumped into his indomitable will to do things his way when he was convinced he was right."[3] Early in his dealings with Congress the President was accused of being a dictator. "When he wanted a bill introduced in Congress he frequently drew it up himself, and if it hesitated on passage he summoned the leadership—and it passed soon thereafter," an Associated Press story observed.[4]

Wilson was brilliant, learned, and stubborn. To that fatal combination, he added the habit of breaking precedents. He revived the custom Washington and Jefferson pursued of delivering messages in person to Congress. He smashed the tradition that a president should not leave the United States and went to Europe while in office. He carried to greater heights the earlier dreams of workers for world peace by fighting to the death for his League of Nations. Perhaps he was, like Shelley, "a beautiful and ineffectual angel, beating in the void his luminous wings in vain" for a country recently victorious in a great war. But despite failure, Wilson held firmly onto his idealism. Upon receiving the Nobel Peace Prize in 1920 he observed, "The cause of peace and the cause of truth are of one family. Whatever has been accomplished in the past is petty compared to the glory of the promise of the future."[5]

The break between Lodge and Wilson did not occur until several years after the latter took office. At their first meeting in Washington in 1913, Lodge remarked, "You may not recall, Mr. President, but I met you for a moment some years ago, at a college commencement, when you were president of Princeton."

To which Wilson replied, "Oh, I remember you long before that. A man never forgets the editor who publishes his first article."[6] Lodge, editor of the *International Review,* in the 1870's had accepted for publication a treatise on government written by Wilson, then a Princeton student.

Their parting came in 1916 when Lodge charged that Wilson wrote a postscript to his second so-called Lusitania note to Germany stating that the previous American pronouncements "were not to be taken seriously." Wilson eventually denied the charge. Lodge accepted the denial though stating his source was apparently "unimpeachable," and cordial relations between the two proud and stubborn men were forever broken off. From there on the breach widened rapidly. Wilson might have healed it and saved his League of Nations, according to widespread rumor, if he had sent Lodge to represent the United States at the Versailles peace treaty conference. It was a cherished ambition of the Senator, who wanted to climax a career devoted to international affairs by being a vital figure at the greatest peace conference up to that time.

"In the Versailles conference he would have saved Europe as well as America lamented mistakes," Low commented in his *Forum* article.[7] Certainly Lodge, working with Wilson instead of against him, would have seen that the League was ratified by the Senate. Perhaps even more important, the patrician New England statesman and the Virginia son of a Presbyterian minister together might have been more than a match for Lloyd George, Georges Clemenceau, and Vittorio Orlando. They might have built a practical League of Nations that would have prevented a second World War.

In Time to Come, by John Huston and Howard Koch, opened December 29, 1941, at the Mansfield Theatre. It was a day of gloom for Americans, with the newspapers reporting that the Japanese were attacking Manila and that England was worried about events in India. Buried away among the less important news stories were the remarks of Senator Austin, Vermont Republican. The Washington *Evening Star* of that date quoted the New England solon as saying:

> A stabilized peace in the world can be had only by some established organization or cooperation among nations. It is vital that some means should be adopted to prevent armed tyrants from attacking other nations—our nation. I do not mean to say we should provide for another League of Nations, but there must be some substitute for war.[8]

The significance of the statement lay in the fact that Senator Austin had been one of those opposing the entrance of our country into the League of Nations following World War I.

In Time to Come deals with the futile fight of Woodrow Wilson for the League of Nations. It opens with the President defying tradition and embarking for the peace conference in Europe. It ends with his leaving the White House a defeated and broken man. But the real conflict is between Wilson and Lodge, even though the latter does not appear often in the play. It is the Senator's shadow that lengthens over Wilson as the drama unrolls to its destined bitter end. The irreconcilable dislike of two brilliant, proud, and frustrated men flares out in the scene where Wilson pleads with Lodge to save the League of Nations. Neither has the quality of mercy to yield, and the tragedy marches on.

"I opposed his League," Lodge told M. E. Hennessey of the *Boston Globe* after Wilson's death, "with reservations because I believed it was a bad thing for the United States. His attitude was 'Take it or leave it'—'Sign on the dotted line'."[9] There it was. "Sign on the dotted line." "Take it or leave it." A Lodge of the Boston Lodges, by blood relationship a kin to the Cabots, could never take such orders. He did not sign, and the world's chance for peace was thrown back another World War and no one knows how many more years.

Brooks Atkinson in his December 29, 1941, *New York Times* review of *In Time to Come* said that the authors:

> have written a record of the greatest of lost causes without rhetoric or recrimination. There, by the grace of God, went a chance to prevent the scourge of warfare that is now beating the aching back of the world . . . they have unfolded a great tragedy of ideals and the hero who stood for them, and they have not cheapened it.[10]

Richard Gaines played Wilson, and was praised for his performance. The play, however, was only a moderate success. Whether it was the mood of a people shocked into action by Pearl Harbor or the inherent difficulty of putting on the stage an historical character well remembered in life by too many, the public did not attend in sufficient numbers to make the play a smash hit. But everywhere its message for some kind of organization to end war was accepted as expressing the temper of the times. Isolationism, for the war years at least, gave way to the "One World" concept Wendell Willkie so ably advocated.

If *In Time to Come* is a dramatic story of a lost cause, *The Prescott Proposals* by Howard Lindsay and Russel Crouse is a play pointing out how an already established idealistic world organization might work. While the League of Nations was doomed to failure from the beginning, the United Nations has gradually achieved more general world support since its organization on October 24, 1945, at San Francisco. This widespread acceptance has been attained despite the many defects any such body must initially have. The goal of its adherents must be to widen and deepen the effectiveness of the organization.

Disagreements among countries comprising the United Nations furnish the basic threat to its success. In the play UN delegate Mary Prescott, played by Katherine Cornell, answers critics of the organization.

"The criticism that the United Nations has been used largely as a forum for voicing the differences between nations is a valid one," she admits.

> The purpose of these recent proposals of my government was very simple: that the United Nations explore, in the temperate atmosphere of closed committee meetings, their areas of agreement, in the hope that those areas of agreement may be later extended. We believe that there will be evidence that the present areas of agreement are large enough to reassure all nations, including Russia, that the solution to world problems lies in negotiations rather than war.

Owing its inspiration to the goals set forth by Woodrow Wilson in his vision of a League of Nations, the United Nations had its inception on January 1, 1942, when twenty-six nations signed a declaration pledging themselves to seek world peace and security. Twenty-one other nations later added their signatures to the document and fifty in all signed the UN charter at the San Francisco conference. In addition to being an agency for world peace and security, the charter called for the development of friendly relations and social and economic cooperation among nations, and for the UN to be a center for nations seeking these ends.

The Prescott Proposals, opening December 16, 1953, at the Broadhurst Theatre, intertwines a love story, a sudden death, the basic disagreement between the United States and Russia, and the United Nations. Mary Prescott is visited by Jan Capek, UN delegate from Czechoslovakia, the night before she is to advance her proposals for breaching the gap between hostile countries. He wishes to revive a love affair they had had in prewar Czechoslovakia. Capek hides in Mary's bedroom when the British, French, Pakistan, and Russian ambassadors to the UN appear for a cocktail party. He dies of a heart attack and those present agree to cover up the death.

But one of the ambassadors breaks his word and news of Capek's death appears in the newspapers. All gather again and each claims that he has kept his vow. But when Petrovsky, the Russian ambassador, speaks over the phone in a Russian dialect, the Pakistan ambassador reveals the former had been guilty of giving the story to the newspapers. Petrovsky, defiant, tells the group he is going to tell the world from the UN dais what happened to Capek. He then adds that he intends to ruin Mary and stop her proposed speech. At this point radio commentator Elliott Clark asks Petrovsky, "Did it give you happiness to destroy Nina Simonova?" She was Petrovsky's youthful sweetheart, whom he had betrayed.

The Russian is so shaken that he tells the UN assembly, "Jan Capek died exactly as reported—exactly as you have been told that he died by the distinguished representative of the United Kingdom. He died of a heart attack in the car of the British Ambassador."

The Prescott Proposals abounds with observations and debates about American foreign policy and how to deal with the Russians. Its basic point is that there is hope for understanding and peace if the human side of the Russians can be reached. Mary defends this possibility while Clark insists that the Russians have become dehumanized and cannot be reached.

"Dehumanized is a pretty strong word," Mary protests.

"You think so," Clark answers. "Take the purge trials. Some of them sent their closest comrades, their dearest friends to death. In cold blood. After that you could never see blood get warm again. You couldn't be human. You couldn't live with yourself."

But the answer in the play is that the Russians can be reached, and Petrovsky's speech after he had been shaken by Clark's charge is evidence to this effect.

The radio commentator wants to know why America is unpopular abroad, and he asks Masaud whether this dislike stems from our foreign policy.

"No," the Pakistan ambassador replies.

> It is the confusion in our minds—we who are outside your country. We can understand your fear of Russia as a nation. You must be armed and prepared. We can understand why you must not have a Communist in your State Department, in your atomic plants, and that you would not want them as teachers in your schools. What we do not understand is your fear of the idea of Communism—that if your citizens discover it on a library shelf, hear it from the pulpit, or even from a college professor, that it would be so attractive that democracy could not compete with it. Have your leaders no faith in the idea of democracy?

With the question of world peace so much upon the minds of people everywhere, it is rather astounding that only two plays of any stature on the subject have reached the Broadway stage. *In Time to Come* was produced during the low ebb days of the war. Twelve years later when the conflict with our enemies had been resolved in victory, *The Prescott Proposals* appeared. By 1953 World War II had taken its unsavory place in history, but the anxieties occasioned then by Germany, Italy, and Japan had been replaced by the cold war tensions between Soviet Russia and its allies, and the United States, Great Britain, and France and its supporters. With the United Nations serving as an agency where these conflicts could be ameliorated, playgoers might have expected more productions dramatizing the role for peace the UN could perform. *The Prescott Proposals* was a clever and popular play. There still seems room for more serious dramas about this all-important arena of our contemporary world.

14

POLITICS AND
PERSONALITIES

Out OF THE South came a new Lochinvar
in 1932, astride a horse named "Share-the-Wealth" and waving
a banner bearing the slogan, "Every Man a King." For a few
years Huey P. Long shocked, startled, and amused the nation.
After his tragic death at the hands of an assassin, the country
wondered whether it had seen a disappearing comet or a perma-
nent constellation in the political heavens. Certainly Long made
a deep impress upon his own period. In a sense, he belonged
more properly in the fabulous Twenties, for all the flamboyance,
color, and raucous show of those years were his. He stormed and
waved his arms during speeches. He strutted at the head of the
Louisiana State University band before football games. He
helped musicians compose the song "Every Man a King" and
promptly dubbed himself the "Kingfish" of them all.

Modesty was not one of Long's virtues. This natural born
salesman turned lawyer and then politician trumpeted loudly his
aims, and he wasn't particular what kind of army fell into line
behind him as long as it was large and it was his. Long first came

to national notice when he was elected Governor of Louisiana in 1928. His friends called him the "Al Smith of the South" and his enemies, the "Karl Marx of the Hillbillies."

From the time he talked the Louisiana State Supreme Court Justices into giving him a special examination so he could be admitted quickly to the bar to the day he died, Huey Long displayed consummate skill as a politician and as a showman. He intimidated those he could not persuade, and so feared was he on the hustings that his threats to fight unfriendly colleagues gave many senators pause in their attacks on him. So certain was Long of his destiny that he wrote a book, posthumously published in 1935, called *My First Days in the White House*. In conversations he told friend and foe alike his plans for bringing the country under his personal rule.

Hamilton Basso in an article in *Life* reported:

> [Long] also liked to tell his plan for bringing the United States under his personal rule, how he intended to take all the affairs of government, both civil and military, into his hands, and how he wanted to eliminate Democratic and Republican Parties and form a single monolithic political party with himself as its head. If this sounds like a page out of Hitler's *Mein Kampf*, it is not. Huey Long was an international figure while Adolf Hitler was still a beer-hall joke. His white paper of dictatorship is almost pathetic in its crudity, but it represents nonetheless the first formulation of the totalitarian ideas based wholly on American life and experience.[1]

Such a man would either be forgotten quickly or become a legend. Huey Long became a legend. Articles about him continued to appear after his death. Then, in the 1940's, the novelists took him up. In quick succession came Hamilton Basso's *Sun in Capricorn*, 1942; John Dos Passos' *Number One*, 1943; Adria Lock Langley's *A Lion in the Streets*, 1945, a best seller; and finally, Robert Penn Warren's *All the King's Men*, 1946, a Pulitzer Prize winner. These works took widely differing views of the "Kingfish," becoming more complimentary as the years from his actual life increased. But in 1939 the menace of dictatorship was casting its ever lengthening shadow over the nation, and the major literary effort that year on Long reflected that fear. On March 14, 1939, a play about him was produced with the startling title *First American Dictator*.

The public was acutely conscious of the overseas dictatorship menace in 1939. It had also been treated to Sinclair Lewis' warning of the threat to America in his novel and play, *It Can't Happen Here*. Now came a play dealing with a figure whose actions indicated the menace had arrived. The historian Jeannette Nichols commented that Long "had built up a machine in his own state which had made him governor. In this office he had ordered a subservient legislature so to change the laws of the state as to make him dictator."[2]

First American Dictator appears to be a careful, factual study of Long's career from the time the Louisiana legislature was preparing to impeach him as governor through his subsequent rise to the United States Senate and national reputation. It shows the ruthless methods Long used to gain his will in Louisiana, and points up the inimitable qualities of the man who harangued the United States Senate for thirteen hours on his "Share-the-Wealth" program. In the play Long is shot by Dr. Carl Austin Weiss as he strode through the halls of the Louisiana state capitol because the Governor had fired the older Dr. Weiss as president of the State Board of Health to make way for someone who would play ball politically with him. One reason advanced in real life for the assassination was Long's utterly unfounded charge that the older Dr. Weiss' parents had colored blood. After observing that the amateurishly written and directed play had wasted its opportunities, the *New York Herald Tribune* critic Richard Watts, Jr., said a good play about Long "would be a most chastening drama to anyone who cared about American Democratic liberties."

How far Long would have succeeded in making the nation a larger Louisiana in its subservience to him will forever be a source of speculation. His meteoric career ended suddenly, like a comet in full flight which unexpectedly nose-dives to earth. It appears probable that the menace of Long will be forgotten in the blaze of his spectacular and colorful qualities, attributes that amused a nation still recovering from the low spirits of the depression.

*　　*　　*　　*　　*　　*　　*

About 7:30 o'clock on the evening of August 2, 1923, Warren Gamaliel Harding, twenty-ninth President of the United States, sat in bed at the Palace Hotel in San Francisco listening to his wife read a *Saturday Evening Post* article. Suddenly he shuddered and went limp.

Mrs. Harding ran into the corridor calling for a doctor, but by the time he arrived, Harding had died. So came to an end the career of a man whose genial personality, outgoing good nature, modest self-appraisal, and strong reliance upon his friends had brought him to the political heights and, continuing after his death, to the political depths. For associated with Harding were many who took advantage of his trusting nature, and the scandals they brought to this well-meaning son of Ohio became a stench in the nostrils of the nation. The corruption, bribery, and license these officeholders and cabinet members perpetrated hung, unfortunately, around the shoulders of their leader and will be forever associated with his name.

The one merciful fact was that all the force of his followers' duplicity and milking of the public were brought to light after Harding's death. When he succumbed to the worries and tensions related to these ungrateful members of his administration, Harding still was held in high esteem by the nation. As his funeral train slowly made its sad way across the country to Washington, thousands stood closely packed and sorrowfully silent at stations along the path. They were paying tribute to a good man. Happily that evaluation has stood up even after the scandals had been thoroughly aired. While the President was responsible for the actions of his appointed officers, he, himself, was free from any taint of dishonesty or unfaithfulness to the trust of his office.

This sad episode in our nation's history was resurrected October 1, 1959 with the presentation of *The Gang's All Here* by Jerome Lawrence and Robert E. Lee at the Ambassador Theatre. The play, with Melvyn Douglas doing a superb piece of acting as the president, opens with the famous "smoke-filled hotel room" meeting where the Ohio Senator's nomination for president was decided, moves through the early and later days of his administration, and ends with the revelation of corruption within his administration ranks and his death. There is only the thinnest of disguises between the play and the real Harding and his administration. In the former, the Senator who becomes president is Griffith P. Hastings, and the man who put him over is Walter Rafferty, most obviously the prototype of Harry M. Daugherty, Harding's campaign manager. These are only two of the many parallels developed as the plot advances.

Indeed, the drama begins on perhaps the most familiar scene associated with Harding, the smoke-filled hotel room where the kingmakers of the Republican Party gathered late one night to pick a nominee. The opening days of the 1920 convention in Chicago had confirmed what party leaders feared, that General Leonard Wood and Governor Frank O. Lowden of Illinois would fight each other into the ground. It soon become apparent neither would win nor allow the other to win. In 1924 a similar, but more bitter deadlock split the Democratic Party wide open and made it impossible for its nominee, John W. Davis, to win. Republican leaders saw such an eventuality if the fight between Wood and Lowden were to continue. A recess was called on the balloting, and that night Senators Charles M. Curtis of Kansas, Frank Brandegee of Connecticut, and Henry Cabot Lodge of Massachusetts met in George Harvey's suite at the Blackstone Hotel to decide upon a compromise candidate.

In the play Rafferty, Hastings' backer, is present at the hotel session. While Daugherty, who was Harding's main, and at times only, important supporter, was not at the Chicago meeting, his spirit and his tactics dominated the thinking within the room. Some months earlier Daugherty, explaining his strategy, told newspapermen:

> There will be no nomination on the early ballots. After the other candidates have failed, after they have gone their limit, the leaders, worn out and wishing to do the very best thing, will get together in some hotel room about 2:11 in the morning. Some fifteen men, bleary-eyed with lack of sleep, and perspiring profusely with the excessive heat, will sit down around a big table. I will be with them and present the name of Senator Harding. When that time comes, Harding will be selected, because he fits in perfectly with every need of the party and nation. He is the logical choice, and the leaders will determine to throw their support to him.[3]

This actually, almost to the exact minute, took place in real life. It furnishes the opening scene of the play. During the meeting at the Blackstone Hotel, Harding was called in and told he was being considered as the compromise candidate. He was reluctant to accept the nomination. He sincerely did not want to be president and had allowed Daugherty to further his candidacy on the theory that being prominently considered for the post would make his re-election as senator so much easier. In real life, Mrs. Harding gave impetus to her husband's final decision to accept the nomination. In the play, Mrs. Hastings pursues a similar course.

Daugherty and Harding met in the most prosaic of ways. The latter was having his shoes shined on the streets of Marion, Ohio, when the former went by. Daugherty, a lawyer and rising political power in Ohio politics, observed the handsome man and thought to himself, "Gee, what a President he'd make." Later, in confiding to his friend Jess Smith, he enthused, "Gee, but he'd make a great-looking president; we'll put it over some time, Jess."[4] This remark was used during the first act by Rafferty in pushing the candidacy of his man.

Truly Harding's entire political career owed much to Daugherty. Ever distrustful of his own abilities, the Marion newspaper editor reluctantly took every step for political office. It is doubtful that without Daugherty, Harding would have become Lieutenant Governor of Ohio or United States Senator through his victory of 1914. In the latter campaign he wanted to quit the race after stumping the state for two weeks. Daugherty told him, "Oh, go out and get your shoes shined, get your clothes pressed, get a good meal, and take a little rest." Harding did so, resumed campaigning, and won the election.

At this point we might profitably compare Daugherty with Louis McHenry Howe. Both men early became dedicated to their heroes, and both men had the rare good fortune of seeing their men reach the pinnacle of political success—the White House. But while Howe was supporting a man of great intellectual gifts and strong will, Daugherty had selected one whose fine personal qualities were vitiated by too easygoing a temperament. Mark Sullivan, whose chapters in his *Our Times, The United States, 1900-1925* must be regarded as the definitive story of the Harding debacle, declared Daugherty "did not want the office of Attorney General nor any other relation to Harding for any purpose of corrupt advantage to himself. About Harding, Daugherty was high-minded—though he could be realistic about nearly every other man or thing."[5] The lawyer even told Sullivan that at that time his chief aim was to protect Harding. "I know Harding, and I know who the crooks are, and I want to stand between Harding and them."[6]

It is this view of Daugherty that furnishes the one false note in the play. Near the end, when the festering corruption in his administration breaks out, Hastings confronts Rafferty with the emerging scandal. The latter denounces Hastings without restraint. He is completely cynical and unsparing in his remarks. No reader of Daugherty's relationship to Harding would ever believe Daugherty capable or willing to act in this manner— no matter what the provocation.

Harding's desire to reward his friends by giving them high political office, positions far beyond their humble capacities, led directly to the tragedy. He named Daugherty, who though having the ability to be an outstanding lawyer had never practiced much, as Attorney General; Senator Albert B. Fall of New Mexico as Secretary of the Interior; Dr. Charles E. Sawyer, a homeopathic physician of Marion, his personal doctor; Colonel Charles R. Forbes, head of the Veterans Bureau, and Edwin Denby, Secretary of the Navy. The last two were named as personal whims by Harding. He met Forbes while on a vacation trip to Honolulu, had taken a liking to the man and decided to put him in a spot where as head of the Veterans Bureau he would be in charge of spending 450 million dollars a year. Denby received his post because he had, at forty-seven years of age and while a member of Congress, joined the Marine Corps when World War I started. This quixotic gesture and the fact that Harding was in a hurry to complete his cabinet, plus the recommendation of Secretary of War John W. Weeks, resulted in Denby's appointment as Secretary of the Navy.

This cavalier way of deciding important government posts is cleverly brought out in *The Gang's All Here*. The real life appointments led to graft and scandals. Forbes proved a man without scruples who used his position as head of the Veterans Bureau for graft. He was finally unmasked and forced by Harding to resign. Senator Fall provided the worst scandal, selling government oil reserves to private companies after taking $100,000 from one of the owners, Edward L. Doheny, and $235,000 from another, Harry Sinclair, for his personal use. The gift by Doheny was indeed a small one considering that he told Senator Thomas J. Walsh of Montana, chairman of the Senate investigating committee, his company expected to get at least 250 million barrels of oil from the reserve, adding, "I would say that we will be in bad luck if we do not get $100 million profit."[7] The episode, part of the overall story best known as the Teapot Dome scandal, resulted in Fall going to jail.

Daugherty and Denby were dismissed as undesirable by Calvin Coolidge upon his entering the White House. Here real life differs from the play, for in the latter, President Hastings, before his death, dismisses Rafferty from the cabinet, calls on Senator Hearn to look into the oil land leases, and takes other steps to clean up his cabinet. He gives this information out to a shy young newspaperman who had been sent to see the President while the other reporters went elsewhere.

Two things are accepted as facts in *The Gang's All Here,* the truth of which has not been established in real life. One is the charge that Harding was the father of an illegitimate daughter, and the second was the rumor that he had committed suicide rather than dying a natural death. The second can be briefly dismissed. Harding began his ill-fated trip across the country to Alaska on June 20, 1923. He was extremely tired and worried at the start, and the numerous demands upon him made the journey a nightmare instead of the stimulating experience it should have been. By the time he returned from Alaska to San Francisco on Sunday morning, July 29, he was utterly weary. A few days earlier, at Seattle, Washington, he had called for Dr. Sawyer because he was in great pain. On reaching San Francisco, Harding went directly to his room and to bed in the Palace Hotel. According to Dr. Ray Lyman Wilbur, who was called into consultation by Dr. Sawyer, "His acute illness came to a peak on Monday night with the rapid development of a bronchial pneumonia." In an article for the *Saturday Evening Post* of October 13, 1923, Dr. Wilbur, a former president of the American Medical Association, one-time president of Leland Stanford University and Secretary of the Interior in President Hoover's cabinet, said Harding was "struck down by apoplexy and lost his gallant battle against death from pneumonia just when victory seemed to be his." In the play Hastings takes a potent pill and dies as Mrs. Hastings is reading to him.

Harding's fatherhood of an illegitimate daughter was rumored around Washington, as were whisperings of his affairs with other

women, in the years following his death. In 1927 a book called
The President's Daughter was published, written by a woman
named Nan Britton. In it the writer claimed Harding was the
father of her illegitimate daughter. According to Mark Sullivan
when the President's brother, Dr. George Harding, asked for
definite dates and places concerning their purported meetings,
Miss Britton could not produce concrete proof. She had asked
for $50,000 to support the child, but the Harding family did not
give her the money.

Harding's love of poker and being with the boys is used in
The Gang's All Here to develop not only this personal trait but
to further the plot. While enjoying a game with his cronies,
Rafferty convinces Hastings that signing an executive order
transferring oil lands from the Navy Department to the Interior
was a proper move. In real life this proved to be the great mistake of Harding's career. In May, 1921 he had signed an un-
constitutional executive order making this shift. Back in 1912
Congress had set aside the Elk Hills oil fields in California as a
reserve for future Navy needs. Three years later the so-called
Teapot Dome field was set aside for a similar purpose.

Both fields were put under the aegis of the Secretary of the
Navy. In 1920 the Secretary was permitted to make leases on
the reserves if necessary, but as Mark Sullivan pointed out, "It
was never contemplated, however, that any of the reserves should
be leased as a whole." In order to get around this safeguard,
Fall and those conspiring with him had the authority for handling these oil fields shifted from the Navy Department, where
they could not be touched by them, to the Interior Department,
where Fall had command.

The poker scene in the play was also used to foreshadow the
part that the Hearn committee, a paper-thin disguise for the committee headed by Senator Walsh, played in bringing the denoue-
ment. Higgy interrupts the group to tell them that Hearn was
getting close to the bad things going on in the administration.
Hastings is shocked by the news and taken ill.

Still another parallel between the play and real life was the role of Axel Maley, played by Bert Wheeler. Maley is the worshiper of Rafferty, as Jess Smith looked up with boundless admiration to Daugherty. Smith was essentially a simple person who found going from the obscurity of a little town in Ohio to a position of importance in Washington too much for him. Everyone knew Daugherty was close to Harding, and that Smith was close to Daugherty. People started coming to the simple small-town man for favors. They flattered his ego at first. Gradually the favors moved from unimportant things harming no one to big deals. Carried away by the rapidly moving events, Jess began to play the stock market heavily, and to lose. He took fees, getting successively larger ones, for services to those desiring help. Basically an honest man, he broke under the strain of his misdeeds and committed suicide. The shock hit Daugherty and Harding deeply, for they genuinely liked the lovable, if ineffectual little man. In the play the second act closes with the announcement that Axel Maley had committed suicide, under conditions remarkably resembling those that caused Smith to take his life.

One necessary correction, for the sake of justice, should be made. In *The Gang's All Here* Doc Kirkaby is made something of a buffoon who knows little about medicine. Mark Sullivan points out that Dr. Charles E. Sawyer, while a small town homeopathic physician, was "a keen, perfectly honest, loyal person with independent means, whose coming to Washington was an act of service to Harding and his wife. The service was more than medical—Sawyer was faithful and shrewd for Harding in some important public matters."[8]

The Gang's All Here is a poignant and thoughtful play. Without whitewashing any of Harding's defects and deficiencies, it does justice to the twenty-ninth President by presenting the man as he was. That Harding was betrayed by his friends furnishes the sad part of both play and life. In the former, he despairingly cries when told of the betrayal, "What is a man to do if he cannot trust his friends?" Other chief executives have relied upon their cronies, and on occasion these, too, have failed their president. It is tragic that the failure in Harding's administration reached so high and was so widespread. But the basic goodness of the man and his idealistic hope for the future might be evaluated by a passage from a speech read for him by his secretary, George Christian, at a meeting of the Knights Templar in Hollywood the night he died. It said, "I am a confirmed optimist as to the growth of the spirit of brotherhood. Science and genius are lending their aid to the removal of the obstacles to intercourse and mutual understanding among the peoples of the world. We do rise to heights, at times, when we look for the good rather than the evil in others."[9]

*   *   *   *   *   *   *

The Gang's All Here was a tense and taut play, almost Shakespearean in its ruthless delineation of a man in high place who falls to the depths because he has a fatal flaw. The musical *Fiorello* was the opposite in almost every respect. It had bounce and verve and joy to its songs and plot, and its hero possessed the iron of greatness enabling him to face every obstacle without flinching.

Even the spontaneous manner in which *Fiorello* skyrocketed to Broadway hit status overnight reflected the career of Fiorello LaGuardia, effervescent mayor of New York from 1933 to 1946. The musical, book by Jerome Weidman and George Abbott with music by Jerry Bock and lyrics by Sheldon Harnick, opened November 23, 1959 at the Broadhurst Theatre. It came into town with a modest advance sale of $204,000, a long cry from the $2,325,000 advance greeting for the arrival of Rodger's and Hammerstein's *The Sound of Music* a short time earlier. But *Fiorello,* like its hero, ran roughshod over the odds against it and, greeted by ecstatic reviews in the newspapers, exploded immediately into a top hit. Typical of the critics' reactions was the headline in the *New York Times* of November 25,

"Fiorello Gets Landslide Vote." Brooks Atkinson, revered dean of Broadway critics, went into lyrical rhapsodies about the show, declaring, "There are three ways in which *Fiorello* is the ideal monument to our beloved Little Flower: it is exciting, it is enjoyable, and it is decent."[10]

The musical presents the story of Fiorello LaGuardia—Congressman, Mayor, war hero, and fireband—from his first try as a candidate for Congress to the day he is nominated, on a fusion ticket, to run for mayor of New York for the second time. Through the book, the music, the lyrics, and even the dancing, the political and general history of the period comes alive for the audience. And most alive of all is the tempestuous, sometimes exasperating, always exciting main character. Tom Bosley, a newcomer to Broadway who bears an astonishing on-stage resemblance to LaGuardia, was whisked to stardom in the role—something the little Mayor would certainly have enjoyed.

Fiorello follows faithfully, with unimportant chronological exceptions, the career of LaGuardia, whose first name means "Little Flower" in Italian. He was born December 11, 1882, in New York of an Italian Army bandmaster father and a mother who was three parts Italian and one part Jewish. His father died while LaGuardia was still in his teens, and the young man set himself to the task of supporting his mother and her little family. He entered the consulate service and was sent to the office at Fiume, then a Hungarian seaport on the Italian border. This step, so important in his political and personal life, also served as the impetus for his studying foreign languages. Fiorello here learned German and Italian, and later mastered French, Spanish, Serbian, and Yiddish. In the polyglot Fourteenth Congressional District, where he made his first bid for public office, there were not only numerous Italians and Jews but sprinklings of immigrants from these other countries. His ability to talk to these people in their own language proved a tremendous political-campaign asset for LaGuardia. He only stayed a few years in Fiume, returning to New York where he took a position as interpreter at Ellis Island and studied law at night at New York University Law School.

Fiorello opens shortly after LaGuardia had put out his sign in 1912 as "Fiorello LaGuardia, Attorney at Law." In real life there was a garment strike that year and the new lawyer, having time and being in complete sympathy with the strikers, became a supporter. He gradually won his way to leadership and was one of three arbitrators chosen to settle the walkout. During the strike Fiorello, never one to sit still when there were things to be done, took his place frequently on the picket line. This situation is used effectively in the show to introduce La-Guardia to his first wife, Thea Almerigotti. Their courtship in real life was a hectic one. She was reserved and cool; he was temperamental and volcanic. Thea was a devout Catholic; he was an Episcopalian. In addition, she had been born in Trieste and sorrowed over its loss to Austria deeply. When LaGuardia pressed her to marry him, she answered, "I shall never marry anybody while Trieste is Austrian territory. You may ask me again when the Italian flag once more waves over it."[11]

LaGuardia, who as a Congressman enlisted in the then almost microscopic United States Air Force, was able to play a part in seeing that Fiume and Trieste were returned to Italy at the end of World War I. He was in Paris in 1919 and spoke with Colonel Edward M. House, Wilson's right-hand man, about the issue. The question was brought to the attention of Italian Premier Orlando and through his efforts Trieste and Fiume were ceded back to Italy. As soon as LaGuardia returned home, he proposed to Thea, who, true to her word, accepted him. They were married on March 8, 1919, in New York by Monsignor Ferranti. The entire episode was faithfully followed in the musical.

Fiorello also sticks close to the facts, with a minor exception, in portraying how LaGuardia obtained his nomination for Congress. In 1914 Republican fortunes in the Fourteenth Congressional District were so low that leaders could not find a candi-

date. To run meant automatic, overwhelming defeat. The club-
house local politicians are playing poker and discussing ways of
tricking some unsuspecting Republican into running for Congress when LaGuardia bursts into the room and announces he
will not only take the nomination but beat Tammany Hall in the
bargain.

"Do I get the nomination?" he asks Ben, Republican district
leader.

"Why not?" Ben answers, indifferently.

In real life LaGuardia nearly lost his chance because a politician could not spell his name. When headquarters was called
on the telephone, the man on the other end could not spell
LaGuardia. "Aw, hell," headquarters erupted, "give me someone else. It doesn't matter anyway."[12] But Fiorello was not
going to get this close and then lose out. He wrote his name
carefully on a piece of paper and sent it by messenger to headquarters. The newcomer lost this first try, but it was by a mere
1,700 votes in a district where the Tammany Hall candidate
always had a margin of 16,000 and more votes. The city and the
Republican leaders sat up. So did Tammany Hall. Two years
later LaGuardia again ran for Congress, and this time he upset
the Democratic machine to win by a scant 257 votes. The first
American of Italian ancestry to sit in the House of Representatives, LaGuardia immediately became a national figure.

This astonishing victory is highlighted in *Fiorello* by Ben and
his followers, who sing the hit song "The Bum Won." Ben,
played to perfection by Howard Da Silva, expresses unbelieving
wonder at the election result and, somewhat in disgust, says:

Even without our help,
Look at the way he won.

The other clubhouse henchmen chime in. Julian suggests
perhaps "this is a beautiful dream," adds "I'm in a bad state of
shock," and joins with Ron in speculating "just how the hell it
happened." They wonder "What did we do right" to bring about

the victory, while Stanley observes that although "People can do what they want to" the result gives him an uneasy feeling "it ain't democratic." These reactions are summed up by Ben, who points out that he permitted an amateur to be nominated for Congress and "What does he do? He wins."

LaGuardia was in Congress when the United States entered World War I. A confirmed pacifist, he nevertheless felt the only fair American way to raise an army was by the draft. Accordingly, and over the grim opposition of many within his own district and leaders in Congress, Fiorello supported the draft act. The new Congressman realized he was risking his political future, for the Fourteenth District was known to be overwhelmingly against the measure. LaGuardia wrote a postcard to every constituent setting forth his position and in May, 1917 told 1,000 Italians at the Labor Temple in New York:

> I want to drive it home and impress it upon you,
> if I can, that we are in the midst of the most cruel war
> in the history of the world . . . and those who prefer
> Italy to America should return to Italy. I know there
> are some of you in my district who won't sacrifice
> themselves for any country—and if I thought I owed
> my election to that sort, I would resign.[13]

Many accused LaGuardia of supporting the draft because, as a Congressman, he would be exempt. These people did not know their firebrand. The future mayor of New York quietly took flying lessons and on July 25, 1917, went to the old Southern Building in Washington to enlist. The conversation between LaGuardia and the enlisting officer, Major Benjamin D. Foulois, is told in *This Man LaGuardia,* by Lowell M. Limpus and Burr W. Leyson.

> "Your name?" asked the major.
> "Fiorello H. LaGuardia."
> "Any relation to the Congressman?"
> "Not exactly." The candidate gave his secret in a
> whisper. "You see, I am the Congressman."[14]

Fiorello telescopes LaGuardia's Air Force exploits into two scenes. Part of the second scene is given up to showing actual moving picture shots taken of the flying major. He is seen with King Victor Emmanuel of Italy at the end of the war when the announcement that Trieste and Fiume have been returned to Italy was made. The film then shifts to LaGuardia disembarking from a troop ship in New York as the crowd cheers. The screen goes up, the stage is lighted and actor Fiorello walks down the gangplank to the beautiful Thea.

> FIORELLO: Thea, I brought you a present—a key to the city—Trieste.
> THEA: Oh, Fiorello . . .
> FIORELLO: Now what's the score?
> THEA: Yes.

Dishonesty and corruption and graft were the things La-Guardia hated in general, but his particular all-consuming visible target was Tammany Hall. He regarded the powerful New York City Democrat organization as a disgrace and menace to the city he loved. When the opportunity came in 1929 to run against Mayor James J. Walker, pet of Tammany Hall, Fiorello grabbed it. But times were too good. People were prosperous and indifferent, and the "Little Flower" was decisively beaten. The set-back shook him to his roots. In the musical this defeat is coupled with the death of Thea, not historically correct. She died in 1921, a few weeks before LaGuardia lost the Republican nomination for mayor to Henry H. Curran.

The 1929 Walker victory was eventually to prove the lever by which LaGuardia was propelled into the mayor's office. Jimmy Walker was the antithesis of Fiorello in many ways. Handsome, debonair, well-dressed, wise cracking, a lady's man, the darling of Tammany Hall held a cynical attitude towards politics and his own administration. While the minions of Harding's administration ran roughshod over their responsibilities in the grab for money and power, the President himself possessed a deep moral code that was a major cause of his untimely death. Jimmy Walker had no such code. If there was graft in his administration, he was quite willing to turn his head.

The philosophy of the charming and nimble-witted Walker is well expressed in the show by the song "Gentleman Jimmy," the opening lines of which are:

> Live and let live
> Love and let love
> There are no finer sentiments than these.

Unfortunately this attitude permitted the marauding politicians running the city to dip deeply into its treasury, without a care for the citizens or the future. Corruption finally became so widespread and notorious that leading citizens were alarmed, came together, and demanded that Governor Franklin D. Roosevelt conduct an investigation into the city's affairs. Roosevelt ordered the investigation, and on April 8, 1931, Judge Samuel Seabury, a one-time candidate on the Democratic ticket for governor, was named counsel for the Hofstadter Legislative Committee.

When Judge Seabury questioned Walker, the former was unable to prove that the mayor had taken "crooked money." But when Walker sought to answer Seabury's searching questions, the *Nation* of September 14, 1932, observed "his usually ready wit floundered in a morass of hesitant, stuttering, confused replies." The *Literary Digest* of June 11, 1932, pointed out that the newspapers all agreed the prosecutor had shown Walker had taken "easy money."

Seabury's penetrating investigation and relentless prosecution resulted in the forced resignation of Walker. But the event that brought down the latter's political house of cards was neatly wrapped up in a few words, "little tin box." During Seabury's interrogation of New York County Sheriff Thomas M. Farley, the question of how the latter had $365,000 in unexplained bank deposits came up. The harassed witness, "a great barrel of a man with a soup bowl haircut and cutaway," answered the searching questions by maintaining that the money came from "a wonderful tin box" at home. The explanation not only failed to convince Seabury and others but quickly ballooned into a slogan of corruption for the period. Roosevelt finally removed Farley from office on the ground that "a public official cannot be free of suspicion of money deposited in his bank account above his official salary."[15]

Fiorello takes the one-time cynically popular phrase and in a series of delightful lyrics explains how large sums came into the possession of different politicians through the magic "little tin box." The song, acted out by Ben and the boys in the club-house, stopped the show. A henchman would step forward and ask the question about the mysterious way in which each politician had accumulated his wealth. Then, with a flourish, Ben would make the appropriate reply. When Mr. "X" is asked how he can buy a yacht on a salary of less than $50 a week, Ben replies:

> Any working man can do what I have done
> For a month or two I simply gave up smoking
> And put my extra pennies one by one
> Into a little tin box.

The acquisition of a Rolls Royce by Mr. "Y" on his modest city salary is explained by Ben who points out:

> I've been taking empty bottles to the grocer
> And each nickel that I got was put aside
> Into a little tin box, etc.

As for Mr. "Z," his ability to keep "a dozen women in the very best hotels" despite a low weekly wage is accounted for by the fact that:

> . . . for one whole week I went without my lunches
> And it mounted up, Your Honor, bit by bit.
> It's just a little tin box, etc.

In 1915 a timid young German girl, recently a graduate of
high school, applied for a job with LaGuardia. Marie Fischer
was uncertain and fearful, and her shorthand and typing were
not as good as they might have been. The shy girl could not
understand her volatile and quick-tempered boss. He was impatient at first, but noting Marie's nervousness and obvious
lack of experience, Fiorello curbed his remarks and instead
became a most considerate and helpful boss. The association was
to have a lifelong influence upon LaGuardia. Deeply loyal
from the beginning, Marie suffered silently as she watched
Fiorello's romance and marriage to the beautiful Thea. After
the latter's death, she continued to serve him unobtrusively but
with a keen eye for political issues and men and events. The
ebullient LaGuardia took her for granted, accepting Marie's
services without thought. One day he suddenly saw Marie
Fischer as a woman. He was stunned. But not for long. For
LaGuardia a new insight meant immediate action. The incident is charmingly told in *This Man LaGuardia*.

"Why, she's—wonderful," he whispered to himself. "And what a life I've led her. Worked her like
a slave. No home life. No social life. No. . . ."

She threw him a quick smile. "Good night, Major."
The door closed behind her.

Instantly he was on his feet. No hesitation now.
With him, to think was to act. His mind was made up
in a flash.

"Muh-ree." He ran after her in panic. The sound of
the footfalls in the empty corridor outside reassured
him before the door opened. He met her in the portal.
Again that ready smile.

"Yes, Major. What is it? Forget something?"
He nodded solemnly. She waited expectantly.

"Marie, you're fired."

She reeled as from a blow. The years rolled back
miraculously. She was just Marie Fischer, from
Morris High School again. Uncertain of her stenog-
raphy and afraid of her employer. But there was a
catch in her throat now. Not to be with him any more.

Not to share his work. Not. . . .

"Why, Major." Her voice was trembling. "You don't mean. . . ."

His tones were low and earnest.

"I mean it," he said. "How can I court a girl that works for me?"

There was an instant of utter silence. He broke it at last, and his voice was trembling now.

"Miss Fischer," he began, hesitantly. "May I see you home—and maybe—call on you tomorrow evening?"[16]

The episode was charmingly presented in *Fiorello,* with the entire audience caught up in the beauty of this long-delayed romance. In real life the marriage proved fantastically happy, ending only with LaGuardia's death on February 20, 1947.

Fiorella LaGuardia was one of those rare phenomena in American political life whose sincerity and honesty were never questioned, even by his severest critics. A mark of this quality was to be found in the men he selected to help him run the city. They were, it was generally agreed, far above the average of city administrators. He had other qualities, not all of them attractive, but none of the less desirable traits were more than normal blemishes upon an unusually fine character. In reviewing LaGuardia's first year in office, the *Nation* of January 16, 1935, observed "he has been courageous, choleric, threatening, dilatory, rash and always interesting." It was this last attribute that perhaps drew the attention of the city and the nation to the ebullient little mayor, for everything he did attracted his fellow citizens. His love of chasing fires, to the extent of dropping everything and appearing at a blaze wearing a large fire chief's hat, caught the imagination of fellow Americans and focused attention upon his foibles, and sometimes through them, upon his solid achievements. His other numerous side interests perhaps were not as well known. For example, his close friendship with Albert Spalding, the outstanding violinist, deepened this aspect of LaGuardia's life.

Fiorello is not only entertaining and exciting and decent, but it is also an encouraging tribute to our democratic way of life. For the figure of LaGuardia stands out in real life as it did in the musical, proof that integrity and honesty will eventually win if they are combined with tenacity and courage. We leave him in the show as we left Roosevelt in *Sunrise at Campobello,* the conqueror of major obstacles on the threshold of still greater victories. We should put Wendell Willkie of *State of the Union* with them, for despite his defeat he is defiant of the foes who hack away at our country's great political structure by graft and corruption. The one-time Indiana farm boy went on to greater triumphs following his defeat by Roosevelt. The three, along with many others, prove that defenders of our nation's form of government are plentiful and that, with all its imperfections, it shall not perish from the earth.

15

CURTAIN

THE STUDY of politics in the American drama is the study of our times. There is scarcely a significant area of life in the United States that did not find a place in the political drama. The playwrights roamed far in their search of subjects attractive to prospective audiences, and as a result a careful reading of plays during the twentieth century will provide a panaroma of what took place in our country over the past sixty years.

Some themes appear in every decade, indicating that they are of constant interest to the public. Others flared up in clusters; then died out and never reappeared. The issues and conditions that brought them into being also receded into the background and rarely came to the forefront again. There is one characteristic of the political drama that aids and detracts from it. These plays are always written for the contemporary scene, and even when an historical subject is used it has a current application. This is probably a contributing factor to the popularity of many political plays which upon revival prove dated and dull. The fact that playwrights built their dramas for audiences aware of contemporary issues may account for

219

the comparatively few plays whose dramatic values enable them to rise above ephemeral subjects.

Probably the most enduring theme in the political drama centers around Washington. From earliest days playwrights used doings in the Nation's Capital for their plots. That was a natural development, for the District of Columbia is the political heart of the country, and what takes place there directly affects every part of the nation. Before 1890 and the rise of greater communication channels for the general public, Congress and the Presidency and to a lesser extent the Supreme Court provided one of the few areas having equal interest to every section of the United States. After this date and as we go into the twentieth century, the sources of communication brought in detail to the country what took place in Washington. A play dealing with personalities and events there had a basic audience available that other themes did not possess.

Theatrical productions with Congress as their theme ran the gamut from outright low musical comedy to intensely serious drama. The *Rogers Brothers in Washington* lampooned the nation's top lawmaking body of the nineteenth century; *Both Your Houses* is an indignant study of Congressmen and their cynical actions; *Born Yesterday* is a serious comedy about big business and its efforts to manipulate legislation through buying Senators. Furthermore, Washington has ever been a socially conscious city and this aspect appears regularly. *A Texas Steer, The Governor's Wife,* and *First Lady* represent different periods using this background as the major element in the plot. Finally, the musical comedies *Of Thee I Sing, Let 'Em Eat Cake,* and *I'd Rather Be Right* grew out of the depression and its aftermath.

Outstanding political figures also proved attractive plot material to dramatists. Senator Plumb, Wendell Willkie, Lincoln, Franklin Delano Roosevelt, Warren G. Harding, Huey Long, Woodrow Wilson, and Fiorello LaGuardia inspired plays attractive to Broadway audiences. This is a source playwrights will undoubtedly exploit still further since the theatre-going public has shown great interest in this area.

There has been a plethora of dramas about fascism, naziism, and communism, and as long as these foreign ideologies threaten our country, the chances are more plays about them will be written. These productions have also been varied, ranging from the bitter-sweet *Knickerbocker Holiday* musical to the mystery comedy *Margin for Error*. The threat of an American dictatorship in *It Can't Happen Here,* the poignancy of *Watch on the Rhine,* and the horror of *Darkness at Noon* are examples of this subject. The best political play, *Winterset,* comes out of a case where passions concerning Bolshevism affected the murder trial of two men. But *Winterset* transcends its subject and is a Greek drama with an American setting destined for permanence in our literature. The suspicion remains that few plays dealing with fascism, naziism, or communism will hold audiences once these threats have passed away.

With the possible exception of themes relating to race relations and world organizations for peace, the remaining plays deal with topics no longer of major interest to the general public. *The Lion and the Mouse* and the muckraking period it represents, *The Sultan of Sulu* and American imperialism, *The Man of the Hour* and municipal corruption, *The Governor's Boss* and bossism in state politics, *The Racket* and prohibition, *The High Road* and child labor are examples of dramas whose subjects are past history. To bring them successfully to the stage would require a background course for the audience, and few people are willing to undertake that task in order to appreciate a play.

Broadway productions about two of the world's major themes, race relations and world organizations for peace, have been disappointing in their number. Only two plays of any stature have come out of the former sensitive problem, *The Nigger* and *They Shall Not Die.* The same may be said of the latter, with merely *In Time to Come* and *The Prescott Proposals* putting on the stage the world's longing for peace through cooperation.

Both subjects should provide future dramatists with rich material.

* * * * * * *

Political plays during the twentieth century showed a marked increase in maturity, technique, and power over earlier efforts. Building upon the slight foundation provided by plays of the eighteenth and nineteenth centuries, the twentieth century dramatists brought greater depth of understanding, keen awareness of issues, and a willingness to discuss grave issues in their works. This represented recognition that their audiences were better equipped to understand the problems before them. The widespread communications media of newspapers, magazines, moving pictures, radio, and television had produced this result. With it came a large potential theatre-going public ready to enjoy plays based upon political subjects.

But the widening audience also presented a hazard, for a superficial plot and one-dimensional characters would not satisfy it. The theatregoer of mid-twentieth century demands more than entertainment. He insists upon a good plot and rounded characters, and frequently a philosophy growing out of the action, as well. Two comparisons will illustrate the point. In *The Senator* the main character was inspired by Senator Plumb of Kansas. But the inspiration proved only an external one— how he looked, talked, and acted. There was no attempt to study his thoughts on politics and life. There was no need, for the plot of *The Senator* had little to do with actual events.

On the other hand, the inspiration of Franklin Delano Roosevelt in *Sunrise at Campobello* penetrated deeply. The playwright not only gave us an almost agonizing insight into the man but developed clearly Roosevelt's philosophy through his fight upwards from physical disability. Wendell Willkie in *State of the Union* represented a definite political philosophy Americans in 1945 at once understood. Grant Matthews—a thinly disguised

Willkie—and his struggle to live up to his ideals while compromising for votes during his campaign for the presidential nomination is the main theme of the play. Lindsay and Crouse refused to admit Matthews was the prototype of Willkie, though they did say, "We're what are called liberals, although we don't like the word much. Our political convictions are close to those of Wendell Willkie and Franklin D. Roosevelt."

In musical comedy the change is even more pronounced when *The Sultan of Sulu* is compared with *Fiorello*. The former is a happy-go-lucky take-off on American imperialism, but the satire was neither deep nor penetrating. *Fiorello* is not only the inspiring story of the great Mayor, but it is a sharp attack on the political shenanigans of a period. In such songs as "The Bum Won" and "The Little Tin Box" the arrows go well below the outer skin.

The advance in the political drama may be roughly divided into three periods: before 1900, when the dramatist used political events as window dressing for his plots; from 1900 to 1930, when the playwright attacked specific abuses, and from 1930 to the present, when the author not only attacked abuses but also advocated a philosophy of government for politicians and voters to follow.

The Last Stroke by I. N. Morris (1896), *A Contented Woman* (1897), and *A Texas Steer* (1891), by Charles H. Hoyt are representative examples of the pre-twentieth century political drama. *The Last Stroke* was one of several plays using the political situation in Cuba during the 1890's merely as a pretext for a melodramatic plot. *A Contented Woman* handled the issue of woman suffrage with a light touch. It completely ignored the serious side. *A Texas Steer* exploited the Washington political background as a convenient peg on which to hang amusing situations. But to be fair, we must point out that *A Temperance Town* by Hoyt (1893), and *The District Attorney* by Klein and Harrison Grey Fiske (1895), were serious attempts to attack specific abuses—prohibition in the former and corruption in the latter.

From 1900 to 1930 the dramatist recognized the growing knowledge of his audience with political events and wrote accordingly. In *The Lion and the Mouse* (1905), Klein attacked the trusts; in *The Man of the Hour* (1906), Broadhurst assailed municipal corruption; in *The High Road* (1912), Sheldon brought bad working conditions for women and children under fire; in *The Racket* (1927), Cormack blasted into the open the tie-up of gangsters and politicians during prohibition days. These and similar plays had one thing in common —they attacked specific abuses but never probed below the surface to a fundamental philosophy of government that would make such abuses impossible in the future. They were dramas of protest but not of thought, of continuous action but rarely of reflection. One of the few Broadway productions heralding the approach of the 1930's was *The Road to Rome* (1928), with Sherwood indicating a philosophy of political action that would make future wars unlikely.

The depression and the shadows of an approaching war left their impress upon the playwrights after 1930. Of the six political plays to win Pulitzer prizes between 1930 and 1945, five tried to express a philosophy for political action. They were *Both Your Houses* (1933), *Idiot's Delight* (1936), *Abe Lincoln in Illinois* (1939), *There Shall Be No Night* (1941), and *State of the Union* (1946). The first political play to win a Pulitzer Prize, *Of Thee I Sing*, in 1932, was straight political satire and made no attempt to go deeper.

Plays dealing with domestic politics included *Both Your Houses, Abe Lincoln in Illinois,* and *State of the Union.* They were joined by such plays as *Winterset* (1935), *I'd Rather Be Right* (1937), and *Decision* (1944), in an effort to formulate a lasting creed of political action. *Idiot's Delight* and *In Time to Come* (1941), tried to do the same thing about war, while *There Shall Be No Night, Flight to the West* (1940), *Watch on the Rhine* (1941), *The Rugged Path* (1945), and *The Prescott Proposals* (1953), carried this searching into international areas.

Superior plays resulted from the growing maturity of the political dramatist. With few exceptions, the genre before 1930 lacked that element which lifted a play out of the rut of acceptable entertainment into literature. With the exception of *The Sultan of Sulu, The County Chairman, The City, The High Road,* and *The Road to Rome,* and perhaps a few others, the plays before 1930 are only for the specialist to resurrect. Since then numerous plays dealing with politics equal or far surpass the best produced before the depression.

With the ever-growing spread of moving pictures, dramatists wrote plays that could be fitted into films. This obviously meant subjects possessing a national appeal had a tremendous advantage over those tailored only for a local community. So the playwright, ever alive to the box-office call, inevitably turned to material already familiar to the national audience. This trend has persisted and even increased to the point where stories having an international appeal attract the dramatist. The indications are that future political dramas will move further in this direction.

The political dramatist has never had a better opportunity to present his wares than now. He is at a juncture in our nation's history where the people are politically aware, and willing to hear him, and his influence upon their thinking is great. With a large potential audience whose knowledge is more than adequate for the subject matter to be presented, the playwright concerned with political themes has an excellent opportunity to further this area of the American drama.

APPENDIX

Plays on politics produced on the New York stage from 1890 to 1960. Dates listed refer to the first New York performances.

1890—1899

The Senator—David Demarest Lloyd and Sydney Rosenfeld. January 13, 1890, Star Theatre.

A Texas Steer—Charles Hale Hoyt. November 10, 1890, Bijou Theatre.

The Nominee—Anonymous adaptation of *Le Depute de Bombignac* by Alexander Brisson. January 26, 1891, Bijou Theatre.

The Power of the Press—Augustus Pitou. March 16, 1891, Star Theatre.

A Temperance Town—Charles Hale Hoyt and G. H. Jessup. September 17, 1893, Madison Square Theatre.

The District Attorney—Charles Klein and Harrison Grey Fiske. January 21, 1895, American Theatre.

The King of Peru—Louis N. Parker. May 7, 1895, Garrick Theatre.

The Capitol—Augustus Thomas. September 9, 1895, Standard Theatre.

Ambition—H. Guy Carleton. October 26, 1895, Fifth Avenue Theatre.

The Last Stroke—I. N. Morris. March 23, 1896, Star Theatre.

A House of Cards—Sydney Rosenfeld. March 27, 1896, Fifth Avenue Theatre.

The Law of the Land—Anonymous. April 7, 1895, American Theatre.

A Tammany Tiger—A. Gratton Donnelly. April 20, 1896, Empire Theatre.

The Gold Bug—Glen MacDonough and Victor Herbert. September 14, 1896, Casino Theatre.

A Contented Woman—Charles Hale Hoyt. January 4, 1897, Hoyt's Theatre.

New York—Andrew C. Wheeler and Edward M. Alfriend. February 1, 1897, American Theatre.

The Alderman—William Gill. May 24, 1897, Fourteenth Street Theatre.

McFadden's Row of Flats—Edward W. Townsend. September 27, 1897, People's Theatre.

For Liberty and Love—Lawrence Marston and Albert H. Paine. October 10, 1897, Grand Theatre.

McSorley's Twins—Anonymous. October 25, 1897, Grand Opera Theatre.

His Honor, the Mayor—Charles H. Meltzer and A. E. Lancaster. April 25, 1898, Empire Theatre.

Kate Kip, Buyer—Glen MacDonough. November 7, 1898, Bijou Theatre.

The Village Postmaster—Alice E. Ives and Jerome H. Eddy. November 18,1898, Fourteenth Street Theatre.

An Arabian Girl—J. Cheever Goodwin. April 29, 1899, Herald Square Theatre.

His Excellency, the Governor—Reginald Marshall. May 9, 1899, Lyceum Theatre.

226

1900—1909

The Carpetbagger—Oppie Read and Frank S. Pixley. March 5, 1900, Fourteenth Street Theatre.

The Interrupted Honeymoon—F. Kinsey Peile. March 20, 1900, Daly's Theatre.

The Governor's Son—George M. Cohan. February 25, 1901, Savoy Theatre.

The Price of Peace—Cecil Raleigh. March 21, 1901, Broadway Theatre.

The Rogers Brothers in Washington—John J. McNally. September 2, 1901, Knickerbocker Theatre.

Hon. John Grigsby—Charles Klein. January 28, 1902, Manhattan Theatre.

The Crisis—Winston Churchill. November 17, 1902, Wallack's Theatre.

The Sultan of Sulu—George Ade. December 29, 1902, Wallack's Theatre.

Rival Candidates—I. N. Morris and C. T. Dazey. February 2, 1903, Bijou Theatre.

Running for Office—George M. Cohan. April 27, 1903, Fourteenth Street Theatre.

The County Chairman—George Ade. November 24, 1903, Wallack's Theatre.

His Honor, Mayor of the Bowery—John J. McNally. January 7, 1905, Murray Hill Theatre.

Love and the Man—H. V. Esmond. February 20, 1905, Knickerbocker Theatre.

Fritz in Tammany Hall—John J. McNally. October 16, 1905, Herald Square Theatre.

The Lion and the Mouse—Charles Klein. November 20, 1905, Lyceum Theatre.

The Clansman—Thomas Dixon. January 8, 1906, Liberty Theatre.

George Washington, Jr.—George M. Cohan. February 12, 1906, Herald Square Theatre.

The District Leader—Joseph E. Howard. April 30, 1906, Wallack's Theatre.

A Square Deal—Edward A. Rose. April 30, 1906, Fourteenth Street Theatre.

The Power of Money— Owen Davis. August 20, 1906, American Theatre.

The Stolen Story—Jesse Lynch Williams. October 2, 1906, Garden Theatre.

Sam Houston—Clay Clement. October 16, 1906, Garden Theatre.

The Man of the Hour—George H. Broadhurst. December 4, 1906, Savoy Theatre.

The Undertow—Eugene Walter. April 22, 1907, Harlem Opera House.

Friends of Labor—Julius Hopp. May 21, 1907, Kalish Theatre.

Patsy in Politics—Joe Doe. September 2, 1907, Fourteenth Street Theatre.

On the Eve—Leopold Kampf. December 20, 1907, German Theatre.

The Governor and the Boss—Guy F. Bragdlon and William Postance. April 27, 1908, Blaney's Theatre.

The Offenders—Elmer Blaney Harris. September 22, 1908, Hudson Theatre.

A Gentleman from Mississippi—Harrison Rhodes and Thomas A. Wise. September 29, 1908, Bijou Theatre.

A Citizen's Home—H. H. Boyd. October 9, 1909, Majestic Theatre.

The Nigger—Edward Sheldon. December 4, 1909, New Theatre.

The City—Clyde Fitch. December 22, 1909, Lyric Theatre.

The Next of Kin—Charles Klein. December 27, 1909, Hudson Theatre.

1910—1919

The Boss—Edward Sheldon. January 30, 1911, Astor Theatre.

A Man of Honor—Isaac Landman. September 30, 1911, Weber's Theatre.

The First Lady of the Land—Charles Nirdlinger. December 4, 1911, Gaiety Theatre.

The Governor's Wife—Alice Bradley. September 10, 1912, Republic Theatre.

The High Road—Edward Sheldon. November 18, 1912, Hudson Theatre.

The Fight—Bayard Veiller. September 2, 1913, Hudson Theatre.

The Governor's Boss—James S. Barcus. April 13, 1914, Garrick Theatre.

Back Home—Bayard Veiller. November 15, 1915, George M. Cohan Theatre.

The Earth—James B. Fagan. February 15, 1916, Playhouse Theatre.

Her Honor, the Mayor—Arline Van Ness Hines. May 23, 1918, Fulton Theatre.

Information Please—Jane Cowl and June Murfin. October 2, 1918, Selwyn Theatre.

The Red Dawn—Thomas Dixon. August 8, 1919, Thirty-ninth Street Theatre.

The Challenge—Eugene Walter. August 17, 1919, Little Theatre.

She Would and She Did—Mark Reed. September 11, 1919, Vanderbilt Theatre.

His Honor, Abe Potash—Montague Glass and Jules E. Goodman. October 14, 1919, Bijou Theatre.

The Unknown Woman—Marjorie Blaine and Willard Mack. November 10, 1919, Maxine Elliott Theatre.

1920—1929

O Henry—Bide Dudley. May 5, 1920, Hudson Theatre.

Immodest Violet—David Carb. August 20, 1920, Forty-eighth Street Theatre.

A Man of the People—Thomas Dixon. September 7, 1920, Bijou Theatre.

Poldekin—Booth Tarkington. September 9, 1920, Park Theatre.

Everyday—Rachel Crothers. November 16, 1921, Bijou Theatre.

Extra—Jack Alicoate. January 23, 1923, Longacre Theatre.

Across the Street—Richard A. Purdy. March 24, 1924, Hudson Theatre.

So This Is Politics—Barry Connors. June 16, 1924, Henry Miller Theatre.

Her Way Out—Edwin M. Boyd. June 23, 1924, Gaiety Theatre.

That Awful Mrs. Eaton—John Farrar and Stephen Vincent Benét. December 24, 1924, Morosco Theatre.

The Backslapper—Paul Dickey and Mann Page. April 11, 1925, Hudson Theatre.

Weak Sister—Lynn Starling. October 13, 1925, Booth Theatre.

Still Waters—Augustus Thomas. March 1, 1926, Henry Miller Theatre.

The Judge's Husband—William Hodge. September 27, 1926, Forty-ninth Street Theatre.

Seed of the Brute—Knowles Entrikin. November 1, 1926, Little Theatre.

Loud Speaker—John Howard Lawson. March 7, 1927, Fifty-second Street Theatre.

Revelry—Maurine Watkins. September 12, 1927, Masque Theatre.

The Racket—Bartlett Cormack. November 22, 1927, Ambassador Theatre.

The International—John Howard Lawson. January 12, 1928, New Playwright Theatre.

The Road to Rome—Robert E. Sherwood. January 31, 1928, Playhouse Theatre.

Skidding—Aurania Rouverol. May 21, 1928, Bijou Theatre.

Gods of the Lightning—Maxwell Anderson and Harold Hickerson. October 24, 1928, Little Theatre.

Poppa—Bella and Samuel Spewack. December 24, 1928, Biltmore Theatre.

The Vegetable—F. Scott Fitzgerald. April 10, 1929, Cherry Lane Theatre.

Congratulations—Morgan Wallace. April 30, 1929, National Theatre.

Make Me Know It—D. Frank Marcus. November 4, 1929, Wallack's Theatre.

City Haul—Elizabeth Miele. December 30, 1929, Hudson Theatre.

1930—1939

Waterloo Bridge—Robert E. Sherwood. January 6, 1930, Fulton Theatre.

Girl Crazy—Guy Bolton and John McGowan, music by George Gershwin. October 14, 1930, Alvin Theatre.

Old Man Murphy—Patrick Kearney and Harry W. Gribble. May 18, 1931, Royale Theatre.

Of Thee I Sing—George S. Kaufman and Morrie Ryskind. December 26, 1931, Music Box.

The Decoy—Harrison King. April 1, 1932, Royale Theatre.

Merry-Go-Round—Albert Malz and George Sklar. April 22, 1932, Provincetown Playhouse.

Destruction—Bertha Wiernik. June 30, 1932, Chanin Auditorium.

Men Must Fight—Reginald Lawrence and S. K. Lauren. October 14, 1932, Lyceum Theatre.

Moral Fabric—G. N. Albyn. November 21, 1932, Provincetown Playhouse.

Both Your Houses—Maxwell Anderson. March 6, 1933, Royale Theatre.

The Mountain—Carty Ranck. September 11, 1933, Provincetown Playhouse.

Let 'Em Eat Cake—George S. Kaufman and Moss Hart. October 21, 1933, Imperial Theatre.

Birthright—Richard Maibaum. November 21, 1933, Forty-ninth Street Theatre.

Legal Murder—Dennis Donoghue. February 15, 1934, President Theatre.

They Shall Not Die—John Wexley. February 21, 1934, Royale Theatre.

When In Rome—Austin Major. February 27, 1934, Forty-ninth Street Theatre.

The Shatter'd Lamp—Leslie Reade. March 21, 1934, Maxine Elliot Theatre.

Picnic—Gretchen Damrosch. May 2, 1934, National Theatre.

Judgment Day—Elmer Rice. September 12, 1934, Belasco Theatre.

Jayhawker—Sinclair Lewis. November 5, 1934, Cort Theatre.

Rain from Heaven—S. N. Behrman. December 24, 1934, Golden Theatre.

Till the Day I Die—Clifford Odets. March 26, 1935, Longacre Theatre.

If This Be Treason—Dr. John Haynes Holmes and Reginald Lawrence. September 23, 1935, Music Box.

Winterset—Maxwell Anderson. September 25, 1935, Martin Beck Theatre.

First Lady—Katherine Dayton and George S. Kaufman. November 26, 1935, Music Box.

Jefferson Davis—John McGee. February 18, 1936, Biltmore Theatre.

A Woman of Destiny—Samuel J. Warshawsky. March 2, 1936, Willis Theatre.

Star Spangled—Robert Ardrey. March 10, 1936, Golden Theatre.

Idiot's Delight—Robert E. Sherwood. March 24, 1936, Shubert Theatre.

Lend Me Your Ears—Philip Wood and Stewart Beach. October 5, 1936, Mansfield Theatre.

It Can't Happen Here—Sinclair Lewis and John C. Moffitt. October 26, 1936, Adelphi Theatre.

Now You've Done It—Mary Coyle Chase. March 5, 1937, Henry Miller Theatre.

I'd Rather Be Right—George S. Kaufman and Moss Hart. November 2, 1937, Alvin Theatre.

The Ghost of Yankee Doodle—Sidney Howard. November 22, 1937, Guild Theatre.

Hooray for What?—Howard Lindsay and Russel Crouse. December 1, 1937, Winter Garden.

Siege—Irwin Shaw. December 8, 1937, Longacre Theatre.

Save Me the Waltz—Katherine Dayton. February 28, 1938, Martin Beck Theatre.

Washington Jitters—John Boruff and Walter Hart. May 2, 1938, Guild Theatre.

Abe Lincoln in Illinois—Robert E. Sherwood. October 15, 1938, Plymouth Theatre.

Knickerbocker Holiday—Maxwell Anderson. October 19, 1938, Ethel Barrymore Theatre.

Waltz in Goose Step—Oliver H. P. Garrett. November 1, 1938, Hudson Theatre.

Glorious Morning—Norman Macowan. November 26, 1938, Mansfield Theatre.

American Landscape—Elmer Rice. December 3, 1938, Cort Theatre.

Don't Throw Glass Houses—Doris Frankel. December 27, 1938, Vanderbilt Theatre.

The American Way—George S. Kaufman and Moss Hart. January 21, 1939, Cort Theatre.

First American Dictator—Jor Marcy and Jacob A. Weiser. March 14, 1939, Bayes Theatre.

Tell My Story—Richard Rohman. March 15, 1939, Mercury Theatre.

No Time for Comedy—S. N. Behrman. April 17, 1939, Alvin Theatre.

Margin for Error—Clare Booth Luce. November 3, 1939, Plymouth Theatre.

1940—1949

Another Sun—Dorothy Thompson and Fritz Kortner. February 23, 1940, National Theatre.

The Fifth Column—Benjamin Glaser. March 6, 1940, Alvin Theatre.

There Shall Be No Night—Robert E. Sherwood. April 30, 1940, Alvin Theatre.

Louisiana Purchase—George de Sylva and Morrie Ryskind, with music and lyrics by Irving Berlin. May 28, 1940, Imperial Theatre.

Flight to the West—Elmer Rice. December 30, 1940, Guild Theatre.

Watch on the Rhine—Lillian Hellman. April 1, 1941, Martin Beck Theatre.

Village Green—Carl Allensworth. September 1, 1941, Henry Miller Theatre.

The More the Merrier—Frank Gabrielson and Irvin Pincus. September 15, 1941, Cort Theatre.

Candle in the Wind—Maxwell Anderson. October 22, 1941, Shubert Theatre.

The Man with Blond Hair—Norma Krasna. November 4, 1941, Belasco Theatre.

The Seventh Trumpet—Charles Rann Kennedy. November 21, 1941, Mansfield Theatre.

In Time to Come—John Huston and Howard Koch. December 29, 1941, Mansfield Theatre.

Johnny on a Spot—Charles MacArthur. January 8, 1942, Plymouth Theatre.

The Flowers of Virtue—Marc Connelly. February 5, 1942, Royale Theatre.

The Moon Is Down—John Steinbeck. April 7, 1942, Martin Beck Theatre.

Decision—Edward Chodorov. February 2, 1944, Belasco Theatre.

Take It As It Comes—E. B. Morris. February 10, 1944, Forty-eighth Street Theatre.

The Searching Wind—Lillian Hellman. April 12, 1944, Fulton Theatre.

Up in Central Park—Herbert and Dorothy Fields. January 27, 1945, New Century Theatre.

Common Ground—Edward Chodorov. April 24, 1945, Fulton Theatre.

The Rugged Path—Robert E. Sherwood. November 10, 1945, Plymouth Theatre.

State of the Union—Russel Crouse and Howard Lindsay. November 14, 1945, Hudson Theatre.

Born Yesterday—Garson Kanin. February 4, 1946, Lyceum Theatre.

Flamingo Road—Robert and Sally Wilder. March 19, 1946, Belasco Theatre.

I Like It Here—A. B. Shiffrin. March 22, 1946, John Golden Theatre.

Woman Bites Dog—Bella and Samuel Spewack. April 17, 1946, Belasco Theatre.

A Flag Is Born—Ben Hecht. September 5, 1946, Alvin Theatre.

The Big Two—L. Bush-Fekete and Mary Helen Fay. January 8, 1947, Booth Theatre.

Parlor Story—William McCleery. March 4, 1947, Biltmore Theatre.

Heads or Tails—H. J. Lengsfelder and Ervin Drake. May 2, 1947, Cort Theatre.

How I Wonder—Donald Ogden Stewart. September 30, 1947, Hudson Theatre.

The Gentleman from Athens—Emmet Lavery. December 9, 1947, Mansfield Theatre.

Strange Bedfellows—Florence Ryerson and Colin Clements. January 14, 1948, Morosco Theatre.

The Survivors—Peter Viertel and Irwin Shaw. January 19, 1948, Playhouse Theatre.

Joy to the World—Allan Scott. March 18, 1948, Plymouth Theatre.

Red Gloves—Jean Paul-Sartre. December 4, 1948, Mansfield Theatre.

Goodbye, My Fancy—Fay Kanin. December 17, 1948, Morosco Theatre.

The Smile of the World—Garson Kanin. January 12, 1949, Lyceum Theatre.

Two Blind Mice—Samuel Spewack. March 2, 1949, Cort Theatre.

The Traitor—Herman Wouk. March 31, 1949, Forty-eighth Street Theatre.

Yes, M'Lord—W. Douglas Home. October 4, 1949, Booth Theatre.

Texas, Li'l Darling—John Whedon and Sam Moore. November 25, 1949, Mark Hellinger Theatre.

The Velvet Glove—Rosemary Casey. December 26, 1949, Booth Theatre.

1950—1959

The Consul—Gian-Carlo Menotti. March 15, 1950, Ethel Barrymore Theatre.

Affairs of State—Louis Verneuil. September 25, 1950, Royale Theatre.

Call Me Madam—Howard Lindsay and Russel Crouse. October 12, 1950, Imperial Theatre.

Darkness at Noon—Sidney Kingsley. January 13, 1951, Alvin Theatre.

The Little Blue Light—Edmund Wilson. April 29, 1951, Playhouse Theatre.

Barefoot in Athens—Maxwell Anderson. October 31, 1951, Martin Beck Theatre.

The Grey-Eyed People—John D. Hess. December 17, 1952, Martin Beck Theatre.

The Crucible—Arthur Miller. January 22, 1953, Martin Beck Theatre

The Pink Elephant—John G. Fuller. April 22, 1953, Playhouse Theatre.

Escapade—Roger MacDougall. November 18, 1953, Forty-eighth Street Theatre.

The Prescott Proposals—Howard Lindsay and Russel Crouse. December 16, 1953, Broadhurst Theatre.

Sing Me No Lullaby—Robert Ardrey. October 14, 1954, Phoenix Theatre.

Silk Stockings—George S. Kaufman, with music and lyrics by Cole Porter. February 24, 1955, Imperial Theatre.

The Great Sebastians—Howard Lindsay and Russel Crouse. January 4, 1956, ANTA Theatre.

Good As Gold—John Patrick. March 7, 1957, Belasco Theatre.

The Egghead—Molly Kazan. October 9, 1957, Ethel Barrymore Theatre.

Romanoff and Juliet—Peter Ustinov. October 10, 1957, Plymouth Theatre.

A Shadow of My Enemy—Sol Stein. December 11, 1957, ANTA Theatre.

Sunrise at Campobello—Dore Schary. January 30, 1958, Cort Theatre.

The Next President—presented by Lee Watson. April 9, 1958, Bijou Theatre.

The Girls in 509—Howard Teichmann. October 15, 1958, Belasco Theatre.

The Gang's All Here—Jerome Lawrence and Robert E. Lee. October 1, 1959, Ambassador Theatre.

Fiorello—Jerome Weidman and George Abbott with lyrics by Sheldon Harnick and music by Jerry Bock. November 23, 1959, Broadhurst Theatre.

NOTES

1. TWO WORLDS: PAST AND PRESENT

1. Charles Hurd, *Washington Cavalcade* (New York, 1948), p. 146.
2. *New York Dramatic Mirror* (February 5, 1898), p. 22.
3. *New York Tribune*, January 19, 1890, p. 6.
4. *New York Tribune*, September 6, 1889, p. 6.
5. *Ibid.*
6. *New York Tribune*, January 14, 1890, p. 7.
7. *Dictionary of American Biography* (New York, 1928), 1:659.
8. *New York Herald Tribune*, November 16, 1945, p. 16.
9. *New York Times*, September 28, 1947, p. xi.
10. Arthur Hobson Quinn, *A History of the American Drama* (New York, 1927), p. 146.

2. POLITICS, MELODRAMA, AND THE NINETIES

1. Frank A. Burr, "The Future of Cuba," *Lippincott's Magazine* (July, 1891), p. 84.
2. Henry L. DeZayas, "The Causes of the Present War in Cuba," *Catholic World* (March, 1896), p. 814.
3. Murat Halstead, "Our Cuban Neighbors and Their Struggle for Liberty," *Review of Reviews* (April, 1896), p. 420.
4. H. T. Peck, *Twenty Years of the American Republic, 1885-1905* (New York, 1920), p. 531.
5. *Ibid.*
6. Arthur M. Schlesinger, *Political and Social Growth of the United States, 1852-1933* (New York, 1936), p. 299.
7. *New York Dramatic Mirror* (March 28, 1896), p. 14.
8. *Ibid.*, p. 16.
9. *The Critic* (October 26, 1895), p. 273.
10. Lynn Linton, "The Wild Woman," *Nineteenth Century* (July, 1891), p. 79.
11. Schlesinger, *Political and Social Growth*, p. 224.
12. Linton, "The Wild Woman," p. 82.
13. Max O'Rell, "Petticoat Government," *North American Review*, (July, 1896), p. 102.
14. John Gibbon, "Why Women Should Have the Ballot," *North American Review* (July, 1896), p. 91.
15. Edward J. Wheeler, "The National Prohibition Party and Its Candidates," *Review of Reviews* (September, 1900), p. 332.
16. *Ibid.*, p. 330.
17. Izzy Einstein, *Prohibition Agent No. 1* (New York, 1932), p. 28.
18. Jeannette P. Nichols, *Twentieth Century United States* (New York, 1943), p. 80.

19. *New York Dramatic Mirror* (April 18, 1896), p. 16.
20. *Ibid.* (October 30, 1897), p. 16.
21. *Ibid.* (November 19, 1898), p. 16.
22. *Ibid.*

3. THE FIRST DECADE

1. Nichols, *Twentieth Century United States*, p. 170.
2. *Ibid.*, p. 178.
3. Fred C. Kelly, *George Ade* (Indianapolis, 1947), p. 164.
4. *Ibid.*, p. 168.
5. Schlesinger, *Political and Social Growth*, p. 316.
6. Lincoln Steffens, *The Shame of the Cities* (New York, 1904), p. 5.
7. Ella Winter and Granville Hicks, eds., *The Letters of Lincoln Steffens* (New York, 1938), p. 147.
8. Nichols, *Twentieth Century United States*, p. 72.
9. Ida M. Tarbell, *All in the Day's Work* (New York, 1939), p. 202.
10. Ward Morehouse, *George M. Cohan* (New York, 1943), p. 82.
11. Bailey Millard, "The Merriwold Dramatists," *Bookman* (August, 1909), p. 627.
12. *The Critic* (May, 1906), p. 339.
13. Schlesinger, *Political and Social Growth*, p. 316.
14. Tarbell, *All in the Day's Work*, p. 212.
15. *New York Dramatic Mirror* (December 2, 1905), p. 3.
16. Kelly, *George Ade*, p. 176.
17. *New York Dramatic Mirror* (March 2, 1901), p. 16.
18. *Ibid.* (May 9, 1903), p. 16.
19. *Ibid.* (February 24, 1906), p. 3.
20. *Ibid.* (May 12, 1906), p. 3.
21. *Ibid.* (September 1, 1906), p. 14.
22. *Ibid.* (January 20, 1906), p. 3.
23. *Ibid.* (November 29, 1902), p. 16.
24. Morehouse, *George M. Cohan*, p. 95.

4. THE SHAME OF THE CITIES

1. Winter and Hicks, *Letters of Lincoln Steffens*, p. xii.
2. *Ibid.*, p. xv.
3. *New York Dramatic Mirror* (January 26, 1895), p. 3.
4. *New York Times*, January 22, 1895, p. 5.
5. *New York Dramatic Mirror* (December 15, 1906), p. 2.
6. *Encyclopedia Americana* (New York, 1943), 18:24.
7. *Ibid.*
8. Steffens, *The Shame of the Cities*, p. 303.
9. *Ibid.*

10. Gustavus Myers, *The History of Tammany Hall* (New York, 1901), p. 276.
11. Steffens, *The Shame of the Cities*, p. 293.
12. *Dictionary of American Biography*, 14:245.
13. Charles H. Parkhurst. *Our Fight With Tammany* (New York, 1895), p. 10.
14. Allan Franklin, *The Trail of the Tiger* (New York, 1928), p. 217.
15. Parkhurst, *Our Fight With Tammany*, p. 257.
16. Alfred Hodder, *A Fight for the City* (New York, 1905), p. 29.
17. *New York Dramatic Mirror* (January 1, 1910), p. 5.
18. *Ibid.*, (February 1, 1911), p. 7.

5. WASHINGTON: COCKTAILS AND POLITICS

1. Mrs. Carl Barus, "A Cabinet Afternoon," *Chautauquan* (April, 1891), p. 89.
2. *Ibid.*
3. *Ibid.*, p. 91.
4. Harrison Rhodes, "Washington the Cosmopolitan," *Harper's* (January, 1917), p. 162.
5. *Ibid.*, p. 163.
6. *New York Dramatic Mirror* (December 6, 1911), p. 6.
7. Hurd, *Washington Cavalcade*, p. 197.
8. *New York Times*, November 17, 1935, p. L20.
9. Hurd, *Washington Cavalcade*, pp. 161-2.
10. *Ibid.*, pp. 207-8.

6. CRUSADING TEENS AND FABULOUS TWENTIES

1. *Outlook*, "Editorial" (October 18, 1913), p. 361.
2. Mary K. Maule, "What Is a Shop-Girl's Life?" *World's Work* (September, 1907), p. 9311.
3. Scott Nearing, "The History of a Christmas Box," *Charities and Commons* (December 29, 1906), p. 556.
4. *New York Dramatic Mirror* (February 26, 1916), p. 8.
5. John Landesco, "Prohibition and Crime," in *Prohibition: A National Experiment*, of *The Annals of the American Academy of Political Science* (Philadelphia, 1932), CLXIII:3.
6. *Newsweek* (February 3, 1947), p. 24.
7. Bartlett Cormack, *The Racket* (New York, 1928), p.v.

7. TWO TRIALS THAT SHOOK THE WORLD

1. *Boston Globe*, August 23, 1927, p. 1.
2. Osmond K. Fraenkel, "The Sacco-Vanzetti Case," in Samuel Klaus, ed., *American Trials* (New York, 1931), p. 21.

3. *Ibid.*, p. 3.
4. H. VanRensselaer Wyatt, "The Drama," *Catholic World* (December, 1928), p. 339.
5. Michael A. Musmanno, *After Twelve Years* (New York, 1939), p. 39.
6. Brooks Atkinson, *New York Times,* October 25, 1928, p. 4.
7. *Ibid.,* September 26, 1935, p. L19.
8. *Literary Digest* (April 23, 1927), p. 6.
9. Fraenkel, "*The Sacco-Vanzetti Case,*" p. 19.
10. *Boston Globe,* August 23, 1927, p. 8.
11. William H. King, "Bolsheviki in the United States," *Literary Digest* (February 22, 1919), p. 2.
12. Augusta (Ga.) *Chronicle,* p. 13.
13. Sidney Howard, "Baiting the Bolsheviki," *Collier's* (January 10, 1920), p. 15.
14. Supreme Court Decisions, October Term, 1932, in *United States Reports,* CCLXXXVII:51.
15. Mary H. Vorse, "The Scottsboro Trial," *New Republic* (April 19, 1933), p. 276.
16. Supreme Court Decisions, October Term, 1932, CCLXXXVII:71.
17. John T. Graves, *New York Times,* November 17, 1935, p. E7.

8. THE DEPRESSION, CONGRESS, AND THE NEW DEAL

1. Arthur Krock, *New York Times,* December 27, 1931, sec. E, p. 5.
2. *New York Times,* December 27, 1931, p. xi.
3. *Ibid.,* December 31, 1933, p. 1.
4. Atkinson, *New York Times,* October 23, 1933, p. C 18.
5. Percy Hammond, *New York Herald Tribune,* March 8, 1933, p. 8
6. Atkinson, *New York Times,* March 7, 1933, p. L 20.
7. Krock, *New York Times,* November 7, 1937, p. E 3.
8. *New York Times,* May 15, 1938, p. L 4.
9. *Ibid.*

9. SUNRISE AT CAMPOBELLO

1. *Commonweal* (May 1, 1936), p. 18.
2. Louis McHenry Howe, "The Winner," *Saturday Evening Post* (February 25, 1933), p. 7.
3. *Ibid.*
4. *Time* (September 15, 1941), p. 12.
5. *Newsweek* (September 15, 1941), p. 18.
6. Elizabeth Marbury, "My Crystal Ball," *Saturday Evening Post* (October 13, 1923), p. 130.
7. *Ibid.*

10. NAZIISM AND FASCISM

1. *The Washington Post,* October 20, 1939, p. 1.
2. Clare Booth Luce, *Margin for Error,* introduction by Henry Luce (New York, 1940), p. xix.
3. *New York Times,* October 28, 1936, p. L 30.
4. *The Sunday Star* (Washington), February 16, 1936, p. 2.
5. Nichols, *Twentieth Century United States,* p. 369.
6. Atkinson, *New York Times,* October 28, 1936, p. L 30.
7. Joseph Wood Krutch, "Knickerbocker Holiday," *Nation* (November 5, 1938), p. 487.
8. *Ibid.,* p. 488.
9. Erik W. Modean, "The Church Against Hitler," *The Cresset* (October, 1947), p. 11.

11. EVOLUTION OF A LIBERAL

1. Robert E. Sherwood, *There Shall Be No Night* (New York, 1936), p. xxiii.
2. Demaree Bess, "European Showdown," *Saturday Evening Post* (December 3, 1938), p. 6.
3. Otto D. Tolischus, *New York Times,* October 15, 1938, p. 1.
4. Sherwood, *There Shall Be No Light,* p. xxvii.
5. Mark Barron, *The Evening Star* (Washington), July 21, 1940, p. F 1.
6. Ira Wolfert, *The Evening Star* (Washington), May 11, 1941, p. F 1.
7. Lewis Nichols, *New York Times,* November 15, 1945, p. 25.
8. Burns Mantle, *Best Plays of 1945-46* (New York, 1946), p. 309.
9. Thomas Riggs, Jr., "We Call Upon America," *North American Review* (June, 1936), p. 264.
10. *The Evening Star* (Washington), December 15, 1941, p. B 10.

12. COMMUNISM

1. "Eight Dead Dogs," *Time* (June 21, 1937), p. 24.
2. Harold Denny, *New York Times* (March 4, 1938), p. 12.
3. *Newsweek* (March 22, 1948), p. 38.
4. O. Henry Brandon, "Was Masaryk Murdered?," *Saturday Evening Post* (August 21, 1948), p. 19.
5. *Ibid.,* p. 18.
6. Edward R. Murrow, "Jan Masaryk," *New Republic* (March 22, 1948), p. 8.
7. *Newsweek* (March 29, 1948), p. 38.
8. Arthur Miller, *Collected Plays* (New York, 1957), p. 44.
9. *Ibid.,* p. 47.

13. ONE WORLD

1. *The Evening Star* (Washington), November 10, 1924, p. 3.
2. *Ibid.*
3. Associated Press biography.
4. *Ibid.*
5. *Ibid.*
6. *The Evening Star* (Washington), November 10, 1924, p. 3.
7. Arthur Fell Low, "Living American Statesman: Henry Cabot Lodge," *Forum* (March, 1921), p. 272.
8. *The Evening Star* (Washington), December 29, 1941, p. A 5.
9. M. E. Hennessey, *Boston Globe*, November 10, 1924, p. 3.
10. Atkinson, *New York Times,* December 29, 1941, p. 20.

14. POLITICS AND PERSONALITIES

1. Hamilton Basso, "The Huey Long Legend," *Life* (December 9, 1946), p. 106.
2. Nichols, *Twentieth Century United States*, p. 356.
3. Mark Sullivan, *Our Times, the United States, 1900-1925,* Vol. 6 (New York, 1935), p. 37.
4. *Ibid.*, p. 46.
5. *Ibid.*, p. 150.
6. *Ibid.*, p. 229.
7. *Ibid.*, p. 300.
8. *Ibid.*, p. 141.
9. *Ibid.*, p. 250.
10. Atkinson, *New York Times,* November 25, 1959, p. C 19.
11. Lowell M. Limpus and Burr W. Leyson, *This Man LaGuardia,* (New York, 1938), p. 49.
12. *Ibid.*, p. 31.
13. *Ibid.*, p. 43.
14. Limpus and Leyson, *This Man LaGuardia,* p. 48.
15. Julian S. Mason, "The Scandals of New York," *Current History* (August, 1932), p. 529.
16. Limpus and Leyson, *This Man LaGuardia,* pp. 273-4.

BIBLIOGRAPHY
HISTORIES

Brown, Thomas Allston. *A History of the New York Stage*. New York: Dodd, Mead & Co., 1903.

Myers, Gustavus. *The History of Tammany Hall*. New York: Privately Printed, 1901.

Nichols, Jeannette. *Twentieth Century United States*. New York: D. Appleton-Century Co., 1943.

Peck, H. T. *Twenty Years of the American Republic, 1885-1905*. New York: Dodd, Mead & Co., 1920.

Quinn, Arthur Hobson. *A History of the American Drama to the Civil War*. New York: Harper & Bros., 1923.

——————. *History of the American Drama*. New York: F. S. Crofts & Co., 1943.

Schlesinger, Arthur M. *Political and Social Growth of the United States, 1852-1933*. New York: Macmillan Co., 1936.

Sullivan, Mark. *Our Times, The United States, 1900-25*. Vol. 6, New York: Charles Scribner's Sons, 1935.

GENERAL

Callcott, Mary Stevenson. *Child Labor Legislation in New York*. New York: Macmillan Co., 1931.

Cuneo, Ernest. *Life With Fiorello*. New York: Macmillan Co., 1955.

Einstein, Izzy: *Prohibition Agent No. 1*. New York: Stokes Co., 1932.

Forrest, J. A., and Malcolm, James. *Impeachment of William Sulzer*. Albany: Fort Orange Press, 1913.

Fraenkel, Osmond K. *The Sacco-Vanzetti Case*. ("American Trials Series." ed. Samuel Klaus.) New York: Alfred A. Knopf, 1931.

Franklin, Allan. *The Trail of the Tiger*. New York: Privately Printed, 1928.

Godkin, E. L., and Berheim, A. G. *The Triumph of Reform*. New York: W. T. Hardenbreck, 1895.

Hodder, Alfred. *A Fight for the City*. New York: Macmillan Co., 1903.

Hunt, D. E. *Life and Work of Charles H. Hoyt*. Bulletins of Birmingham-Southern College. January, 1946.

Hurd, Charles. *Washington Cavalcade*. New York: E. P. Dutton & Co., 1948.

Kelly, Fred C. *George Ade*. Indianapolis: Bobbs-Merrill Co., 1947.

Landesco, John. "Prohibition and Crime," *Prohibition: A National Experiment*, in *The Annals of the American Academy of Political Science* (Vol. CLXIII). Philadelphia, 1932.

Limpus, Lowell M., and Leyson, Burr W. *This Man LaGuardia*. New York: E. P. Dutton & Co., 1938.

242   POLITICS IN THE AMERICAN DRAMA

Marcosson, Isaac F. *David Graham Phillips*. New York: Dodd, Mead
& Co., 1932.
Merz, Charles. *The Dry Decade*. New York: Doubleday, Doran & Co.,
1931.
Morehouse, Ward. *George M. Cohan*. New York: J. B. Lippincott Co.,
1943.
Musmanno, Michael A. *After Twelve Years*. New York: Alfred A.
Knopf, 1939.
Parkhurst, Dr. Charles H. *Our Fight with Tammany*. New York: Charles
Scribner's Sons, 1895.
Pitou, Augustus. *Masters of the Show*. New York: Neale Publishing
Co., 1914.
Steffens, Lincoln. *The Shame of the Cities*. New York: McClure,
Phillips & Co., 1904.
Tarbell, Ida M. *All in the Day's Work*. New York: Macmillan, 1939.
——————. *History of the Standard Oil Company*. New York: Mc-
Clure, Phillips & Co., 1904.
Winter, E., and Hicks, Granville (eds.). *The Letters of Lincoln Steffens*.
New York: Harcourt, Brace & Co., 1938.

COMPILATIONS

Dictionary of American Biography. New York: Charles Scribner's Sons,
1928.
Encyclopedia Americana. New York: American Corporation, 1943.
Hoyt, Charles H. *Five Plays*, ed. by Douglas L. Hunt. New Jersey:
Princeton University Press, 1941.
Kaufman, George. *Six Plays*. New York: Modern Library, 1942.
Kronenberger, Louis (ed.). *Best Plays of 1953-59*. New York: Dodd,
Mead & Co., 1959.
Kunitz, Stanley J., and Haycraft, Howard. *Twentieth Century Authors*.
New York: H. W. Wilson Co., 1942.
Mantle, Burns, and Sherwood, Garrison P. *Best Plays of 1899-1909*.
New York: Dodd, Mead & Co., 1933.
Mantle, Burns. *Best Plays Series*. All Volumes 1919-20 to 1945-46.
New York: Dodd, Mead & Co., 1920 to 1946.
Nathan, George Jean. *The Theatre Book of the Year, 1934-44*. New
York: Alfred A. Knopf, 1944. Also 1944-45, 1945.
Payson's New York and Brooklyn Theatrical Album. New York: F. G.
Gardner & Co., 1886.
Strang, Lewis C. *Famous Actors*. (First and Second Series.), Boston:
L. C. Page Co., 1900, 1902.
——————. *Famous Actresses*. (First and Second Series.), Boston:
L. C. Page Co., 1900, 1902.

PERIODICALS

"A. Mitchell Palmer, 'Fighting Quaker'," *Literary Digest* (March 27, 1920).

Aikman, Duncan. "Chicago Laughs and Big Bill Loses," *Outlook* (April 25, 1928).

Alsop, J., and Catledge, T. "The 168 Days," *Saturday Evening Post* (September 18, 1937).

Angoff, Charles. "Maxwell Anderson's Knickerbocker Holiday," *North American Review* (December, 1938).

"Another View of Woman Suffrage," *Review of Reviews* (December, 1925).

"Around the World," *Living Age* (September 15, 1927).

"Awful Dangers of Woman Suffrage," *Ltierary Digest* (October 23, 1920).

Bailey, Millard. "The Merriwold Dramatists," *Bookman* (August, 1909).

Barus, Mrs. Carl. "A Cabinet Afternoon," *Chautauquan* (April, 1891).

Basso, Hamilton. "The Huey Long Legend," *Life* (December 9, 1946).

Blind, Karl. "Czarism at Bay," *North American Review* (October, 1904).

Brandon, O. Henry. "Was Masaryk Murdered?," *Saturday Evening Post* (August 21, 1948).

Burr, Frank A. "The Future of Cuba," *Lippincott's* (July, 1891).

Cahan, Abraham. "Russian Nihilism of Today," *Forum* (June, 1901).

"Cardinal Gibbons and the Roman Catholic Church in America," *Outlook* (October 10, 1903).

Carmer, Carl. "Maxwell Anderson," *Theatre Arts* (June, 1933).

Cason, Clarence E. "Black Straws in the Wind," *North American Review* (July, 1933).

Catholic World. (April, 1933), (October, 1941).

"Chicago's Recent Growth As a Financial Center," *Literary Digest* (September 22, 1928).

Child, Maude P. "Capital Society," *Saturday Evening Post* (February 20, 1926).

Clapper, Raymond. "Cuff-Links Club," *Saturday Evening Post* (February 25, 1933).

Collins, Peter W. "Bolshevism in America," *Current Opinion* (March, 1920).

Colum, Mary M. "Life and Literature," *Forum* (June, 1936).

Commack, Thomas H. "Nearly Every Prospect Pleases," *Outlook* (July 25, 1928).

Comonweal. May 1, 1936.

Conger, Charlotte M. "The European Legations at Washington," *Munsey's* (June, 1892).

Cothran, Ben. "South of Scottsboro," *Forum* (June, 1935).

Creel, George. "The Kitchen Cabinet," *Collier's* (June 17, 1933).

———————. "The Heroes," *Collier's* (February 10, 1945).

Critic. (October 26, 1895).

DeZayas, Henry L. "The Causes of the Present War in Cuba," *Catholic World* (March, 1896).

Demaree, Bess. "European Showdown," *Saturday Evening Post* (December 3, 1938).

DeVoto, Bernard. "The Pulitzer Prize Winners," *Saturday Review of Literature* (May 8, 1937).

Dow, Neal. "The Effectiveness of Prohibition," *Forum* (March, 1887).

Downing, Francis. "Loyalty Affidavits," *Commonweal* (August 26, 1949).

Ecab, James H. "The Russian Remedy," *Arena* (June, 1902).

"Eight Dead Dogs," *Time* (June 21, 1937).

Evans, Elizabeth G. "Foreigners," *New Republic* (June 8, 1921).

Forrest, H. F. "The Overthrow of Prohibition in Vermont," *Outlook* (March 7, 1903).

"The Fortune Survey," *Fortune* (January, 1939).

Hacher, Louis M. "The Rise and Fall of Prohibition," *Current History* (September, 1932).

Halstead, Murat. "Our Cuban Neighbors and Their Struggle for Liberty," *Review of Reviews* (April, 1896).

Hamilton, Clayton. "Charles Klein," *Forum* (March, 1909).

Harper, Ida Husted. "The American Woman Gets the Vote," *Review of Reviews* (October, 1920).

Howard, Sidney. "Baiting the Bolshevist," *Collier's* (January 10, 1926).

Howe, Louis McHenry. "The Winner," *Saturday Evening Post* (February 25, 1933).

Howe, M. A. DeWolfe. "Causes and Their Champions," *Ladies Home Journal* (April, 1926).

Johnston, Charles. "The Americanizing of Russia," *Harper's Weekly* April 25, 1903).

Kane, Harriet T. "Every Man a King," *Reader's Digest* (September, 1941).

Kennedy, John B. "Lords of the Loop," *Collier's* (April 3, 1926).

Kenny, Herbert A. "A Summing Up," *Catholic World* (September, 1957).

Kirchwey, Freda. "Masaryk," *Nation* (March 20, 1948).

Krivitsky, W. G. "Why Stalin Shot His Generals," *Saturday Evening Post* (April 22, 1939).

"Lined with Despair," *Time* (March 14, 1938).

Linton, Mrs. Lynn. "The Wild Women," *Nineteenth Century* (July, 1891).

"Living in War-Swollen Washington Is a Serious Problem," *Literary Digest* (April 27, 1918).

Low, Arthur F. "Living American Statesman: Henry Cabot Lodge," *Forum* (March, 1921).

MacDonald, William. "The Execution of Sacco-Vanzetti," *Current History* (October, 1927).

Mandeville, Ernest W. "Prohibition in Chicago and Cincinnati," *Outlook* (May 6, 1925).

Marbury, Elizabeth. "My Crystal Ball," *Saturday Evening Post* (October 13, 1923).

Markham, Edwin. "The Grind Behind the Holidays," *Cosmopolitan* (November, 1906).

Mason, Gregory. "William Sulzer and the Invisible Government," *Outlook* (October 18, 1913).

Mason, Julian S. "Scandals of New York," *Current History* (August, 1932).

Masters, Edgar Lee. "Chicago," *Century* (July, 1928).

Maule, Mary K. "What Is a Shop-Girl's Life," *World's Work* (September, 1907).

"McCarthy Era," *Nation* (August 27, 1955).

McFaul, Right Rev. James A. "Catholics and American Citizenship," *North American Review* (September, 1900).

"Mild-Mannered Mr. Volstead," *Literary Digest* (December 27, 1919).

Modean, Erik. "The Church Against Hitler," *Cresset* (October, 1947).

"Murder of the Russian Imperial Family," *Current History* (October, 1920).

Murrow, Edward R. "Jan Masaryk," *New Republic* (March 22, 1948).

Musgrave, Percy. "Big Business Is Very Happy," *Nation* (September 7, 1929).

Myers, Gustavus. "The Secrets of Tammany's Success," *Forum* (June, 1901).

Nearing, Scott. "The History of a Christmas Box," *Charities and The Commons* (December 29, 1906).

Nelson, Henry L. "Washington Society," *Harpers* (March, 1893).

New York Critics Review. (1941-1959).

New York Dramatic Mirror. (January, 1890-December, 1920).

"Official Attitude of the United States Toward Russia," *Current History* (February, 1921).

O'Rell, Max. "Petticoat Government," *North American Review* (July, 1896).

Palmer, A. Mitchell. "The Case Against the Reds," *Forum* (February, 1920).

"Passing of Joe McCarthy," *Time* (May 13, 1957).

Peffer, W. A. "Prohibition in Kansas," *Forum* (April, 1901).

Pierce, Edwin C. "The True Politics for Prohibition and Labor," *Arena* (November, 1891).

Ratcliffe, S. K. "Senator Lodge," *Living Age* (May 3, 1919).

"The Recrudescence of Nihilism," *Harper's Weekly* (August 13, 1904).

"Russia and America," *Living Age* (July 23, 1904).

Schmidt, Godfrey P. "Senator McCarthy, A Martyr for Civil Liberties," *Catholic World* (September, 1957).

Schmidt, Karl. "The Billy Sunday of the Theatre," *Everybody's* (March, 1919).

Selden, Charles A. "Four Years of the Nineteenth Amendment," *Ladies Home Journal* (June, 1924).

"Senator Lodge's World Court Plan," *Outlook* (May 21, 1924).

Skinner, Richard D. "The Steps," *Comonweal* (May 19, 1933).

Smith, Arthur D. Hovden. "Roosevelt's Pilots—Colonel House and Colonel Howe," *Scribner's* (January, 1933).

Sorenson, Per. "Kaj Munk, a New Danish Dramatist," *Theatre Arts* (November, 1939).

"The South and the Scottsboro Ruling," *Literary Digest* (April 13, 1935).

"The Soviets Clean House," *Nation* (November 2, 1946).

"Stalin's Purge," *Current History* (July, 1937).

"Thank God," *Time* (March 21, 1938).

"Verdict on Walker," *Literary Digest* (June 11, 1932).

Villard, Fanny B. "Susan B. Anthony," *Nation* (February 14, 1920).

Villard, Oswald Garrison. "Al Smith—Latest Phase," *American Mercury* (February, 1935).

Vorse, Mary H. "The Scottsboro Trial," *New Republic* (April 19, 1933).

Warner, Arthur. "Sacco-Vanzetti—A Reasonable Doubt," *Nation* (September 28, 1921).

Wheeler, Edward J. "The National Prohibition Party and Its Candidates," *Review of Reviews* (September, 1900).

Whittaker, Charles. "Why Workmen Drink," *Harper's Weekly* (August 7, 1915).

Wilbur, Dr. Ray Lyman. "Last Illness," *Saturday Evening Post* (October 13, 1923).

Winkler, John K. "Izzy and Moe Stop the Show," *Collier's* (February 6, 1926).

Wyatt, H. Van Rensselaer. "The Drama," *Catholic World* (December, 1928).

NEWSPAPERS

Boston Globe
Evening Star (Washington)
New York Herald Tribune
New York Sun
New York Times
New York Tribune
Washington Post

INDEX

* The names of characters in plays are set in small capitals to distinguish them from actual persons.

† Where a character is known by only one name, the title of the play is given to aid identification.